Education, Ps)
Transformation

Series Editors
Jan Jagodzinski
Department of Secondary Education
University of Alberta
Edmonton, Alberta, Canada

Mark Bracher
English Department, Kent State University
Kent, Ohio, USA

Within the last three decades, education as a political, moral, and ideological practice has become central to rethinking not only the role of public and higher education, but also the emergence of pedagogical sites outside of the schools-which include but are not limited to the Internet, television, film, magazines, and the media of print culture. Education as both a form of schooling and public pedagogy reaches into every aspect of political, economic, and social life. What is particularly important in this highly interdisciplinary and politically nuanced view of education are a number of issues that now connect learning to social change, the operations of democratic public life, and the formation of critically engaged individual and social agents. At the center of this series will be questions regarding what young people, adults, academics, artists, and cultural workers need to know to be able to live in an inclusive and just democracy and what it would mean to develop institutional capacities to reintroduce politics and public commitment into everyday life. Books in this series aim to play a vital role in rethinking the entire project of the related themes of politics, democratic struggles, and critical education within the global public sphere.

More information about this series at
http://www.springer.com/series/14964

Dennis Atkinson

Art, Disobedience, and Ethics

The Adventure of Pedagogy

palgrave
macmillan

Dennis Atkinson
Department of Educational Studies
Goldsmiths University of London
London, United Kingdom

Education, Psychoanalysis, and Social Transformation
ISBN 978-3-319-87361-9   ISBN 978-3-319-62639-0   (eBook)
DOI 10.1007/978-3-319-62639-0

This Palgrave Macmillan imprint is published by Springer Nature
The registered company is Springer International Publishing AG
The registered company address is: Gewerbestrasse 11, 6330 Cham, Switzerland

ACKNOWLEDGEMENTS

A number of people have read and commented on versions of the chapters in this book or upon the presentations I have given in various locations upon which some chapters are based. Equally, there are others with whom I have learned a great deal in conversation. I want to thank them for their time, conversations, comments and suggestions. They are Paul Dash, Alex Moore, jan jagodinski, John Baldacchino, Rosalyn George, Gerald Raunig, Jusso Tervo, Kevin Tavin, Catarina Martins, John Johnston, Carolina De Palma Silva, Esther Sayers, Arunthathi Mahendran, Tony Brown, Michaela Ross, and Fernando Hernandez. Many of the chapters are based upon presentations and seminars over the last three or four years, and I want to thank the students and audiences who participated. A version of Chap. 4 was published in the AD Magazine published by the National Society for Art and Design in the UK. I would also like to thank the artists whose work appears in the book for allowing me to use images of their work. Thanks to Palgrave Macmillan for the continued support and advice.

The book circles around the problematic of developing effective pedagogical strategies that support and extend the different ways in which children and students learn in line with their changing and evolving sensibilities in this world. In doing so, there is a tendency towards repetition that may be disappointing or frustrating to some. However, I would ask that such repetition be viewed in terms of differentiation, as the text explores the central problematic through a series of, always incomplete, meditations that are developed through the various perspectives that I have chosen.

CONTENTS

LIST OF FIGURES

CHAPTER 1

Introduction: The Pragmatics and Ethics of the Suddenly Possible

*Standing inside a waterfall is a very different experience from
standing outside and reflecting upon it.*

The main reason for writing this book stems from what I see as a persistent under-valuing of the educational force of art in education by governments around the world. In recent decades, in my country and others, the time allocated for art in schools has been cut significantly to allow greater emphasis upon what are often called the STEM subjects—including science, technology and mathematics—that are viewed as central for economic ambition and competition. Though the arts do make a significant contribution to economic performance in many countries, this book is not concerned with justifying the arts in education along such socio-economic lines. Rather, its aim is to formulate a more fundamental advocacy for art practice as an ethico-aesthetic and political process that has generative potential for producing new modes of becoming and new forms of coexistence. In other words, the force of art can take us beyond the human as is constituted into new modes of becoming.

The nature and force of art practice is what I call disobedient: disobedient to established parameters of practice, practices of thinking, seeing, making and feeling. We might also say that the process of what I have called real learning (Atkinson 2011) is itself disobedient; it too has the potential to take us beyond the human. The book explores the notion of disobedience in art

© The Author(s) 2018
D. Atkinson, *Art, Disobedience, and Ethics*, Education, Psychoanalysis,
and Social Transformation, DOI 10.1007/978-3-319-62639-0_1

practice and pedagogic work and the need for an ethics of relevance and creativity commensurate to such disobedient processes.

The phrase 'the pragmatics of the suddenly possible' is taken from an essay by Susan Buck-Morss (2013), where she writes about the idea of communism. On reading her essay, the phrase leapt off the page and immediately resonated with the notion of real learning as an existential event on which I had been working, where real learning is conceived as a leap into a new or modified ontological state whose affects and relations produce an expansion of acting and thinking. I will qualify and then relinquish this term shortly. This emphasis upon learning is future oriented, but not exclusively because it emerges from an embedded past. I am interested in exploring pedagogic strategies that might be able to respond effectively to the 'unknown' in learning processes, suggested by the notion of the suddenly possible, which emerges as the ontogenesis of learning evolves. The idea of the pragmatics of the suddenly possible resonates for me with Deleuze's distinction between the actual and the virtual, a kind of dual ontology in which an infinitely differentiated domain, the virtual, (unknown) precipitates processes of actualisation. Learning therefore is not conceived solely as a process migrating towards established identities of learners or teachers or even established bodies of knowledge but as a process characterised by the idea of the not-known and that-which-is-not-yet; it is a process of adventure. The idea of the not-known is beautifully depicted by Spinoza's statements from the *Ethics* (III P2), indicating that we do not know what a body is capable of or what a mind is capable of thinking. This suggests that learning involves the human and the non-human, in the sense of that which lies beyond how we understand the human, and that the process and practice of learning engages the domains of finitude and infinitude. If these ideas are embraced by pedagogic work, then such work is not only concerned with the induction of learners into valued bodies of knowledge and practice, where the emphasis is placed upon the finite knowledge to be learned, but it has to embrace a more complex and uncertain position of trying to understand the different ways in which children and students learn and the outcomes of such learning, which may not be known (infinite). Put another way, rather than pedagogic work being viewed in mechanical or instrumental terms where emphasis is placed upon the attainment of a known world of knowledge and practice, it has to be viewed as an *adventure* in which modes of learning and their outcomes may be unclear, but which need to be addressed. In the current epoch of education in schools in England, the USA and elsewhere, there is a strong emphasis upon the former position characterised by the notions of attainment, audit and inspection. Under such a regime, the level of examination success or assessment tests defines effective teaching and learning. This forms the chief criterion that determines the educational quality of a school and the quality of teaching.

In a passage from an earlier essay, Buck-Morss (2010, p. 70) provides a telling comment upon what she finds narrow-minded and perhaps doctrinaire about this educational scenario.

> There is a blindness to institutionalised education that passes down the authority of tradition, a mental timidity, born of privilege or just plain laziness, that cloaks itself in the heavy bombast of cultural heritage and historic preservation. It generates enormous resistance to trespassing conceptual boundaries or exceeding the limits of present imagination, rewarding instead the virtues of scholastic diligence, disciplinary professionalism and elitist erudition, all escape routes from the pragmatic necessity of confronting the new. Indeed extreme discomfort is caused by the truly new, the truly 'contemporary', that which Nietzsche called the 'untimely' – those aspects of the present moment that simply do not fit our established traditions or modes of understanding.

My concern with the current educational climate in many countries, which I think is driven mainly by economic ambition, is that what children and students *should learn,* dominates the educational project to the extent that too little consideration is given to trying to understand *how children and students learn* and the pedagogical obligations and values for supporting each individual 'how'. Being able to respond to the different ways in which they learn may often involve what Buck-Morss calls confronting the new. It involves the gentle but profound advice given by Alfred North Whitehead (1968, p. 116), 'Have a care, here is something that matters'. Thus, it may be the case that there is an inherent blindness of education to the untimeliness of events of learning as manifested in the different ways in which children and students learn.

This book, set in the context of school art education but applicable to other sites of learning and teaching, is one attempt to argue for a rebalancing of the current educational project and its dogmatic emphasis upon the acquisition of particular domains of knowledge and skills. The current emphasis in educational policies upon science, technology and mathematics reduces the time for engaging with the arts in the school curriculum. I argue for a refocusing upon learners and their different ways of entering into and engaging with the process of learning, which I view as a process of building or growing a life. The phrase *the pragmatics of the suddenly possible* captured my attention because of its deeply practical resonances with the potentialities emerging in processes of learning and what these might be capable of producing. I am interested therefore in those occasions or encounters, in teaching or learning, where learners and teachers become aware of the suddenly possible within their specific modes of existence so that 'learning' or 'teaching' (a form of learning) and their potential are suddenly viewed in a new light; that is to say, where one's understanding of what learning or teaching are becomes expanded, leading to new or modified capacities to learn or to teach. Put in another way, with particular reference to teaching, what becomes suddenly possible can be conceived as also involving what Judith Butler (2005) terms 'becoming undone', which precipitates periods of uncertainty when confronted, for example, by a student's work that is difficult to grasp and where previous pedagogic practice is challenged. In such moments, we risk ourselves in encounters with others and their practice. We have an opportunity to question the self-sufficiency of established knowledge and practice that we *are* and try to embrace the potential of the unknown and, in doing so, expand our capacities to act and our understanding of practice. The book is therefore concerned with thinking about the different sensibilities that are required when confronting and responding to events of learning. Such pedagogical situations seem to create a contrast between what we might call the transcendent enunciators that inform pedagogic work, such as methodologies, bodies of knowledge and skills, theories of learning, modes of assessment, and how a learning encounter matters for a learner which concerns the immanence of a particular learner's mode of learning. We might view this contrast as a contrast of values.

The specific educational context for my explorations is the domain of art education. Historically, economic forces, such as the demand for skilled workers in industrial ceramics and other industries, have equally affected this domain. It has also been influenced or determined by specific ideologies and their respective methodologies that proclaim a particular purpose for school art education and the education of teachers in this domain. I am thinking here of movements such as Basic Design (de Sausmaurez 1964), Visual culture art education (Freedman 2003; Tavin 2016) Discipline Based Art Education (Eisner 1988), Critical and Contextual Studies (Taylor, 1986), Multicultural Art Education (Mason 1995; Chalmers 1996; Dash 2010), a/r/tography (Irwin, de Cosson 2004), that are concerned with the theory and practice of art. These innovative movements have expanded the field of art education in schools and other institutions, as well as research in art education, and can be understood as establishing transcendent positions according to which art educational practice is conceived and valued, or put another way, they create a series of parameters and criteria that determine particular approaches to art educational practice. Such parameters are usually necessary for formulating appropriate pedagogic aims and methods of procedure.

However, I want to work from a relatively inverse position, that is to say, to relax the transcendent force of established parameters of practice in order to respond to the immanence and value of local practices of learning that emerge, for example, from the 'suddenly possible' that may transgress the framings and values of transcendent forces. But, one may argue, how is this position possible when pedagogic work relies upon series of criteria and methods, evolved from traditions or more recent developments, to be able to respond to the processes and outcomes of students' work? What I am suggesting or speculating is the notion that we engage in pedagogic work such as responding to the immanence of children's and student's learning processes *without criteria*. A pedagogy without criteria that is able to respond effectively to the difference of learning processes and their immanent values that in some cases may expand our understanding of learning in art and of what art is. This does not mean that I am advocating a pedagogy of 'anything goes'. I am not. I am suggesting a relaxing of parameters and criteria that underpin particular forms of learning and practice so as to enable those forms of learning and their outcomes that may be marginalised or ignored, to be recognised. The same applies to teaching. This involves a process of experimentation and invention. In many contexts, in recent decades, the practice of teaching has been subject to a series of competencies or standards whose purpose is to define and monitor good teaching. For some, this is viewed as a positive and constructive approach to improving teacher quality. For others, the idea of standards, which of course is difficult to dispute, has produced a rather mechanical and prescriptive approach to what they see as a creative enterprise. The latter view, which I adopt, would subscribe, I think, to a Spinozan interpretation: that we do not know fully what teaching is or can become.

I have already hinted at the impact on educational practices of what many term neoliberal economics (Ball 2009), and it is difficult to envisage pedagogic work beyond the influence of market capitalism. The interesting thing is, of course, that mainstream educational practices as we have known them for the last century or longer emerged through and are direct consequences of capitalist economics although, in qualification, during times when capitalism reflected a more liberal-economic dimension that embraced the importance of social welfare in contrast to recent decades where the emphasis has been almost entirely upon economic prosperity and competition. The book is set against this political-economic background and its effect upon education but its aim is to consider a different approach to politics or the political, a dissensual politics, advocated by Ranciere and others, in which educational practices are conceived in a rather different light, where emphasis is placed upon the notion of building a life, a process of invention and creation involving the emergence of the new within local processes of learning. We might call this approach a *dissensual pedagogy* where the notion of dissensus refers to situations in which something is produced in a world (teaching and learning) that is in some way heterogeneous to its existing patterns, so as to open up new possibilities and transformations of a world and of co-existence. It is through such dissensual relations that expanded understandings of learning and teaching may emerge. I am using the term disobedience in a similar way to refer to events of practice that run counter to established frameworks and practices.

The book will therefore consider approaches to pedagogic work based upon the notion of building a life rather than focussing upon a particular kind of life that is predicated, for example, upon economic ambition, where life is captured and exploited by capital, its territorialising and re-territorialising *dispositifs*. Whilst we are subject and complicit to the power of capitalist modes of being, and we recognise that education is largely a preparation for life in such a world nevertheless the book argues for a way of thinking about teaching and learning that moves the emphasis towards the different ways in which learning and its outcomes might emerge. This advocates that learners should not be denied modes of experiencing that constitute and expand what it is to be human. Thus the arts, which are currently being marginalised in the school curriculum in many countries, should be recognised as playing an important part of learning experiences along with other modes of learning such as science, language, technology and mathematics. A challenge within art education itself concerns trying to respond effectively to the different ways in which learning encounters are manifested in their outcomes and to the evolving sensibilities of learners in their changing social milieus. This raises the challenge of ethics proposed by Spinoza, the capacity to expand what our bodies and our minds are capable of.

I am not suggesting that art should be viewed as an instrument for learning. It is not. Though a kind of learning may emerge through the experience of art practice or engaging with art, it is more an ontological force of becoming that often involves unlearning. This issue raises the paradoxes of art and education that are made even more entangled and confused by the term art education. In themselves, art and education are generic terms that require unfolding into *actual local practices*. I would suggest that an important effect of art both in terms of its practice and in terms of engaging with it is that it can produce a destabilisation, or what Deleuze and Guattari call a deterritorialisation, that opens up a potential for new ways of seeing, thinking, feeling or making. Such disruptive processes *may* lead to new ways of learning, but not always. This ontological force can often be marginalised or occluded within the schooling or the institutionalising of art education where practice may become instrumentalised, or even homogenised. In such spaces, preconceptions about practice often cast a normative canopy over practice, whereas the great value of art practice is its force to challenge thought to think, to be disobedient, to disturb vision to see, to destroy practice in order to make. Similarly, if we understand education as a process through which individuals engage in building a life, without presuming or pre-ordaining a particular kind of life, then it becomes paradoxical when the latter prospect dominates the purpose of education.

This book can be conceived as a series of connections and meditations through which I explore practices of learning and pedagogic work; connections linking domains of philosophy, pedagogy, art practice and learning. It is not directly concerned with an analysis or comparison of current approaches to learning in the domain of art education, but more with a sense of adventure; a process of exploring in which any fixed coordinates of learning and teaching are relaxed. An adventure in which things and relations are undetermined, where we are confronted with the unexpected or the unforeseen; where we travel beyond knowledge and without established criteria. On such an adventure, thinking, in the words of Deleuze, is viewed as an experimenting, not a judging predicated upon established modes of practice or knowledge. Such thinking raises issues relating to ethics, aesthetics and politics that are grounded in established codes, representations and knowledge that constitute the human, in order to move beyond these into a domain of the non-human through which understanding of becoming human is expanded.

This adventure therefore does not relate to an already constituted 'I' or a 'we' or a 'practice' or 'art', but to a people and practices yet-to-come and to the possibility of collectives or publics yet-to-come. In relation to sites of learning, this adventure questions the recent and current organisation of education in schools in England, the USA and elsewhere, and poses questions about future organisations and pedagogic work in order to forge new connections and modes of living, new possibilities beyond the artifices in which we have come to believe when they fail to respond to or marginalise onto-epistemic and affective differences. But such manoeuvres towards radical change are never straightforward and very difficult to achieve. To inaugurate change beyond established identities and representations, there has to be a firm belief that something positive will emerge even though outcomes are not clear. We require, as Rajchman (2000, p. 7) writes, 'to remain attentive to the unknown knocking at the door'. In making these introductory remarks, I am reminded of a work entitled *Pacific* (1996) by the Japanese artist Yukinori Yanagi. In general terms, the work consists of a large rectilinear grid of small rectangular boxes each with a clear perspex front. Transparent plastic tubes link the boxes. Each box contains a national flag made of synthetic coloured sand. A colony of ants was introduced through a tube at the bottom of the rectilinear structure and proceeded to move through the flag boxes and their inter-connecting tubes. In time, the lines of movement made by the ants defaced or destroyed the flags; they dissolved each national identification and their imaginary boundaries through the lines of migration. An important motivation for this book concerns a questioning of established identities, boundaries, hierarchies, systems and codes of representation that operate in the domain of education and which facilitate but also control and limit our capacities to act, feel and think. The task is to try to think pedagogic work beyond such facilitations and restrictions in order to extend capacities for building a life.

This is not a book, therefore, that discusses the variety of art practices in which students and teachers engage and develop nor does it advocate a new genre of art educational practice. Rather, the book aims to discuss and explore a number of pedagogic sensibilities that emerge from the adventure of pedagogic work in this field. Such sensibilities include ethical, political and aesthetic adventures that lead towards and constitute achievements that are not posited in advance, but which emerge in the struggles of pedagogic work and inquiry. Such adventures may lead to new potentials for becoming and the opening of new worlds of pedagogic practice. These adventures and sensibilities (ethical, political, aesthetic,) do not provide pedagogic work with a prescribed 'method' predicated upon particular identifications, but should be viewed as meditations and experiments that ensue from the relations and experiences of pedagogic work. Learning (and teaching) in this context of experimenting towards a future from an embedded past; towards building a life and modes of co-existence, requires risking possibilities, ways of thinking, seeing and acting where success is not guaranteed (but where failure is a form of learning) that act as lures for the opening up of new experiences. Pedagogic work is therefore fallible. A pedagogical imperative for a teacher when approaching such modes of learning is to heed the advice of Whitehead, mentioned earlier, 'Have a care, here is something that matters'. This *situates* an ethics of inquiry and prioritises the notion of relevance or the adventures of relevance (Savransky 2016) that are undertaken by addressing the question of mattering to each learner's mode of inquiry and the subsequent obligational constraints that emerge for a teacher from such modes and their respective values.

I mentioned above that I would qualify my use of the term *real learning* that I used extensively in an earlier publication. In that book (Atkinson 2011), real learning is conceived as a leap into a new or modified ontological state whose affects and relations produce an expansion of acting and thinking. In this book, I have decided to replace the term (except in Chap. 4), with the notion of *event/s of learning*, where the event is viewed as a multiplicity consisting of what Deleuze and Guattari call virtualities and actualities. That is to say, events of learning arise from a realm of the virtual, of the infinite, what Guattari calls a *chaosmosis*, and they precipitate particular actualisations or phases of consistency according to the evental context. Events of learning are composed of human and non-human, organic and inorganic forces and relations. The notion of the non-human refers to phases of becoming that lie beyond the influence and capture of transcendent framings that already constitute the human. Such events of learning lie in contrast to what we might call normative learning, which can be viewed in terms of realisations of established patterns of possibilities. These ideas will be discussed in more detail in later chapters.

Process and Becoming

I suggest that any exploration of processes of learning and teaching needs to consider how human subjects who undergo such processes might be conceived. Throughout this book, this subject is not understood in essentialist terms, which is to say as an independent and autonomous being existing in a separate objective world. Nor is the subject viewed in terms of a dualism between mind and body or between thinking and feeling. Rather, subjectivity, or subjectivation, the process of forming of a subject, is conceived in relational terms, whereby what we call a subject is viewed as a temporal phase consisting of a number of relational processes in and of a world composed of a series of intensities, thoughts, affects and actions. The notion of 'becoming with and of a world' is central to the process of subjectivation discussed in the book and the process of becoming is conceived as constituted through several registers, including feeling, thinking, attuning or mattering, making, seeing and risking. Becoming with a world is a relational becoming that includes relations between human and non-human actants. In Whitehead's terminology, such relational becoming is called *prehension,* which, in simple terms, refers to a taking account of something or somebody by all participants involved in such a relation. In terms more apposite to Spinoza's (1996) work, such becoming refers to an ability to affect and to be affected. These reciprocal relations of becoming precipitate the process of ontogenesis. The notion of the human subject therefore has to build in the ideas of the inhuman and the more-than-human, which is to say that which lies beyond the human as *is,* to which the process of becoming, as a future oriented process, must be exposed.

Another way of conceiving the subject as a process of becoming that is employed in the book is to view it as a composition of finitude and infinitude. Seamus Heaney alludes to this when he writes:

> And it is that double capacity that we possess as human beings – the capacity to be attracted at one and the same time to the security of what is intimately known and the challenges and entrancements of what is beyond us. (Heaney 2002, p. 48)

This brief quotation seems to capture the territory of pedagogic work and relations with which I am concerned: to try to comprehend and respond effectively to the particular securities, insecurities and relevances of individual learners, their ways of knowing, their capacities for affecting and being affected, their ways of acting, seeing and thinking; whilst also presenting them with learning encounters that extend these capacities.

References

Atkinson, D. (2011). *Art, equality and learning: Pedagogies against the state.* Rotterdam/Boston/Taipei: Sense Publishers.

Ball, S. J. (2009). Privatising education, privatizing education policy, privatizing education research: Network governance and the 'competition state'. *Journal of Education Policy, 24*(1), 83–99.

Buck-Morss, S. (2010). The second time as farce…Historical pragmatics and the untimely present. In C. Douzinas & S. Zizek (Eds.), *The idea of communism* (pp. 67–80). London/New York: Verso.

Buck-Morss, S. (2013). A commonist ethics. In S. Zizek (Ed.), *The idea of communism 2* (pp. 57–75). London/New York: Verso.

Butler, J. (2005). *Giving an account of oneself.* New York: Fordham University Press.

Chalmers, G. F. (1996). *Celebrating pluralism: Art education and cultural diversity.* Los Angeles: Getty Foundation.

Dash, P. (2010). *African Caribbean pupils in art education.* Rotterdam/Boston/Taipei: Sense Publications.

De Sausmaurez, M. (1964). *Basic design: The dynamics of visual form.* London: Studio Vista.

Eisner, E. W. (1988). *The role of discipline based art education in America's schools.* Getty Centre for Education in the Arts.

Freedman, K. (2003). *Teaching visual culture: Curriculum, aesthetics and the social life of art.* New York: Teachers College Press.

Heaney, S. (2002). *Finders keepers, selected prose 1971–2001.* London: Faber and Faber.

Irwin, R. L., & de Cosson, A. (2004). *A/r/tography: Rendering self through arts-based living inquiry.* Vancouver: Pacific Educational Press.

Mason, R. (1995). *Art education and multiculturalism.* Corsham: NSEAD.

Rajchman, J. (2000). *The Deleuze connections.* Cambridge, MA/London: MIT Press.

Savransky, M. (2016). *The adventure of relevance: An ethics of social inquiry.* London: Macmillan.

Spinoza, B. (1996). *Ethics.* London: Penguin.

Tavin, K. (2016). *Angels, ghosts and cannibals: Essays on art education and visual culture.* Helsinki: Aalto University Publications.

Taylor, R. (1986). *Educating for art: Critical response and development.* Harlow: Logman.

Whitehead, A. N. (1968). *Modes of thought.* New York: The Free Press.

CHAPTER 2

Restoring Pedagogic Work to the Incipience and Immanence of Learning: Disobedient Pedagogies

Neo-liberal Agendas in Education: Privatisation and Marketisation

Since the introduction of state systems of education in England, the USA and other countries, two recurring initiatives can be detected; one that is grounded in the need to design an education system that fuels and sustains economic growth and the ability to compete successfully in market economies, and one that is immersed in a more humanist and communal tradition grounded in the notion of a public good. In England and elsewhere, in recent years under consecutive governments, the former project has dominated government policy, a key priority being to educate students in those subjects that will service and maintain economic competitiveness.

In the late 1980s, the government took central control of the curriculum in England and introduced a National Curriculum (5–16 years) for school subjects in which learning targets were established for each year group, accompanied by formalised methods of assessment. The National Curriculum went through several changes throughout the 1990s and into the first decade of the new millennium. The strong emphasis upon the assessment of learning was consolidated and intensified by the introduction of OfSTED (Office for Standards in Education), the government inspection service that conducts regular inspections of schools to assess the quality of learning, teaching and school management. There are severe consequences for teachers, managers and schools if they fall below the required standards.

© The Author(s) 2018
D. Atkinson, *Art, Disobedience, and Ethics*, Education, Psychoanalysis, and Social Transformation, DOI 10.1007/978-3-319-62639-0_2

Primary and secondary students are subject to a constant stream of tests to assess their progress from the age of seven onwards.

Teacher education has followed a similar route whereby teacher training courses (no longer called teacher education) are inspected by OfSTED according to a set of teaching standards, and if the quality of these programmes falls below the expected standard, they can be closed. More recently, the government has opened up a number of training routes for people to train to be a teacher. This has introduced competition into the domain of teacher training, but where competition is engineered by government—in the sense that it controls the number of student allocations available to some routes. From 2010, the government has made a determined effort to move the training of teachers from its more traditional home of university education departments into schools. The universities now play a much smaller part in teacher training than was once the case mainly because government argues that what student teachers require is more practice in schools and less theory from the university. Critical reflections on pedagogy are viewed as unnecessary distractions from real classroom experience.

So to sum up, the knowledge that learners are expected to acquire is laid out by statute and the quality of teaching is inspected according to a set of government standards. In this particular *dispositif* (the power to capture, orient, determine, model and control the behaviours, ways of thinking and speaking of living beings) of education we might say that teachers/teaching and learners/learning as pedagogic subjects and practices are heavily prescribed. The neo-liberal ideology underpinning this didactic and regulated approach to education is grounded in the pursuit of economic ambition and competition. Thus, what are called the STEM subjects (Science, Technology, Mathematics), viewed as essential to achieve this ambition, are given priority and the arts are becoming more marginalised and superfluous, to the extent that the time spent in lower secondary schools doing art has been cut by as much as 50 per cent and in the proposed new English Baccalaureate art has been excluded altogether.

State education in English schools has undergone a rapid move towards marketisation and privatisation. Many secondary and a growing number of primary schools have become Academies, giving them independence from the control of local education authorities so that free-market principles are adopted in their management. Funding for Academies comes directly from government, but also partly from private business or charities, which increases the influence of business on school management. Some Academy chains are run by private companies and therefore managed by those with a background in business rather than teaching or education. Schools have become independent employers; they compete for pupils, parents become consumers, school funding is geared to success rates and teachers' salaries are geared to performance. Advocates of this move towards privatisation and marketisation argue that by introducing competition and business principles of management it reduces what they see as the inefficiency of local education authority management. It is interesting to note the increasing interest of 'big business' to develop fiscal opportunities in the 'education market,' particularly those companies concerned with technology. Those opposed to the intervention of business principles in education argue that such intervention is changing the makeup of the curriculum, where strong emphasis is placed upon the STEM subjects that will equip learners with the knowledge and skills they will require in the world of employment. Consequently less emphasis is placed upon the humanities and the arts. In other words a form of internal segregation emerges where particular forms of knowledge, skills and learning are privileged over others and, by implication, where those learners with an interest in such knowledge and skills become privileged. This is not to imply that the emphasis upon the STEM subjects did not exist before the emergence of a neo-liberal agenda for education. Since the beginning of state education, the sciences, mathematics and language were always viewed as what we might call 'core subjects,' but in England and elsewhere, there was always a provision for the arts and humanities under the guiding principle of a broad and balanced curriculum.

The impact on school management, teaching and learning of today's neo-liberal *dispositif* is a governmentality (Foucault) of individual and school performance, the governing of modes of thought and action towards specific pedagogised identities that respond to the requirements of economic ambition and competition. This results in a highly prescribed conduct of conduct constructed through the signifiers of performance, assessment, progress and achievement, which anticipate known pedagogic subjects (teachers and learners).

In the US context, Elliot Eisner, writing in 2002, makes the point that in such an economist market-driven approach to education where such signifiers dominate and determine the way in which educational institutions function, they colonise working discourses and reconfigure education as praxis. He writes:

What we are now doing is creating an industrial culture in our schools, one whose values are brittle and whose conception of what's important narrow. We flirt with payment by results, we pay practically no attention to the idea that engagement in school can and should provide intrinsic satisfactions, and we exacerbate the importance of extrinsic rewards by creating policies that encourage children to become point collectors. Achievement has triumphed over inquiry. I think our children deserve more.

At university level Henry Giroux (2011) comments:

[T]he pedagogical nature of education [was] viewed by many members of the American public and intellectual classes as central not only to the civic mission of the university [...] but also to the functioning of a just and democratic society.

However under the onslaught of a merciless economic Darwinism and theatre of cruelty that has emerged since the 1980s, the historical legacy of the university as a vital public good no longer fits the revamped discourse of progress in which the end goal is narrowed to individual survival rather than the betterment of society as a whole. In fact, the concept of social progress has all but disappeared amid the ideological discourse of a crude market-driven presentism that has a proclivity for instant gratification, consumption and immediate financial gain. (p. 147)

The effect of the neo-liberal *dispositif* of state education in England, the USA and elsewhere raises an interesting aspect of the perennial debate about education and the commons, often framed by the contentious issue of private versus public education. There are those who believe that private education should be available to those who choose to pay for it and, by extension, is denied to those who cannot afford it. The implication being that private education is of a higher quality than that provided generally by state schools. Others argue vociferously that access to good education should not be determined by income, but that it should be available to all, irrespective of income. However, in the current context of increasing privatisation and marketisation of state education, the principle that education should be free and available to all, that learners should be able to develop their individual interests and potentials—in tandem with those 'necessary' skills and forms of knowledge such as numeracy and literacy (including digital literacy), in order to build a life—becomes rather uncertain and more distant. If some modes of learning, such as the arts, are marginalised or cut from the curriculum, if funding for what we call special educational needs is reduced, then the notion of education as part of the commons becomes questionable in the sense that education becomes a process through which some forms of building a life are privileged over others, and where some may be limited or denied. Even though the principle of income, which facilitates privilege, does not or should not apply to state education, the increasing influence of business upon state education and the wider neo-liberal agenda has created a form of privilege whereby some modes of learning and learners are valued more than others. (This discussion does not take account of other forms of privilege, as explored by Bourdieu and others, that relate to the social/domestic background cultures in which learners are situated and which, they argue, can influence attitudes to and capacities for learning.)

In the more global context of education, the reading and justification of education through the register of economic ambition and competition is a pervasive image of thought (Deleuze) that has developed international proportions. Economies of performance in the form of statutory assessments (SATS), effectiveness and improvement programmes, inspection regimes, audits and league tables, as well as the marketisation of schools, have hegemonised educational contexts from the crèche to the university (Apple 2005; Stronach 2010). The general effect and outcome of such economies has been to create a normalising and homogenising series of educational practices to constitute teaching and learning, as well as their respective objects, teachers and learners. The main value of a school (as well as teacher quality) is drawn according to a register of academic performance and results (DfE 2013, 2014) while other educational/pedagogical values, in relative terms, tend to be sidelined. The key criterion for effective teaching and a successful school is the examination pass ratio. The effect is to reduce any discussion of pedagogy to the margins simply because it is clear what good teaching is.

In England competition between schools in terms of examination results is crystallised in the form of a national league table, and, on an international scale, national examination results are subjected to similar hierarchical statistics, with little or no reference to mediating national or social contextual factors. As Stronach wryly suggests, we now have an Olympic Games of educational performance. 'TIMSS [has become] the Olympic Games of international educational assessment' (p. 2), where 'the game appears to be the same for all' (p. 22, see also MacAloon 1984). Stronach explores the contrast, but also the unavoidable, necessary imbrications and tensions between economies of performance and ecologies of practice. These terms have some resonance with the notions of normative learning and local curations of practice I have used (Atkinson 2011); they refer to the difference between relevance, histories, haecceities, memories, ideals and values of each teacher's and learner's practice (ecologies) that tend to be occluded by economies of performance that emphasise assessment and targets, and the specific routes to attain these. There are those who subscribe to such economies, who believe the rigid disciplinary structure of programmes of study, assessment and performance indicators provide teaching and learning with a clear pedagogical mandate. There are others who feel uneasy, frustrated or 'deprofessionalised,' perhaps inauthentic, but who are able to deal with the tensions. There are some who are starved of intellectual curiosity within the current economies of performance and who welcome communal opportunities to debate and research their experiences of pedagogic work. This last point is expressed frequently by Master's students who are engaged in a critical reflection of their professional context. But there are always unavoidable tensions between the ontogenesis of professional ecologies of practice and the politics of performance indicators.

This book challenges the neo-liberal *dispositif* of education and its prescriptive agenda on a number of levels. In contrast to the notion of prescribed pedagogised identities that are required to service the needs of economic ambition and competition and which are held in place by controlled curricula, assessment and inspection regimes, it advocates a principle of teachers and learners *yet-to-arrive*. This principle advocates a more uncertain pedagogical adventure characterised by novel modes of engagement and relevance that emphasise a subject-yet-to-come and where the notion of the not-known is immanent to such adventures. In this opening chapter, the tension between these two modes of pedagogical existence is illustrated through a discussion of a contemporary art project entitled *Rogue Game*.

In the domain of art in education, the book considers events of learning in relation to the *force of art* to precipitate ontogenesis: new ways of seeing, thinking and making and the creation of new worlds. The book is therefore advocating an alternative approach to pedagogic work than that which is driven by economies of performance, one that is grounded in subjects-yet-to-come, which in turn raises issues of politics, ethics and aesthetics of pedagogy. Some of these issues were raised in an earlier book (Atkinson 2011), in which I developed the notion of pedagogies against the state as a way of trying to reflect upon the demands of pedagogic work where learning is viewed in less predictable and contingent terms.

RESTORING PEDAGOGIC WORK TO THE INCIPIENCE AND IMMANENCE OF LEARNING

What I want to do in this opening chapter is to try to think beyond the domination of education by prescribed pathways and outcomes in order to consider the *eventfulness of learning* through art practices and their different lines of becoming. The term 'art education' is indeed a questionable notion when taking on board the idea of the force of art (Ziarek 2004), which travels beyond established conceptions of art and its practice. I will offer an alternative approach to knowledge, learning and teaching in art education, an approach that is more uncertain, less prescribed, grounded in the notions of the not-known and subjects-yet-to-come. Pedagogical work is therefore not conceived as a teleology of prescribed routes and end points (a transcendent framing), but more in terms of an adventure responding to *the immanence of local events of encounter*. An adventure that tries to respond effectively to the different ways in which learners learn and which may expand our understanding of what learning is and what art practice is. In Walter Benjamin's sense, this may constitute a *mutual translation* in which the teacher's reaching out to the learner's form of expression can change the teacher's framework of understanding. Pedagogical work in this mode, being less certain than the former prescriptive mode and which tries to remain open to the immanence of each learner's potentialities, often involves *becoming undone* on the part of the teacher and then trying to learn new ways of relating to learners and their ways of learning. The event of becoming undone introduces the issue of ethics, which will be discussed throughout this book and particularly in Chaps. 6 and 10. Rather than approaching learning and teaching with a fixed set of criteria that constitute these processes, I am advocating a relaxation of prescription and an approach to pedagogic work characterised by the phrase *beyond knowledge and without criteria*. In such moments what a learner produces can actually expand our understanding of both art and learning. This echoes the well-known aphorism by Paul Klee: 'Art does not reproduce the visible but makes visible.'

I am interested in how learners, through their local generative pathways of events of learning, which involve a shift into new or modified ontological, epistemological and affective states, learning that defines a problem of existence and appearance, *make visible* and how, as teachers, we respond to this making visible and how this making can expand our understanding of learning and of art practice. In the words of Ingold (2015) this pedagogic work involves a *joining with* learners 'in an on-going exploration of what the possibilities and potentials of learning might be (157).' This notion of *joining with* the worlds of individual lines of becoming or in Nancy's (2000) terms of *being-with*, I would argue, changes the view of pedagogy away from advocating the acquisition of prescribed knowledge and skills towards teachers *developing ways of living attentively with learners* and thereby facilitating the continuous weaving of their mutual lines of life. To live attentively to these different lines of learning, I argue, is to hold in abeyance the force of prescriptive pedagogies and their transcendent criteria and restore pedagogic work to the incipience and immanence of learning. So rather than seeing pedagogic work as the passing on of fixed bodies of knowledge, it would be more concerned with creating the conditions for events of learning to be set in motion which lead to transformation and the invention of new worlds. This constitutes an ethico-political as well as an ethico-aesthetic project and one that lies at the heart of my concern (Shaviro 2014, pp. 24–26).

I am thinking of ethics, politics and aesthetics in relation to the project of education as a process of building a life. This process can be viewed as a process of *transduction* (Simondon) rather than an *induction* to prescribed knowledge. Transduction in Simondon is equivalent to the process of individuation (or ontogenesis). It is characterised by an initial genetic element (like the formation of a crystal in physical individuations), a catalytic nuclei (Guattari 2006, p. 18), or a generative event that propagates across a domain—in this case a human domain—and in the process the event trans-forms or reconfigures the domain. Here, we might say that the human becomes exposed to the non-human, to unknown vistas and ways of becoming that might take us beyond the confines of the human. So we can think of what I have called events of learning, referring to a shift into new or modified onto-epistemic phases, not simply as a reconfiguration of previous experiences, but as a process of transformation, the genesis of a new world or reality whereby previous experiences and life become transformed. This transductive process, I would argue, involves an indissol-ubility of knowing (not knowledge), ethics and aesthetics, as intimated in the notion of the forming of new worlds, or the process of building a life.

Susan Buck-Morss (2010, p. 77), argues that a persistent dilemma confronts institutionalised education systems; the collision of tradition with the new, 'the truly new, that none of our knowledge traditions has anticipated (Ibid. p. 77),' or put in Nietzsche's terminology, the *untimelines* of the present. The tendency to force the new into the 'Procrustean bed of tradition' thus destroys its global newness and potential (its truth in Badiou's terminology or its immanence in Deleuze's terms) and this constitutes, for her, a period of political danger. I repeat the quote from my Introduction:

> There is a blindness to institutionalised education that passes down the authority of tradition, a mental timidity, born of privilege or just plain laziness, that cloaks itself in the heavy bombast of cultural heritage and historic preservation. It generates enormous resistance to trespassing conceptual boundaries or exceeding the limits of present imagination, rewarding instead the virtues of scholastic diligence, disciplinary professionalism and elitist erudition, all escape routes from the pragmatic necessity of confronting the new. Indeed extreme discomfort is caused by the truly new, the truly 'contemporary', that which Nietzsche called the 'untimely' – those aspects of the present moment that simply do not fit our established traditions or modes of understanding.

This book constitutes an attempt to reflect upon the *untimely* in pedagogical work and in learning encounters—those moments in which a teacher is confronted with a learner's practice that does not fit the former's parameters of practice and understanding, those moments in which a learner breaks new ground in ways of seeing, thinking or making. In many ways this throws up a paradox in that, generally speaking, institutional policies of education, curriculum content and structure, teaching programmes, assessment procedures tend to demand homogeneity, linearity: clearly planned routes or aims for learning; whereas the existential territories of events of learning or the untimely of learning refer to heterogeneous local contingent processes. The former are often blind to the latter.

ART AND LEARNING, EVENTS OF BECOMING

I have already mentioned the contrast between transcendent frameworks that structure and determine learning and teaching and the immanent processes of local learning practices. This difference can be conceived in terms of the difference between hylomorphic modes of pedagogic practice and more processual modes. Hylomorphism refers to the imposition of form on matter as when, for example, particular modes of learning or teaching are imposed upon learners or teachers to determine their conduct. In contrast, trying to respond to the immanence of learning in its own terms relates to a more processual pedagogic practice. In the field of moral practice, moral judgements function according to hylomorphic principles when they are used to determine how to act. The difference between moral codes and ethics as understood in this book is that a moral perspective asks what should be done and refers back to established codes, whereas ethics considers in each particular situation what it is possible to do. The link between transcendent framings and hylomorphism becomes evident.

In the field of art education in schools and elsewhere, we can detect traces of hylomorphism and transcendent framings when we consider curriculum or course content, teaching methodologies and assessment practices. This can range from teaching and assessing particular techniques to viewing a student's practice through the lens of a favoured approach to practice. It is not easy to put such practical or conceptual 'influences' aside in pedagogical work, for how else, some would argue, are we to proceed without the guidance of established modes of practice?

A wider historical overview illustrates the broadening conceptions and practices of art education in schools, as it has developed a number of genres according to a range of theoretical and practical influences and innovations. A similar claim can be made for the development and evolution of art school practices. I will not go into detail here but merely mention these influential developments in school art education to which I referred in my Introduction. These include the psychological and developmental explorations of children's art work, investigations of the language of art and the dynamics of visual form, a concern for the expressive force of art, advocacy for the critical, creative and aesthetically informed learner, the development of multicultural and inter-cultural art education and the pursuit of visual culture art education. These genres of art education in schools serve different interests and exert different pressures upon pedagogical practices and the production of teachers and learners. They constitute specific ideological formulations of art education that effect a particular material production of practice and subjectivity. Put another way, each of these educational discourses encouraged the formation of new teaching and learning publics in their field. They produced different pedagogising forces and their respective identities. These art education programmes do not claim to identify the sole purpose of art education, but extend its compass as a consequence of responding to changing socio-cultural and historical factors, which 'at the time' were considered to be pedagogically important and relevant. Many of these genres presuppose traditional notions of the art object and technical skill, as well as ideas of self-expression...notions that have become redundant in more contemporary participatory or inter-active art practices.

My central point is that these historical developments each generated their respective criteria for practice, that is to say frameworks according to which learning and practice are conceived. Put another way, each of these developments generate transcendent operators according to which teaching and learning are understood, and I think it is important to develop a constant vigilance upon their effects and affects on pedagogical work.

I want to consider a kind of *pedagogical inversion* to these transcendent framings so that rather than viewing art education, learning and teaching in the field through such established lenses that 'pedagogise' through their epistemological frameworks, I want to soften these lenses and focus on the immanence of learning; to adopt a pedagogical position which views learning in terms of how the contents of this vital process *matter* for a learner. What I am attempting therefore is not to view learning and teaching by circumscribing these processes within established parameters (though this is very difficult to avoid) but to try to work with the immanence of learning events—a task which may expand our frameworks of understanding what learning, teaching and art practice can become.

Put another way, how does a learning encounter matter for a learner and how is this manifested differently through the force of art? Can we relax the transcendence of tradition, or put another way, can we be eternally vigilant to its power of control? Is this a form of necessary disobedience? I use the term, force of art, to refer to a deeply affective force particular to art's event that precipitates ontogenetic potentials for building a life.

What I am proposing then is to relax prescribed categories of and propositions about art education, to subdue their ideological framing and try to view the processes of practice in which learners engage as 'acategorical' events (which of course is another ideological framing) that is to say as 'evental' practices whose singularity cannot be categorised in any terms but their own. I am using the term singularity to refer to that which is singular, that which differs from the regular. So the aim is not to view these singular events according to already established criteria, though this is difficult to avoid, but to try to approach them *without criteria*. This suggests that the 'thisness' of art practice, its internal resonance, is a coherent 'as-it-is' event that has the potential to extend how we conceive art and learning; a singular event that has universal implications. We are therefore not concerned with prescribed subjects of teaching and learning, but with subjects-yet-to-come.

I will now turn to the context of art and learning and consider the incipience of learning, immanence and the not-known through the notions of the force of art and poietic materialism, which will be dealt with in more detail in subsequent chapters, and then offer some initial thoughts regarding the kind of pedagogies or perhaps anti-pedagogies that might be commensurate with the idea of learning grounded in the not-known and subjects-yet-to-come. These are pedagogies I have termed pedagogies against the state, but which also embrace pedagogies of encounter, pedagogies of relevance and negotiation.

I have often referred to a couple of visual practices to illustrate the themes with which I am concerned, and at the risk of repetition, I will use them here. I think they are relevant to think about learning in terms of encounters, lines of becoming, and the task of building a life. The first is a video of a young boy painting and the second is an art project called *Rogue Game*. Both these practices illustrate for me the force of art, a vital force of inventive transformation which is resistant to the capture of identity, though its outcomes frequently are not.

Luca Painting

Some years ago I came across a video of a young boy called Luca (3 years) engaged in painting, and I referred to this video in a previous book (Atkinson 2011). Briefly Luca engages in a series of painting processes that involve a number of inventive phases flowing together. He paints a storm, a windmill, a train going backwards and forwards and then coming to a dead end and crashing. He paints around his hand, makes hand prints and then paints his hand and forearm. As the painting continues we witness periods of sustained concentration as well as glimpses of surprise, fascination and uncertainty. The temporality of Luca's practice as it proceeds seems to involve what Susan Buck-Morss (2013) calls a *pragmatics of the suddenly possible* (in contrast to a pragmatics of inscription), a very powerful phrase I think, which has implications for the practice, ethics, aesthetics and politics of pedagogic work. Luca passes through a series of little events of real learning, little epiphanies that simply evolve with no clear sense of direction or end point. It is as though there is no commanding plan-leading action, but rather an *aspirant imagination* (Ingold 2015) feeling a way forward and improvising a pathway through an as yet unformed world. It might be described as an *undergoing of action in relation*, where there is no separation between the actants but a kind of *correspondence* of body movements, imaginings, paint, brush, paper; a becoming-with, a generation and a dis-solution, a process on the edge of the not-yet-known. We might think of the flow of events of learning as being on the edge of time, as consisting of a tension between that which exists and that which-is-yet-to-arrive.

Another way of thinking about this complex heterogeneity is through the notion of multiplicity used by Deleuze and Guattari. For them a multiplicity does not denote a set of multiple entities or relations, but an open and infinite process that involves actualities and virtualities with ever-expanding potentials. Put another way, it suggests a process not concerned with an ontology of *what is*, or a collection of *what is's*, but an ontogenesis of becomings, a stream of 'and-and-ands.' It refers to an immanence of life, its intensities and relations rather than a series of identities. If we transfer such events of learning into the context of pedagogic work, then pedagog-ical relations can be viewed as a series of 'becoming-withs' that develop contingent choreographies.

This video, which has resonance with the wider domain of art practices in schools and other institutions, raises for me the issue of how such practices become captured and pedagogised by curriculum and assessment dis-courses, what we might call transcendent operators or transcendent enun-ciators, that regulate, orient and control such practices and turn them into pedagogised objects. Such capture seems to involve an unconscious desire to involve a transformation of the heuristics of the different lines and times of learning into algorithms of audit.

These transcendent operators may overlook or ignore ways of conceiv-ing, ways of making, ways of seeing that are not commensurate to them but which nevertheless constitute events of learning for the child or student. We might therefore think of learning processes in terms of *local correspondences* (becoming-with, a mutual shaping) whose relevance functions at different speeds and intensities according to how things matter for a learner. Learn-ing as a *becoming-with-correspondence*, sometimes aberrant, that unsettles what is expected.

A pragmatics of the suddenly possible requires that we relax the force of the transcendence of external criteria in order to pay close attention to the immanence and incipience of learning and its expressions, which could be occluded if we allow transcendent forms to dominate, and sometimes we do not recognise when this is happening. I need to make a distinction between external forms of transcendence, such as assessment criteria or established conceptions of practice, and those that emerge from the imma-nence of practice that can be conceived as forms of *necessary transcendence*.

These external forms can be conceived in Deleuzian terms as molar cate-gories, which can frequently occlude the myriad of minor becomings that constitute local learning processes. It seems to be a matter of overcoming the blindness of transcendent operators that constitute educational praxis in the form of assessment, teaching methodologies, educational aims that define the purpose of education and so on, *to the untimeliness of learning and its potential*. If this blindness is to be averted, the teacher needs to become a *nomadic operator*, a navigator of places and territories that form and in-form local processes of learning whilst also remaining eternally vigilant towards those transcendent operators that capture and channel pedagogic strategies. Such nomadic practice does not assume or prescribe particular kinds of learners (or teachers), but works from an expectation of developing more effective learners (and teachers) through engaging with the local incipience and relevance of each learner's mode of learning.

ROGUE GAME

The only thing that is given to us and that *is* when there is human life *is the having to make it...Life is a task.* (Ortega y Gasset 1941, p. 200)

Life and learning can be conceived as an ongoing series of encounters. There are times when, for example, in a classroom when a learner produces something, a way of thinking, seeing or making, that fall beyond a teacher's framework of understanding. I remember experiencing such events partic-ularly when confronted with drawings that I found difficult to comprehend. The pedagogical question then is 'how do I proceed?'

The art project *Rogue Game* that I came across in about 2010 seems to me to deal precisely with this question, but in an entirely different relational context. For me *Rogue Game* was a case of art forcing thought to think as it made me think about the issue of how to proceed when confronted with mystery in classrooms or other social situations. *Rogue Game* is organised by the Turkish artist Can Altay in collaboration with Sophie Warren, Jonathan Mosley from Bristol and Emily Pethick from London. It has already gone through four iterations. Altay has produced a number of works dealing with interventions in the everyday spatial architectures and practices of cities in Turkey and elsewhere. Dwelling on the notion of a pragmatics of the suddenly possible, *Rogue Game* raises for me a number of issues including the tensionalities between the known and the not-known, identity, the tactics of becoming-with, Spinoza's notion, which I will discuss in the

Fig. 2.1 *Rogue Game* (With kind permission from Sophie Warren and Jonathan Mosley in association with Can Altay)

next chapter, alluding to the idea that we do not know what actions a body is capable of, or what thoughts are capable of being thought.

The work takes place in a sports centre, outside area or a gallery, where the markings that designate different games such as badminton, basketball or five-a-side soccer overlap. Participants for three or four games are asked to play their respective game simultaneously on the overlapping game areas. They have to negotiate playing their game while trying to manage interruptions and interventions from the other games that inevitably invade their territory, this management of disruption constitutes the *Rogue Game* (Fig. 2.1).

Each game abides by its code or rules of practice through which player identities are constituted. Each game is prescribed by a designated playing area that regulates the space of play. In the *Rogue Game*, however, players also need to respond to the intermittent disruptions from other games. Thus, in the *Rogue Game*, players' identities are less well defined, there are no rules or conventions. Players' identities become reconfigured according to the new relationalities and tactics that emerge as the *Rogue*

Game develops. The *Rogue Game* forces constant reterritorialisings of practice; it involves collisions and negotiations of space and rules, whereby the games interweave. It is as though new rhythms of play emerge and reconfigure, and this makes it possible to view the playing area according to new horizons of playing together. As Can Altay (2015, p. 208), states, '*Rogue Game* posits the struggle of a "social body" within a set of boundaries that are being challenged.'

Because the *Rogue Game* has no rules that pre-constitute relations between players, we are therefore encouraged to consider the 'thisness' of such relations and their potential outcomes. Such relations are therefore viewed as intra-active (Barad 2007), a process whereby bodies and strategies become constituted in the *thisness* of relation in contrast to pre-established identities or codes. Here *intra-action* contrasts with *inter-action* in that the latter involves pre-constituted entities that come together to inter-act. The intra-active nature of *Rogue Game* draws our attention to the continual presence of a functioning disequilibrium or metastability.

In chemistry and physics, the notion of metastability refers to a physical state of stability that can be destabilised by small changes or disturbances. In general terms, metastability relates to states of tension that, given the right kind of push or disturbance, can unleash potential energy that creates a transformation. So we can think of individuals in terms of relational processes existing in their particular milieus as metastable states containing potential energies that may be discharged given the right kind of push or disturbance.

Because there are no established tactics informing practice in the *Rogue Game*, its manoeuvres are informed by relations-in-transition and a thinking-in-action (*phronesis*) that denotes a knowing-how and a knowing-when. In the *Rogue Game* the players have to continue to play, to individuate constantly within their social milieu, which also constantly individuates. Thus, to be a player in the milieu of the *Rogue Game* is to learn how to become in a rather uncertain world of becoming, where individual (psychic) and social becomings are entwined, where the relations between 'I' and 'we' are precarious and constantly being renegotiated, but also where the horizons of cohabitation are expanded.

DISJUNCTIVE SYNTHESES

Rogue Game illustrates the tensionalities between practices of the known and the not-known. I am using it to draw analogies with such tensionalities in practices of teaching and learning, where established forms of address, forms of knowledge, rituals of practice and theories of learning constitute pedagogical 'knowns' and where unexpected responses from learners, mis-alignments between a teacher's expectations and what actually happens, the thisness or singularities of learning and their explosive ontogenetic character constitute the 'not-known,' where practice runs counter to received wisdom, where practice is, in Nietzsche's terms, 'untimely,' travelling on a path with no clear destination, and where practice and its outcomes can appear as disobedient.

The pedagogical aspect of *Rogue Game* concerning its dissensual dynamics (Ranciere), whereby heterogeneous games collide in the same space, encourages us to reflect upon the architectures, divisions, regulations and boundaries of pedagogical spaces, to consider the 'rules and relations of existence' that regulate and legitimate particular epistemologies and ontologies. In education the 'games' or *dispositifs*, of subject discourses and practices and their specific organisation and regulation of knowledge can be contrasted with the collection of heterogeneous ontological worlds of students and their respective ways of thinking, feeling, seeing and doing. The homogeneous organisation of knowledge and curriculum content can be contrasted with the heterogeneity of the living realities of students.

We tend to think of the temporality of the classroom in homogeneous terms…the art practices of children or students taking place in the same time. But really, this teaching-learning context consists more of a heterogeneity, a disjunctive synthesis of different times of living and their different lines of becoming, each on the edge of time. How does a teacher cope with the complex diversity of this disjunctive synthesis?

Returning to Buck-Morss's phrase *the pragmatics of the suddenly possible* and applying it to pedagogical work and processes of learning, we might say that processes of learning and art practice are, in a nutshell, concerned with *the politics, ethics and aesthetics of the suddenly possible.* How might we consider this idea in relation to pedagogic work and learning? What might a pedagogy of the suddenly possible look like? Is this a pedagogy of precarity?

Summarising briefly what has been discussed so far, I have described the political background and current neo-liberal agenda for education operating in many countries, an agenda driven by prescribed approaches to teaching and learning and teacher education. I have also mentioned historical developments in art education and their particular pedagogical agendas, which have expanded its field and modes of practice and established new parameters according to which practice and outcomes are understood.

In contrast to the notion of prescribed pedagogies that tend to presuppose what teaching and learning are, I introduced a pedagogical reversal through which a key question is how does a learning encounter matter for a learner and how does a teacher respond effectively to this? I used the example of *Rogue Game* as a device for thinking about the idea of a pragmatics of the suddenly possible, when, for example, in pedagogical work, we become undone by what confronts us. How can we respond to the unexpected, the appearance of something new? Here pedagogical work is viewed as an adventure continually evolving as it responds to the different affects and potentials of becoming, where the processes and outcomes of a learners practice sometimes force us to think and extend our practice. In such moments of becoming undone, it seems that pedagogical work requires a kind of *disobedience* towards the parameters of practice and thought that hold us.

THE FORCE OF ART, POIETIC MATERIALISM AND INTRA-ACTION

What is this force of art? Put briefly, it is a deeply *affective* force, particular to art's event that precipitates ontogenetic potentials for evolving what it is to be human in its various relationalities. It generates new ways of making, seeing, thinking and feeling. This force, it seems to me, is prior to its capture or application by various critical perspectives, motives or agendas. Though these may initiate and propel art practice, they do not prescribe or control its force, which has the potential to pass beyond them and open up worlds that become possible as the work unfolds, but which, beforehand, were 'unknown.' The force of art, like the evental force of learning, is restless, inventive and experimental, and has the potential to recompose our lives. The *Rogue Game* interrupts the space of prescription and identity and allows us to contemplate new potentials for becoming, from prescribed to contingent collectives or communities. It provides a momentum for critique coupled with invention, a space reminiscent of what the Greek word *kairos* suggests: a temporal point of invention and innovation, an opportune moment, where being is endlessly constructed. The force of art has ontogenetic potential and so, in relation to thinking, it is not a case of thought coming to think art but of *art forcing thought to think*. We might think of the affective force of art in terms of a *poietic materialism*, where the notion of poiesis refers to the process of appearing, the appearing of new possibilities for making, seeing, thinking, feeling.

KAREN BARAD, INTRA-ACTION AND INTRA-RELATION

Many in the fields of social enquiry, including educational research and philosophy, have taken up the work of Karen Barad on the notions of intra-action and intra-relation. These notions have some resonance with the *Rogue Game* and its constant iterations of practice. In relation to an ethics and aesthetics of pedagogical work and practice, her formulations on what she terms *onto-epistem-ology* have some profound implications, which I want to mention briefly before finally offering some thoughts about what might be called disobedient pedagogies, discussed more fully in Chap. 9. Barad (2003, p. 829) writes:

> There is an important sense in which practices of knowing cannot be fully claimed as human practices, not simply because we use non-human elements in our practices but because knowing is a matter of part of the world making itself intelligible to another part. Practices of knowing and being are not isolatable, but rather they are mutually implicated (*indissolubility of ethics and knowing*). We do not obtain knowledge by standing outside of the world; we know because "we" are *of* the world. We are part of the world in its differential becoming. The separation of epistemology from ontology is a reverberation of a metaphysics that assumes an inherent difference between human and non-human, subject and object, mind and body, matter and discourse. *Onto-epistem-ology* – the study of practices of knowing in being – is probably a better way to think about the kind of understandings that are needed to come to terms with how specific intra-actions matter (my italics in brackets).

The idea of 'part of the world making itself intelligible to another,' reminiscent of the cosmology of Alfred North Whitehead that will be discussed in Chap. 5, has powerful implications for learning in that it is concerned with the specific onto-epistemic events of learning, their composition and their correspondences that include human and non-human actants. Here we are confronted not with a world of separate entities that inter-act but a world of processes of folding, unfolding and refolding that produce differential becomings. Furthermore I want to say that such onto-epistemic events are indissoluble from ethics in the sense that knowing forges new ways of being/becoming, of building a life.

The complexities of Barad's work are formidable and my grasp is limited, but I want to mention some key concepts. As already mentioned in the discussion of *Rogue Game*, the term *intra-action* is distinct from inter-action and in one sense this difference is indicative of Barad's metaphysics, which in a nutshell is a metaphysics of relation and process. For Barad, similar to Whitehead, Deleuze and others, we do not live in a world of separately inter-relating or inter-acting entities, but in a world of intra-acting and intra-relating processes. Intra-action invokes a radical shift in the meaning of causality, in that the relational process of intra-actions is agential, it actually produces iterations of determinate boundaries, properties and meanings.

We usually think of a learning encounter as a series of inter-actions between a learner and the particular focus of learning. In art practice, for example, we tend to think in terms of a separation between a maker, the subject matter of practice and the means or materials for accomplishing this practice, (over and above the separations of mind and body, knower and known). These are established conventions and criteria (transcendent framings) through which we comprehend and determine practice as well as the practice of assessment. But in Barad's notion of intra-action, we have to think of a learning encounter as a specific *phenomenon* consisting of a series of ongoing intra-relations, composed of specific material engagements of human and non-human processes within a specific phenomenal space *prior to any differentiation* between learner, materials, bodies and so on. The apparatus of assessment, for example, that makes such differentiations—in the form of a discursive-material practice—is therefore not to be viewed as an external device (hylomorphic discourse) that measures pre-existing entities, such as the ability of a learner or teacher for example, but is to be viewed as a *material performance* that *produces* the very construction of ability. In Barad's metaphysics, humans are not independent entities with inherent properties, but relational processes that enable particular material (re) configurations of the world whose boundaries, properties and meaning are constantly shifting (stabilising and destabilising) thus, according to Barad, enabling 'specific material changes in what it means to be human' (Ibid, p. 820).

A material practice of learning through making a drawing enables particular material (re)configurations of the world whose boundaries, properties and meaning are constantly shifting (stabilising and destabilising), thus enabling specific material changes in what it means to make a drawing. The process of mattering through making a drawing is thus an intra-active becoming or, in other words, a continual iterative performance. In the world of intra-action agency is not something which is attributable to subjects or objects, but to a series of ongoing relational processes that (re) configure boundaries and meaning that in turn can 'contest and rework what matters and what is excluded from mattering' (Ibid, p. 827), what is relevant or becomes relevant in particular contexts of practice.

The pedagogical imperative therefore is to initiate learning encounters, in the museum, in the school, in the university and other sites that encourage learners to ask questions and formulate their ways of learning and the materialisation of their world in this world—to become disobedient learners—in the sense of being encouraged to go beyond what might be expected. This is an ethical, epistemological, ontological and political process, but it is more than that, the materialising of new worlds by learners is fundamentally an aesthetic process, a process of creativity and invention. And as teachers, working alongside and witnessing such new materialisations, our own understanding of learning and practice is expanded.

WHAT KIND OF PEDAGOGIES DO WE REQUIRE THAT CAN RESPOND TO THE ITERATIONS OF BECOMING?

Does my very limited presentation of Barad's work, to which I will return in Chap. 6, offer us any insights for extending our ideas and practices concerned with learning and teaching in art education? Can we begin to think pedagogic work beyond the established and prescriptive entities of teacher, learner, knowledge, art practice and so on, which tend to impose a form of *onto-epistemic invalidation* on those ways of knowing a learner evolves from his or her experiential relations and which are different or at odds with official or dominant knowledge forms. Can we engage with a local or vernacular intra-active scenario of pedagogic work that puts such categories aside? What might this look like? What kind of pedagogies might we need?

We might adopt some initial guiding, but not absolute principles: (1) to set up *learning encounters* rather than prescribed pathways of learning; (2) to work *attentively* with learners and the relevance of their ways of learning; (3) not to allow transcendent enunciators (criteria, established knowledge) to dominate how we respond; (4) to be alive to the unexpected.

A few years ago I considered the notion of *pedagogies against the state* as a way of trying to think about more effective, responsive and relevant approaches to each learner's state of learning, as well as the wider episte-mological and political states that impact upon the former. Thus, the term 'state,' as I used it, is ambivalent; it refers to local ontological states of learning, the epistemological state of bodies of knowledge that constitute the curriculum and the political state of government educational policy. Pedagogies against the state is therefore a call for pedagogies that work against themselves; anti-pedagogies or disobedient pedagogies, in that they cannot afford to become captured by particular transcendent values and modes of practice, or particular approaches to learning and teaching, but are open to embracing the different ways in which students learn and teachers teach. This is particularly important in a world where the sensibilities that learners are evolving may be incommensurate to those of their teachers. One outcome of adopting a disobedient pedagogy is that by viewing learning as an onto-epistemic event that can open new vistas and potentials, there is an obligation to expand our grasp of what learning and teaching *are* or can become. We might then extend Barad's term *onto-epistem-ology* to integrate an ethical dimension, an *ethico-onto-epistem-ology,* which of course is a bit of a mouthful. And the outcome of this *ethico-onto-epistem-ology*—the study of relevance in practices of learning and becom-ing—is a new or modified aesthetic phase. I am using the word aesthetics to denote the vital creative forming of processes of becoming.

In making this claim for an ethical imperative for pedagogical work, I am suggesting that 'ethics' does not refer to established codes of conduct or ways of thinking, but to the struggle to formulate ways of going on when we find ourselves, in Butler's terms, 'becoming undone' where, in a pedagogical encounter, for example, there is no clear pathway ahead, but where there is a need to respond with responsibility. Ethics is therefore indissoluble from *knowing* (not knowledge) in its iterative intra-actings. Butler (2005) writes:

> Perhaps most importantly, we must recognize that ethics requires us to risk ourselves precisely at moments of unknowingness, when what forms us diverges from what lies before us, when our willingness to become undone in relation to others constitutes our chance of becoming human. To become undone by another is a primary necessity, an anguish to be sure, but also a chance – to be addressed, claimed, bound to what is not me, but also to be moved, to be prompted to act, to address myself elsewhere, and so to vacate the self-sufficient "I" as a kind of possession. If we speak and try to give an account from this place, we will not be irresponsible, or, if we are, we will surely be forgiven. (p. 136)

To add an important rejoinder, the 'chance of becoming human' seems to me to inaugurate a 'becoming more than human,' what Deleuze and Guattari would perhaps state as 'becoming other.' That is to say, it is a chance to pass beyond how we understand what it is to be human, to pass beyond anthropocentrism and beyond anthropomorphism.

It is through the encounter of 'becoming undone' that the pedagogic parameters of a teacher may be disturbed sufficiently so as to 'make visible' forms of learning and art practice previously not recognised as such. Equally, for a learner, the challenge of becoming undone during a learning encounter may release potentials for inventing new ways of making and thinking, but this process is likely to require the attentive support of the teacher. Such encounters then are not grounded in an idea of prescribed pedagogised subjects (learners or teachers) but in the notion of subjects-yet-to-come or a that-which-is-not-yet—becomings on the edge of existing. Such encounters involve a virtual on the verge of being actualised.

What we need then are pedagogies that are open to the thisness of real learning, pedagogies that can be fed and nourished by a pragmatics and ethics of the suddenly possible (the unexpected). Such pedagogies would then be pedagogies of the event, pedagogies against the state, disobedient pedagogies, in their particular places of practice.

The notion of disobedient pedagogies, which will be discussed more fully in Chap. 9, relates to an advocacy for those pedagogies that do not antic-ipate a prescribed onto-epistemic subject (teacher or learner), which in turn invokes an onto-epistemic invalidation of those practices of learning or teaching that do not fit the prescription. In the neo-liberal agenda for education, which I have already mentioned, the pedagogical subject of prescribed pedagogies is conceived almost completely in terms of produc-tivity relating to economic ambition. Within this specific onto-epistemic prescription of learning and teaching, art practice tends to register little significance and is therefore viewed as superfluous to requirements—hence the proposal to exclude art in secondary schools from the proposed English Baccalaureate. In this context art education faces a struggle for survival.

Disobedient pedagogies in contrast to those prescribed by government adopt the Spinozan notion that we do not really know what a body is capable of or what thoughts are capable of being thought, coupled with the notion of a pragmatics and ethics of the suddenly possible. Such a pedagogical stance when confronting disobedient objects or aberrant ways of learning/practising may open up new possibilities for practice and new ways of understanding learning, new ways of understanding art. It seems important therefore to ask, for whom is the practice of learning relevant? Is it the learner, the teacher, the government? Each of these implies different agenda. This negotiation of relevance or the morphology of relevance is important in asking how something matters for a learner. Different agendas assume different ontological, epistemological, ethical and political grounds, and different kinds of knowledge.

I will conclude this Introduction with a very brief description of a workshop with primary student teachers, which has a gentle but disobedient nature in relation to the standards of teacher competence that govern and regulate teacher training in England. The workshop was organised by my colleague John Johnston at Goldsmiths University. At the beginning of their year of training the students were asked to describe their backgrounds and their reasons for wanting to become teachers to their student colleagues. This involved a process of communal story telling that opened up a process of mutual learning, of sharing values, aspirations and anxieties relating to the desire to teach and the task ahead. Working together, each student then designed a symbol that represented their reasons for wanting to be a teacher and which hinted at their state of being at the beginning of the course. They were asked to put this symbol on their cell phones and to remind themselves of their reasons for wanting to teach during significant moments during teaching practice.

During teaching practice the students met on several occasions to discuss how they were getting on, to discuss and share issues and so on. At the end of their course, they were asked to produce a short text that articulated a specific moment or experience in their teaching practice which they found particularly inspiring or distressing. These moments again constituted a sharing of experiences, a dialogical space that opened up a critical discussion and sharing of what it is to be a teacher from their different existential territories and experiences of teaching. The students added their text to their initial symbol. The combined image and text represented their personal reasons for becoming a teacher, a kind of personal pedagogical icon. The individual symbols were brought together in a large tapestry that indicated the multiplicity of reasons for becoming a teacher and the multiple modes these becomings manifested. It demonstrated the importance of an evolving public of teachers and their collective knowings, values, practices, the multiple inventive and varied pathways of becoming a teacher, which stand in sharp and distinct contrast to the official route prescribed by the standards of teacher training demanded by government.

REFERENCES

Altay, C. (2015). Rogue Game: An architecture of transgression. In L. Rice & D. Littlefield (Eds.), *Transgression: Towards and expanded field of architecture*. London: Routledge.

Apple, M. W. (2005). Globalizing education: Perspectives from below and above. In M. Apple, J. Kenway, & M. Singh (Eds.), *Globalizing education, policies, pedagogies, and politics*. New York: Peter Lang Publishing.

Atkinson, D. (2011). *Art, equality and learning: Pedagogies against the state*. Rotterdam/Boston/Taipei: Sense Publishers.

Barad, K. (2003). Posthumanist performativity: Toward an understanding of how mater comes to matter. *Signs: Journal of Women in Culture and Society, 28*(3), 801–831.

Barad, K. (2007). *Meeting the universe halfway: Quantum physics and the entanglement of matter and meaning*. Durham/London: Duke University Press.

Buck-Morss, S. (2010). The second time as farce…historical pragmatics and the untimely present. In C. Douzinas & S. Zizek (Eds.), *The idea of communism* (pp. 67–80). London/New York: Verso.

Buck-Morss, S. (2013). A commonist ethics. In S. Zizek (Ed.), *The idea of communism 2* (pp. 57–75). London/New York: Verso.

Butler, J. (2005). *Giving an account of oneself*. New York: Fordham University Press.

DfE. (2013). *Reforming the accountability system for secondary schools*. London: Crown Copywrite.

DfE. (2014). *School and college performance tables*. London: Crown Copywrite.

Eisner, E. (2002). *What can education learn from the arts about the practice of education? John Dewey Lecture*. Stanford: Stanford University.

Gasset, O. (1941). *Towards a philosophy of history*. New York: W.W. Norton & Company.

Giroux, H. A. (2011). *Beyond the swindle of the corporate university*. London: Pluto Press.

Guattari, F. (2006). *Chaosmosis: An ethico-aesthetic paradigm*. Sydney: Power Publications.

Ingold, T. (2015). *The life of lines*. London/New York: Routledge.

MacAloon, J. (Ed.). (1984). Olympic games and the theory of spectacle in modern societies. In: *Rite, drama, festival, spectacle. Rehearsals toward a theory of cultural performance*. Philadelphia: Institute for the Study of Human Issues.

Nancy, J. L. (2000). *Being singular plural*. Stanford: Stanford University Press.

Shaviro, S. (2014). *The universe of things: On speculative realism*. Minneapolis/London: University of Minnesota Press.

Stronach, I. (2010). *Globalizing education, educating the local: How method made us mad*. London/New York: Routledge.

Ziarek, K. (2004). *The force of art*. Stanford: Stanford University Press.

CHAPTER 3

Spinoza and the Challenge of Building a Life

INTRODUCTION

The idea of subjectivity has been a central concern of enquiry in the fields of philosophy and the social sciences for many years and, since the 1970s, it has generated a huge volume of academic literature, including an international academic journal entitled *Subjectivity*. My own interest was stimulated by texts such as *Changing the Subject: Psychology, Social Regulation and Subjectivity* (Henriques et al. 1984) which led me into the works of many other writers that explore, in very different ways, issues of power, ethics, politics and aesthetics relating to subjectivity and practice. But what is subjectivity; is there such a thing? How can we comprehend the human subject? How does a subject come into being? Such questions seem important in terms of having some understanding of how human subjects come into being and continue to become, particularly in the realm of education and, more specifically, in processes of teaching and learning with which this book is concerned. Gaining some understanding of processes of becoming, how such processes emerge, would seem important for pedagogic work in which a central aim is to help students to become more effective learners, and more widely, more effective human beings; where learning is viewed as much more than an accumulation of facts or skills but includes also an expansion of affective processes towards the world and others that include feeling, sensitivity, concern, creativity, perspicacity and adventure. The aim of this and subsequent chapters is to look at some theoretical work on how subjectivity is conceived and then consider how such conceptions and

© The Author(s) 2018
D. Atkinson, *Art, Disobedience, and Ethics*, Education, Psychoanalysis,
and Social Transformation, DOI 10.1007/978-3-319-62639-0_3

theories might be helpful for developing how we might engage in peda-gogic work and its development. I want to make a distinction between the terms subjectification and subjectivation. The former relates to the power of external social processes according to which subjectivities are moulded, most typically within schools and other institutional contexts. This echoes Foucault's earlier work on institutions such as prisons, asylums, hospitals and other sites, within which subjects appear and are formed according to their respective discourses, bodies of knowledge and practices. I am using the term subjectivation to refer to modes of thinking, seeing, making and feeling that emerge immanently within human relations with the world and which form local curations of becoming or local refrains of becoming. These local processes may arise within institutional contexts but may not subscribe to the latter's codes or values.

In this chapter, the key thinker is Spinoza whilst in Chap. 5 I will consider the philosophy of Whitehead and its implications for pedagogical work. Chapter 7 will examine some ideas from Deleuze and Guattari that have relevance for pedagogical work. Does the philosophical work of these thinkers help us to expand our comprehension of pedagogical work as well as the way in which we understand learners/learning and teachers/teaching? Do these thinkers provide ideas that allow us to enter into a critical and productive engagement with established pedagogical policies and practices in order to develop ones that are more effective? Of course, the answer to such questions may be negative or viewed as irrelevant if we believe, as some do, that they are superfluous because we already have a clear idea how and what children should learn and how and what teachers should teach. I think that those who hold such beliefs tend to view teaching and learning as processes that should follow *prescribed practices* in which the identities of teachers and learners are already inscribed. This chapter takes a contrary position, arguing, in the spirit of Spinoza, that we don't know what a body is capable of doing or thinking; we don't know what teaching or learning are capable of. If this premise is transferred to pedagogical work then, rather than being dominated by prescribed practices and knowledge, it has to be future oriented, that is to say, it has to have a concern with that which is not-yet-known and with learners and teachers-yet-to-come. This premise does not exclude established knowledge and practice, but views it in a relational tension in which such knowledge suffuses with future potentials in the worlds of each learner and teacher. The outcomes of such fusions are not always predictable and may (or may not) lead to an expansion in our understanding of what learning (or teaching) is. In this sense, both learning and learning about learning can constitute dynamic expansive processes of adventure and creativity.

BENEDICT DE SPINOZA

In the *Ethics* (1667, 1996), Spinoza considers human beings as existing in relation to all other entities and beings. They do not have a privileged existence above such beings. Bodies are composed of an infinite number of parts and the relations of motion and rest or different velocities between parts constitute the particular individuality of a body. Mind and body are not conceived as separate entities, as in the philosophy of his near contemporary Rene Descartes, nor is mind considered as dominant over the body, rather mind and body are conceived as different modes of a single substance; they are inter-dependent vital processes that constitute a multiplicity producing different modes of existence, mental, physical, affective. A crucial and far-sighted point made by Spinoza about the inter-relation of mind and body from Part III, Proposition II, of the *Ethics* is, 'For indeed, no one has yet determined what the body can do…' and, by inference, O'Sullivan (2013, pp. 13–14), following Deleuze, comments that as well as 'the body surpassing the knowledge we have of it, thought likewise surpasses the consciousness we have of it'. These points on the relation between mind and body resonate with a later passage in the Preface to Part IV of the *Ethics*, where Spinoza writes about the relation between singular creative acts and the prejudice of universal or transcendent models according to which the former are judged. In relation to pedagogic work, Spinoza's point concerning the capture or over-coding of individual creative practices by dominant models of practice is a key issue with which this book is concerned. Similarly, his idea that we don't know what a body is capable of doing or what a mind is capable of thinking is an important leitmotif for the following chapters.

For Spinoza, all physical entities have different degrees of sentience and all entities, human and non-human, organic or inorganic, persist and strive to persist in and according to the essence of their own being. This striving to persist and the consciousness of it he called *conatus*. So we can think of human beings, each in their own ways, as existing and becoming in their respective relational modes to other things (ideas, beings, entities, feelings, memories) in the world driven by this striving (affected by its relations). It is crucial not to view this striving in terms of individualism, but as a relational process of becoming, a kind of *correspondence* functioning at different speeds and slownesses, in a world. Equally, we can conceive of trees, vegetables or animals as striving to persist in their respective modes of being and becoming.

The more acting and thinking flow from creative endeavours to persist in one's being, the more active we are. The more we are acted upon by external bodies, pressures, regulations or controls in whatever form, the more passive we become. For Spinoza, active behaviours stem from adequate ideas, which I will discuss shortly, whilst passive behaviour emerges from inadequate ideas and the more we are affected by the latter the more we are subject to processes of bondage or enslavement, which is the subject of Part Four of the *Ethics*. Put in other terms, the more we become subjected to transcendent forces the more inactive or inauthentic we become. So the *Ethics* provides a kind of handbook for living and the ethical task is to try to live according to a creative understanding, what Spinoza terms *virtue*, through the application of adequate ideas supported by what he calls joyous passions, that can lead to an expansion of our capacities to act and think. In striving for this expansion of life we have to try to avoid the excesses of over-indulgence of seemingly joyful passions and, more importantly, to overcome or minimise the harmful affects of inadequate ideas, that lead to sad passions and precipitate a decrease in our power of living. External forces of which we have inadequate ideas, for example, the impact of immigrants and refugees that generates a desire to exclude them, often produces intolerance that sometimes turns into hatred. Such passions do not accord to others the sentiments and values that we ourselves desire and thus, according to Spinoza, lead to a diminution of our capacities to act and think (see *Ethics* Part IV Appendix).

Deleuze held Spinoza in extremely high esteem as a philosopher but, in his day, he was 'maligned and hated'. In order to grasp this negative reception Deleuze insists that we have to consider Spinoza's practical theses through which he administers a 'triple denunciation: of 'consciousness', of 'values' and of 'sad passions' (17 SPP)'. Through the notion of *parallelism*, Spinoza rejected any primacy of mind over body on the contrary; mind and body are simply different aspects of the same underlying process of being. Spinoza's conception of the body offered a new model for thinking about processes of being and becoming. But Deleuze (1988, p. 18) asks:

> What does Spinoza mean when he invites us to take the body as a model? It is a matter of showing that the body surpasses the knowledge that we have of it, *and that thought likewise surpasses the consciousness we have of it.*

These ideas of body and thought illustrate that Spinoza's notion of the body embraces the ideas of finitude and infinitude; that our knowledge of what a body can do is only a finite fragment of its infinite potential, and that our potential for thought likewise is way in excess of conscious awareness (see *Ethics* Part III Prop. 2 Scholium). Thus, Spinoza's idea of the body is an appeal to the power of its future potential, which is given a kind of precedence over established ways of thinking and acting. The notions of actual and virtual developed by Deleuze connote similar notions of finitude and infinitude. Put another way we might say that Spinoza's emphasis is upon the creative process and immanence of becoming rather than upon formed habits of being and their respective transcendent forces. Of course, the process of becoming is a relational process and the quality of relations or relational encounters will determine whether they lead to growth, restriction or diminution. The nature of such relations is fundamental for Spinoza, who views them in terms of joy or sadness. Put briefly, when a body encounters another body and enters a relation of agreement that extends its capacity to act, this constitutes a mode of joy, a mode that increases its capacity to affect and to be affected. Spinoza is employing the notion of affect to identify this power of acting and thinking. Conversely, if a body enters into a relation that is disagreeable, then this is likely to diminish its power to act and to think. These relational processes constitute the process of life, which consists of a constant variation of increases and diminutions in the power to act according to the ideas that we have and the affects we experience. Our ideas and affects are constantly succeeding each other in the process of experiencing, according to where we are, who or what we meet, what we do, what we see, and so on. Sometimes our relations to where we are or who we meet might be uplifting; at other times, they may be depressing. Such perceptions are not of the 'objects or people in themselves' but our ideas or 'imaginations' of them and the ways in which they affect us as well as our power to affect. Thus, such experiences do not consist only of ideas, but also the force of affect that introduces a constant variation, a variation of my force of existing and power of acting. This force of affect is what Spinoza deals with in Parts III and IV of the *Ethics*, where he provides a detailed description and discussion of the different kinds of affects and their power to influence human behaviour, to increase or decrease our capacity to act and to think. Life consists of a multiplicity of what might be termed a continuum of affective encounters between the two affective poles of sadness and joy, which constitute the two major passions for Spinoza supplementing the desire to persevere in being.

For Spinoza, bodies and minds should not be viewed as substances or as subjects, but rather, as modes, which are constituted according to different velocities or flows. We can think of such velocities as *rhythms*, and these rhythms are affected by other bodies or things as well as affecting other bodies. So, if we conceive a learner or teacher as a series of rhythms and capacities for affecting and being affected, we move away from more essentialising discourses of subjects and substances and replace such ways of thinking with ones that are concerned with the relations of affects and capacities. Deleuze (Ibid, p. 125) indicates that such ways of thinking produce an ethology, that is to say a study 'of capacities for affecting and being affected that characterises each thing'. We can perhaps see the importance of this notion for pedagogic work, which is concerned with expanding the different rhythms and capacities of each learner. Such rhythms 'constitute a particular individual in the world' (Ibid, p. 125). From a pedagogical viewpoint, we might ask how these rhythms are affected by different learning encounters. Are these rhythms strengthened and extended or are they diminished? How can we expand the rhythms and capacities that constitute a learner? What kind of pedagogical publics are required to expand individual rhythms and capacities in a world of increasing change and instability? How can a teacher engage with a learner while preserving and expanding the learner's relation to his or her world? Such questions highlight a conflict between forms of transcendence that govern or organise teaching and learning according to established bodies of knowledge, curriculum methodologies or regimes of assessment, and the immanence of internal rhythms of composition arising from learning or teaching encounters. Such flows of immanence may pass beyond transcendent organising forces so that the notion of building a life in pedagogic work suggests a process in which learners are encouraged to go beyond established parameters of knowledge and practice.

THE THREE KINDS OF KNOWLEDGE

In the *Ethics* (P 40, Schol. 2), Spinoza describes three kinds of knowledge, the first relates to knowledge accrued from 'random experience', knowledge emerging from our actual being in a world, a world of encounters through which we come to exist and experience. Such knowledge, as Lord (2010, p. 79) states, consists of 'imagination, opinion or empirical knowledge'. It is knowledge that is confused and grounded in inadequate ideas. The processes of reaction or response as when a body is affected by others that surround it typify this knowledge in that we don't have a full understanding of our bodies or those bodies that affect us, human or non-human. It is not a systematised knowledge, but that which arises through the immediacy and contingency of experience. Our bodies are made up of a multiplicity of parts and their relations that are constantly changing and in turn produce changing capacities to affect and to be affected. We are driven by a desire to exist, and existence is a matter of this struggle in which we are continually striving for effective relations to extend our capacity to exist, to act and to think. These modes of existence and the affective composition of encounters lead either to 'greater or lesser perfection' (SPP 21). Those objects or people that we encounter that agree with our nature 'determine us to form a superior totality', whilst those that disagree 'jeopardise our cohesion' (ibid.). The first kind of knowledge is inadequate in the sense that what we experience are affections stemming from relations with other bodies or things without comprehending the broader picture of causation, of ourselves and of the other; where the full picture is obscured. One example of such inadequate knowledge might be gleaned from the semiotics and affects of advertising which, playing on our desires for objects, such as a particular piece of clothing, obscure the reality of sweat-shop labour. Put in other terms, this example illustrates the point that we are often unaware or ignorant, or we turn a blind eye, to the real source of our subjectification by advertising's technology of desire and dwell in the pleasure of goods. Another example given by Spinoza and reiterated by Deleuze in his lecture on Spinoza (1978–1981) is the effect of the sun on my body. I feel the effect of the sun but, as long as I remain in this state of affection, I know little of the causes, the relations between these two bodies whereby one produces a particular effect upon the other and how this occurs. Another way of expressing this situation is that in this form of knowledge, we exist as it were in a series of encounters without developing a full understanding of their cause.

If we consider the two passions of joy and sadness then, in relation to the notion of inadequate knowledge, such passions are passive. Forces such as advertising that generate desires for particular products can precipitate joyful passions. Such desires are not self-authored, but produced through the technologies of capital to which we acquiesce. The passive nature of sad passions can be witnessed in the domain of religious confession where the priest relies upon the guilt of his gathering. Religion for Spinoza was a process of social control. We might equally state that many traditional forms of pedagogic work rely upon the passivity of learners to acquiesce to the practices and regulation of established knowledge that are deemed important by government. Equally, such government prescriptions of knowledge and learning depend upon the passivity of teachers. So the question is, if desirable, how can we move beyond these passive affects of joy and sadness towards more active and adequate understandings of ourselves and our world? Another way of thinking about inadequate knowledge is through the idea of consciousness itself, which Descartes privileged over the body; Spinoza thought that this constituted a transcendent illusion that obscured access to real or adequate knowledge. This illusion is manifested, for example, in mistaking effects for causes.

The second kind of knowledge for Spinoza is reason or the development of what he calls 'common notions'. Rather than simply understanding the effect of a body on another, the second kind of knowledge involves a comprehension of the composition of relations, an understanding of causation that does not arise in the immediacy of experiential relations but as a consequence of reflection upon such relations. Spinoza writes:

> ...from the fact that we have common notions and adequate ideas of the properties of things...This I call reason and the second kind of knowledge. (*Ethics* Part II P40 Schol. 2)

It is through reason and common notions that we are able to gain a more comprehensive understanding of our world and ourselves. So, it is important to continue to have encounters with other bodies, human or non-human, to experiment, to have adventures, in order to extend our capacity to think, to see and to feel.

The first kind of knowledge involving imagination and inadequate ideas forms a large part of our cognitive make-up. Our experiences of the world are frequently confused and uncertain, though we often think the opposite. We watch the news on television or mobile tablets and form opinions about what we are hearing even though we have mostly inadequate knowledge of what is being described. Teachers respond to their students' work or questions sometimes with an inadequate grasp of the way a learning encounter matters for a student. We live largely in a social world where, frequently, things or events get lost in translation.

The second kind of knowledge concerns the attempt to comprehend our reasons for acting or responding in a particular way and so building a picture of our world and of our capacities and those of others. It seems to involve a combination of noticing aspects of our actions and then reflecting upon them in a space that is detached from the space of action that is being reflected upon, but, crucially, such noticing and reflection involve the body and its changing relations and affects—it is not a purely abstract space. We might call this kind of knowledge hypothetical, experimental, practical or speculative, but whatever its conclusions or outcomes, it will never produce a *complete* understanding of events in which we are involved or that compose us but nevertheless it can expand our capacity to act and think more effectively. When we experience successful relations, that is to say, when our bodies agree with or attune with other bodies and their capacities (physical or mental bodies in the form of ideas), this constitutes a common notion or a concept (or a general idea; Deleuze SPP, 54), that allows us to partly understand our relations in and to a world. It is through the development of common notions or concepts that we gain knowledge of structures and relations and, in this sense, common notions are viewed as adequate ideas. Spinoza tells us that when we come into a positive relation (a creative composition) with other bodies, this generates the affect of joy and this affect has the potential to produce more common notions thus expanding our capacity to act and think. This process is not linear or homogenous but one characterised by leaps and different speeds. We might say that this second kind of knowledge allows us to move towards an ethics of living.

Therefore, the second kind of knowledge leads to an understanding of the relations and capacities that form different modes of existence. It is by acquiring this second kind of knowledge that a body can extract itself from the passive state of the passions of joy or sadness and enter into a self-authored active state to achieve (or not) joyful encounters which leads to a third kind of knowledge that we might call a self-authoring of life, where the parallelism of body-mind becomes an auto-poietic force. This is not an easy process for how do we distinguish between actions and ways of thinking that are self-authored and those that are informed by external transcendent sources? In answer to this question, it is important not to forget the relational nature of existence depicted by Spinoza and the importance of developing joyful encounters in which our bodies and minds engage in affirmative relations. The aim is therefore to extricate ourselves from passive passions (living according to effects and manipulations of external desires such as those promoted by advertising, or those transcendent forms promoted by institutions such as schools or universities) as far as is possible and, in doing so, become more active and independent, to live life more authentically and expand our capacity to act and think. This has resonances with Lacan's seminar on ethics in which he appeals to us to reject the service of goods and the controlling and regulating influences of desires generated by them. It also seems to chime with the idea of avoiding the imperatives of transcendent forces such as moral codes, the allure and force of identity, normalising conventions, and so on, that reduce or marginalise the essence and the power of acting that we are, or, put another way, more in line with Deleuze, the immanence and power of our becoming.

Spinoza's third kind of knowledge is extremely difficult. It seems to involve a grasp of the infinite or the eternal nature of our being in the struggle to build a life. Whereas the second kind of knowledge consisting of common notions provides pragmatic strategies for living and co-existence, for composing actual relations and experimenting, the third kind of knowledge seems to relate to a grasp of the intensities that constitutes our being. In his lecture on Spinoza's affects Deleuze (24/01/78 LS) tells us:

> What Spinoza calls singular essence, it seems to me, is an intensive quality, as if each one of us were defined by a kind of complex of intensities which refers to her/his essence, and also of relations which regulate the extended parts, the extensive parts. So that, when I have knowledge of (common) notions that is to say of relations of movement and rest which regulate the agreement or disagreement of bodies from the point of view of their extended parts, from the point of view of their extension, I don't yet have full possession of my essence to the extent that it is intensity. (my bracket)

The third kind of knowledge seems to involve an understanding of this singular essence or degree of power, the intensity of the rhythms that compose our particular modes of being.

Each of us experiences different affections, affects and thresholds of intensity but how might we gain some understanding of these and is such understanding important in spheres of teaching and learning? How might we understand this idea of essence of which Spinoza writes in the *Ethics*? Deleuze (LS,12/12/1978) tells us that essence needs to be considered in terms of three dimensions: the eternal, instantaneity and duration. The eternal is the modality of essence in-itself, instantaneity is the modality of *affections (affectio)*, the immediacy of instants of affections such as our initial perception of a person, the impact of a shower of rain or encountering a new art work. Duration characterises the dimension of *affect (affectus)* that is enveloped by an affection, it defines the lived passage from one state to another and this passage, the passage of affect, can be understood as consisting of an increase or a decrease of one's power or level of intensity.

Deleuze gives the example of being inside a dark room when someone enters and turns on the light. Here the two states of dark and light are very close together and the passage from one to the other is fast, but it affects the whole body. *Affection* concerns the immediate transformational mode as it hits us from being in the dark to being in the light, whilst the *affect* is the lived temporal passage from one to the other. We can think of other examples of being 'in the dark' such as when we endure phases of incomprehension and then something happens or someone says something that transports us into a new state of comprehension that increases our capacity to understand. Equally, someone may make an interjection that decreases our power to understand and make the situation more confusing. This increase or decrease in power relate to the particular forces of affection and affect.

From the pedagogic perspective of events of learning that I adopt in this book, a grasp of the intensities of affectations and affects of a learning encounter that expand or decrease capacities of thought and action seem to constitute an understanding of a body's-mind's power; a kind of self-assurance of learning. An interesting point made by Deleuze relates to the increase in power through the affect of joy that produces a new individual. I read a passage from a text or consider an artwork, and the subsequent affections and affects increase my capacity to act, to think in a new way. My previous 'self' and the text or painting form sub-parts of this new person. Deleuze states:

> To increase one's power (puissance) is precisely to compose relations such that the thing and I, which compose the relations, are no more than two sub-individualities of a new individual, a formidable new individual. (LS 20/ 01/81)

It is this composing of new relations and their joyful affects that increases our power to act (forming a new individual) and it is this degree of power that constitutes our essence and which is eternal:

> "This power of being affected is the power of being affected of our essence," and "this is a kind of auto-affection whereby essence is affected by itself (Deleuze, LS 24/03/81)."

The degree of power of which we are composed is an intensity that varies according to affections and their affects in relation to the circumstances and relations in which we find ourselves. Simon O'Sullivan (2013, p. 22) nicely describes this essence as a 'kind of autopoietic point around which a given subjectivity might cohere'. It seems to me that these notions of essence and intensity that make up Spinoza's third kind of knowledge resonate to some extent with Foucault's (1992:10–11 Use of Pleasure Vol. 2) notions of techniques of the self and the arts of existence. These relate to the ability not only to establish ways of living and thinking, but also to work and transform oneself—in relation to others—as if 'the self' was a continually evolving work of art. Becoming is therefore a process composed of finite and infinite relations; the former relate to Spinoza's second kind of knowledge whilst the third kind of knowledge relates to our infinite potential. We might view the second kind of knowledge as preparing the ground for the third, which expands the auto-poietic core of our existence. A question verging on the education of the self might be, have you fully developed the essence, the intensity that you are (see O'Sullivan, p. 25)?

To bring together these ideas from Spinoza and Deleuze in relation to subjectivity, it is clear that if we take them on board, then we cannot conceive the subject in essentialist terms but rather in terms of a series of modes of relations of existence and variations of intensity that are constantly changing, evolving, becoming. Individuals are produced through a complex process of forces, relations and intensities, and what we understand in everyday terms as a subject is only a finite fragment or as O'Sullivan (ibid, p. 27) writes, 'a selective abstraction and retroactive appropriation of certain parts of the process'; it is a phase of finitude in the realm of infinitude. A body for Spinoza is composed along two axes: the first is a body constituted by an infinite number of parts and relations, of relations of motions and rest, and these define the individuality of a body. The second axis is that constituted by the intensity of affect, the ability to affect and to be affected and this also determines a body in its individuality. In the process of becoming, we do not know in advance what affects we are likely to experience or how we might affect particular situations; we do not know beforehand in a particular encounter what we are capable of doing or thinking. Which particular circumstances affect a body so that it increases its capacity to act and think, which circumstances have a reverse affect? Such questions seem important in the domain of pedagogical work. Deleuze (SPP, p. 126) writes:

> How do individuals enter into composition with one another in order to form a higher individual, ad infinitum? How can a being take another being into its world, but while preserving or respecting the other's own relations and world?

I think these questions strike at the heart of pedagogic work that is concerned with responding effectively to the different ways in which children and students learn. Such processes are composed of different backgrounds, modes of being and compositions of understanding as well as different spheres of intensities that determine the individuality of learners. Here, the notions of transcendence and immanence, which will appear in other chapters, are crucial. To envisage and implement a pedagogic project in which teachers and learners are required to initiate and follow specific routes of learning, where the route takes priority, is a project determined by a transcendent pedagogical and moral (also political) plan. To acknowledge that learners take different routes—in order to learn—that are dependent upon their particular relations and sensibilities to their world and to work from these local spheres of difference and intensity is to embrace a pedagogy grounded in immanence.

Spinoza is concerned with questioning the obedience that is demanded by different orders of society and the consequent production of sad passions. His writing for me invokes the idea of *disobedience*, a possibility of breaking through the subjectification of transcendent forces in order to produce expanded capacities for co-existence. Deleuze writes:

> The best society, then, will be one that exempts the power of thinking from the obligation to obey, and takes care, in its own interest, not to subject thought to the rule of the state, which only applies to actions. As long as thought is free, hence vital, nothing is compromised. When it ceases to be so, all the other oppressions are also possible, and already realised, so that any action becomes culpable, every life threatened. (Ibid, p. 4)

We might say that Spinoza views becoming as a series of on-going encounters that have extensity and intensity. O'Sullivan (23) makes the point that though the world of consumer capitalism, or what jagodinski (2010) terms 'designer capitalism', involves the affective, it is a passive affect—as in the world of advertising and its operation of desire I have already mentioned. Such passivity suggests a process of exploitation in which we are not the authors of our affects. O'Sullivan goes on to argue that active affects and Spinoza's third kind of knowledge pass beyond this passivity because such knowledge cannot be commodified. However, as O'Sullivan points out (n 17, p. 230) our current educational systems are largely a child of capitalism introduced historically to feed its increasing demands for particular skills and knowledge, as defined in Spinoza's second kind of knowledge. These points raise an important issue apropos education and its relation the second and third kind of knowledge. Do we want the process of education to be committed entirely to the acquisition of the second kind of knowledge, of causation and adequate ideas, which of course is important, or should education also go beyond such knowledge and try to develop the third kind, an auto-poietic knowledge of the immanence and intensities of becoming, or in more simple terms, an on-going active and creative understanding of self and our capacities in relation to those of others that expands our modes of co-existence?

Such creative understanding, which is echoed in the work of Whitehead that will be discussed in Chap. 5, suggests a subject that is simultaneously grounded in habits (finitude) of understanding and practice but also able to transcend the world of habit in order to extend the capacity to affect and be affected, to act and to think (infinitude). Translated into local learning processes, each learner can be conceived as a collection of habits of thinking, feeling, acting and so on that are formed through on-going relations in the world. Such habits involve sedimentations of memory of which some become useful within actual functioning realities. Habits may be reinforced or weakened according to their effects in particular learning encounters. What I term events of learning (Atkinson 2011) occur when a learning encounter projects the learner beyond the capture of habit into a new or modified ontological and epistemological phase where capacities to act are expanded. An important question for pedagogic work is therefore what kind of strategies can a teacher initiate to engage with the finitude and rhythms of each learner's mode of learning so as to project the learner into a space of infinitude whereby the learner's potential expands his or her rhythms and capacities to act?

A brief aside in passing on this point of the question of pedagogic work. Tim Ingold (2014) reflecting on the relationship between ethnography and learning insists on anthropology as a practice of education, he writes:

> ...it is a practice dedicated to what Kenelm Burridge (1975: 10) has called *metanoia*: "an ongoing series of transformations each one of which alters the predicates of being." (p. 388)

The process of altering the predicates of being in order to expand capacities to think, to act, to feel, to see, to co-exist, can be viewed as a fundamental aim of education and learning, (and of Spinoza's three kinds of knowledge). Ingold reasserts a much older quest of education that seems quite distant from its current manifestation in schools and elsewhere: to *lead* novices into a world rather than 'instilling knowledge into their minds'. In sharp contrast to the latter stance, Ingold asserts that, 'instead of placing us in a position or affording a perspective, education is about pulling us away from any standpoint – from any position or perspective we might adopt' (p. 389). This point relates closely to the notion of transcendence that will be discussed in later chapters, particularly to those transcendent operators or enunciators that condition and regulate ways of acting, seeing and thinking. When considering many of our current systems of education, these points suggest that a common tendency is to generate passive affects, in which learners become exploited, rather than being encouraged to develop their own lines of intensity and capacity. They return us to Spinoza's discussion of the sad passions and three critical targets of Spinoza's *Ethics*: the slave, the priest and the tyrant who rely upon the sad passions of others for their continued existence.

The combination of Spinoza's second and third kinds of knowledge facilitates a transformation or expansion of the subject; it extends its knowledge of causation and its self-knowledge, its degree of power. Knowledge of causation includes not only that applied to natural science, but also to knowledge of transcendent operators, those social forces that impact upon and subjugate, explored, for example, by Foucault in his work on knowledge and institutions, or by Althusser in his investigation of ideological state apparatuses. Such transcendent operators include moral codes that impose systems of judgement. Moral laws invoke obedience to their codes. Ethics for Spinoza is concerned with an experiment of action and thought: what are my capacities for action in this particular situation, not how ought I to act.

One of the key statements made by Spinoza, which I emphasised earlier, refers to the indissolubility of mind and body and their joint infinite potential. In the *Ethics*, he writes (Ethics, Part 3, P2, Schol.):

For indeed, no one has yet determined what the body can do, that is, experience has not yet taught anyone what the body can do from the laws of Nature alone, insofar as Nature is only considered to be corporeal, and what the body can do only if it is determined by the mind. For no one has yet come to know the structure of the body so accurately that he could explain all its functions...

Again, no one knows how, or by what means, the mind moves the body, nor how many degrees of motion it can give the body, nor with what speed it can move it.

The implication that we don't know what a body is capable of or what thoughts can be thought is, I believe, a foundational position of pedagogic work if we are to respond effectively to the different ways and rhythms in which children and students learn and experience their world. Spinoza's theory of affects in Part Three of the *Ethics* gives a detailed series of statements that indicate that what we are capable of doing and thinking emerges from the different relations (with objects, with beings, with ideas), and their affects that we experience and how we conceive them. This points to the importance of learning encounters, and how they matter for each learner. What I am coming around to in repeating this pivotal statement by Spinoza concerning the infinitude of the body and mind and its importance for pedagogic work is the notion of ethics relating to such work. It seems clear that if we take Spinoza's words on board, then ethics, as mentioned above, is not concerned with established ways of doing and thinking, with what we should do, but with the question of what we can do, with the indeterminate potential of actions and thoughts that are not-yet or yet-to-come. Thus, ethics can be viewed as indissoluble from ontogenesis and ontogenesis can be viewed as a series of material encounters whose affects lead to an 'expression of living' (an expression of learning').

When we consider the infinitude of the body-mind in relation to art practice and education, for example, to new technologies that involve digital worlds, questions arise concerning how such technologies can be used, how they affect action and thought and how through their use and application we become able to affect. How does the affect of such technology influence or change the ways in which we act, think and feel? What kinds of 'hidden' affects do such technologies create? Do such technologies exert forms of passive desires whose real intentions are hidden?

PERFECTION, APPETITE, AND VIRTUE

At the risk of some repetition, I will conclude my discussion of Spinoza with a brief reference to the Preface to Part IV of the *Ethics*, entitled *Of Human Bondage Or The Powers of the Affects*. In this section, Spinoza makes some interesting remarks on the notions of perfection, appetite and virtue that I think are relevant for pedagogical work. He writes:

> If someone has decided to make something, and has finished it, then he will call this thing perfect – and so will anyone who rightly knows, or thinks he knows, the mind and purpose of the work. [...] But if someone sees a work

whose like he has never seen, and does not know the mind of its maker, he will of course, not be able to know whether that work is perfect or imperfect.

This statement clearly has implications for pedagogic work where the task is to understand the learning practices of students and their intentions. However Spinoza proceeds:

> But after man began to form universal ideas, and devise models of houses, buildings, towers, and the like, and prefer some models of things to others, it came about that each one called perfect what he saw agreed with the universal idea he had formed of this kind of thing, and imperfect, what he saw agreed less with the model he had conceived, even though its maker thought he had entirely finished it.

Universal models therefore become transcendent templates according to which the notions of perfect and imperfect are conceived, irrespective of the 'perfection' immanent to the making process in which body, ideas and materials interweave. In the application of such models, we are likely to obscure a learner's singular appetite for the process of learning. In the world of assessment of learning, it may be the case that, in the process of assessment, we are not conscious of conceiving the immanence of learning and its local reasoning according to universal models of learning. In such states of unawareness, that which is deemed imperfect or lacking as adjudged by assessment discourses and practices becomes so because it does not accord with the universal model. However, in the immanence of the learner's practice and how something matters for a learner, it may lack nothing. Such judgements can have negative impacts upon a student's capacity to act and think and upon how he or she values their work.

Spinoza equates the power to act through striving to persevere in one's being and being conscious of this striving (conatus), with the notion of virtue.

> Virtue is human power itself, which is defined by man's essence alone, that is, solely by the striving by which man strives to persevere in his being. So the more each one strives, and is able, to preserve his being, the more he is endowed with virtue. And consequently, insofar as someone neglects to preserve his being, he lacks power. (Ethics, Part IV P20)

Our lack or increase of power is dependent upon our capacity to reason and understand, but also upon the affects of sad or joyful passions. Our capacities for acting, thinking and feeling need to be constantly nourished and, in the Appendix to Part IV, (XXVII) of the *Ethics*, Spinoza places a metaphorical importance upon food; these are his enlightened words:

> The principal advantage we derive from things outside us – apart from the experience and knowledge we acquire from observing them and changing them from one form into another – lies in the preservation of our body. That is why those things are most useful to us which can feed and maintain it, so that all its parts can perform their function properly. For the more the body is capable of affecting, and being affected by, external bodies in a great many ways, the more the mind is capable of thinking. [...] So to nourish the body in the way required, it is necessary to use many different kinds of food. Indeed, the human body is composed of a great many parts of different natures, which require continuous and varied food so that the whole body may be equally capable of doing everything which can follow from its nature, and consequently, so that the mind may also be equally capable of conceiving many things.

If we replace the term food with encounters that feed and challenge learners, then we might see their importance in pedagogical work and in local practices of learning in which a learner's capacity to affect and be affected is extended. To nourish learning it is therefore important to experience encounters of different kinds. This point has importance when we consider not just the art curriculum in schools, but the full curriculum and the need to provide learners with wide and varied experiences in their task of building a life. Pedagogic work is therefore concerned with learning about how what learners encounter affect them, how it empowers or dilutes their capacity to act and experiment with emerging assemblages of practice. From a teacher's perspective, it also concerns learning about how working with learners and their encounters affects a teacher's capacity to experiment and act.

This book is concerned with the domain of art in education, with advocating the importance of the force of art to transform and expand ways of seeing, thinking, acting and feeling. This force, which will be dealt with in Chap. 8, has pedagogic potential to effect new onto-epistemic phases. It is not concerned with the closure of knowledge, with those forms and frameworks that hold us (and which of course are important), but with events of disclosure; a disclosure of seeing, knowing and feeling; hence the huge significance of Spinoza's words that encourage us to experiment with ideas and ways of making that may lead to unknown capacities to think and to act.

REFERENCES

Atkinson, D. (2011). *Art, equality and learning: Pedagogies against the state.* Rotterdam/Boston/Taipei: Sense Publishers.

Burridge, K. (1975). Other people's religions are absurd. In W. E. A. van Beek & J. H. Scherer (Eds.), *Explorations in the anthropology of religion: Essays of Jan van Baal* (pp. 8–24). The Hague: Martinus Nijhoff.

Deleuze, G. (1978–1981). *Lecture transcripts on Spinoza's concept of affect.* http://www.webdeleuze.com/php/sommaire.html. Cours Vincennes.

Deleuze, G. (1988). *Spinoza, practical philosophy.* San Francisco: City Light Books.

Foucault, M. (1992). *The use of pleasure, The history of sexuality* (Vol. 2). London: Penguin.

Henriques, J., et al. (1984). *Changing the subject: Psychology, social regulation and subjectivity.* London/New York: Methuen.

Ingold, T. (2014). That's enough about ethnography! *Journal of Ethnographic Theory, 4*(1), 383–395.

Jagodinski, J. (2010). *Visual art and education in an era of designer capitalism.* London/New York: Palgrave Macmillan.

Lord, B. (2010). *Spinoza's ethics.* Edinburgh: Edinburgh University Press.

O'Sullivan, S. (2013). *On the production of subjectivity: Five diagrams of the finite-infinite relation.* London/New York: Palgrave Macmillan.

Spinoza, B. (1996). *Ethics.* London: Penguin.

CHAPTER 4

The Force of Art and Learning: Building a Life

> Force is not to be confused with power. Force arrives from the outside
> to break constraints and open new vistas. Power builds walls.
> Brian Massumi

A learner builds a life, a life in relation with 'others'; it is a relational struggle. A girl takes a stick and makes a mark in the sand; hand, arm, brain, visions, imaginings, stick, sand, resistance, movement, pausing, shaping: an on-going series of relational forces precipitating wanderings, pondering, lines and shapes. Territorialising—deterritorialising—reterritorialising on different planes, a proliferation into not-yet-known spaces and times, rich in potential.

Others approach and join in; shouts, questions, permissions, gestures. A series of new relations emerge that include thinking together, agreeing, disagreeing, arguing, discussing, suggesting, acting, supporting, responding... a constellation of actualisations, potentialities, hidden and overt connections that may spark innumerable lines of practice and working together. Participation is a constant production of a whole never achieved, playing-a-part-together. Not something already established in which a 'we' participate, but rather, a building together on a number of connected-disconnected and shifting planes; a building together in which space and subject emerge, a shifting multiplicity.

© The Author(s) 2018   59
D. Atkinson, *Art, Disobedience, and Ethics*, Education, Psychoanalysis,
and Social Transformation, DOI 10.1007/978-3-319-62639-0_4

A politics of difference, an ethics of thisness, an aesthetics of building a world: all perhaps embraced by the German word *bildung* which entails a critical experimentation of our selves and our social relations.

Our current dispositif of education affecting schools and universities invokes participation grounded on a pre-conceived and highly regulated venture governed by economic prosperity and ambition. A dispositif of prescribed subjectivities (learner, teacher), and prescribed bodies of knowledge. Real learning in the sense of experimentation has no prescriptive force, it is restless, disobedient and awaits subjects-yet-to-arrive. Real learning is a deterritorialisation, a disobedient force opening up potentials for new or modified ways of doing, making, seeing, thinking, feeling; a potential to generate new peoples. Is it possible or desirable to conceive spaces of teaching and learning beyond their current organisation? Economic performance is important, but should it be the driver of education? Education is a process better conceived as facilitating learning encounters (no hierarchy between teacher and learner) and supporting each learner's struggle to build a life.

This struggle functions on many levels and includes learning in a number of practices, of which art practice is one that develops learning and knowing according to its particular modes of practice. The force of art enables learning through its force of disobedience. Disobedience does not denote opposition, but a possibility for an opening, resisting normalising forces and the subsumption to established modes of practice/thought. The force of art does not emanate from a prior subject, but through this force a subject, or more accurately, a subjectivation and a world emerge. The coming into existence of art practice through its force makes a difference to the world it helps to compose. Negotiating how something matters for a learner involves intellectual, ethical, political as well as aesthetic considerations in order to gain some grasping of relevance and potential of a learning encounter: how it is felt, conceived, enfolded…without imposing a ready-made conception of what is happening whereby how *this matters here and now for a learner* becomes something else.

Problematisations can be viewed as a matter of invention and, in pedagogical contexts, they can inspire the adventure of pedagogy to expand our comprehension of what art, teaching and learning can become. It's a matter therefore of not closing down what we confront according to established frameworks, but of remaining open to the not-known. Knowledge here may be de-limiting, whereas processes of knowing remain open to that which does not fit. Knowing here is indissoluble from ethics. Sometimes all you meet are walls and then it's about trying to reveal your own foundations. The force of art, as Paul Klee stated, does not reproduce the visible but makes visible, and this making visible is the pedagogical force of art; the composing of new possibilities, new ways of seeing, making, feeling and thinking.

Pedagogic work involves a *joining with* learners in an on-going exploring and experimenting with what the possibilities and potentials of learning might be. It involves that which is not yet known. This notion of *joining with* the worlds of individual lines of becoming or, in Nancy's (2000) terms, of *being-with*, I would argue, modulates the view of pedagogy transfixed by an advocacy for prescribed knowledge and skills to embrace the idea of teachers *developing ways of living attentively with learners* and thereby facilitating the continuous weaving of their mutual lines of life. To live attentively to these different lines of learning, I would argue, is to hold in abeyance the force of prescriptive pedagogies and their transcendent criteria and restore pedagogic work to the incipience and immanence of learning. This would seem to require what Susan Buck-Morss (2013) calls a pragmatics of the suddenly possible.

Rather than seeing pedagogic work only as the passing on of fixed bodies of knowledge or practice, yet without rejecting their importance, it would equally be concerned with creating the conditions for real learning to be set in motion, which lead to transformation and the invention of new worlds. This constitutes an ethico-political as well as an ethico-aesthetic project.

Disobedient pedagogies in contrast to those advocated by Government adopt the Spinozan notion that we don't really know what a body is capable of or what thoughts are capable of being thought, coupled with the notion of a pragmatics and ethics of the suddenly possible. Such a pedagogical stance when confronting disobedient objects or aberrant ways of learning/ practising may open up new possibilities for practice and new ways of understanding learning, new ways of understanding art. It seems important therefore to ask, for whom is the practice of learning relevant, is it the learner, the teacher, the government. . .these imply different agendas. This negotiation of relevance or the morphology of relevance is important in asking how something matters for a learner.

In an essay entitled Something *To Write Home About*, the Irish poet Seamus Heaney reflects upon his childhood days walking between Castledawson and Ballaghy. He remembers crossing a ford on the river Moyola and has vivid memories of standing on the stepping-stones, feeling giddy at the thought of falling in but standing stock-still as he took in the vastness of the sky above. 'Nowadays', he remarks, 'When I think of that child rooted to the spot midstream, I see a little version of the Roman God Terminus, the God of boundaries.' There was an image of Terminus in the Temple of Jupiter on Capitol Hill and the interesting thing, Heaney comments, is that the ceiling above the image was an open cupola, suggesting that although Terminus is the God of earthly boundaries, it's as if by means of the open cupola he requires access to the boundlessness of the sky above. Heaney writes:

> As if to say that all boundaries are necessary evils and that the truly desirable condition is the feeling of being unbounded, of being king of infinite space. And it is that double capacity that we possess as human beings – the capacity to be attracted at one and the same time to the security of what is intimately known and the challenges and entrancements of what is beyond us. (Heaney 2002: 48)

Heaney's words seem to me to be deeply resonant with the adventure of learning. The stepping stones that constitute his boyhood experiences invite him to change the terms and boundaries of his understanding...they 'do not ask you to take your feet off the ground but they refresh your vision by keeping your head in the air and bring you alive to the open sky of possibility that is within you' (2002: 58).

When I reflect on these words in relation to processes of human learning, they seem to point towards finite moments of understanding in learning experiences, but also to the 'immanence of infinitude' in these finite moments which involves the potential of new ideas, new practices, new ways of seeing, new values, and so on. It is as if, when thinking about learning in the context of art practice, the importance for the learner is not only the finite occasions of practice: the drawing, the painting, the video, the construction, the performance, but perhaps of more significance, is the immanence of infinitude within each of these moments and the potential for what Alfred North Whitehead termed 'the creative advance into novelty'. A key aspect of learning therefore is the importance beyond itself of a learner's expression. We might rephrase this as 'the importance to learning of the not-yet-known'. This suggests that in our work with learners, we are *concerned* with the notion of learners-yet-to come and correlatively with an appeal for appropriate, relevant and commensurate pedagogical strategies, teachers-yet-to-come. We are dealing with the finitude and infinitude of learning and teaching.

REFERENCES

Buck-Morss, S. (2013). In S. Zizek (Ed.), *A commonist ethics in the idea of communism 2* (pp. 57–75). London/New York: Verso.

Heaney, S. (2002). Something to write home about. In *Finders keepers: Selected prose 1971–2001* (pp. 48–58). Princeton: Recording for the Blind & Dyslexic.

Nancy, J. L. (2000). *Being singular plural.* Stanford: Stanford University Press.

CHAPTER 5

Whitehead's Adventure

Have a care, here is something that matters.
A. N. Whitehead, Modes of Thought, (p. 116)

INTRODUCTION

In the film, *The Dead Poet's Society,* the main character, the maverick teacher of English Mr. Keating, played by Robin Williams, challenges his affluent students to 'seize the day' (*carpe diem*), to embrace the present and make their lives extraordinary. His pedagogical aim is to encourage his students to become independent thinkers and not just to accept established ways of thinking and doing. At the beginning of a literature lesson he instructs his students to take their textbooks and tear out the initial pages of instruction. Bewildered, tentative and bemused they begin to do so and deposit the pages in the litterbin. I think the importance of this scene lies not in the students 'seizing the day', but in the event of disobedience through which they begin a new pedagogical journey. It is the event of disobedience that seizes them and opens up new vistas and a new series of questions and narratives. Seizing the day presupposes a 'subject who seizes', whereas the event of disobedience precipitates a new subjectivation.

Turning to the final moments of the film, *Boyhood*, written and produced by Richard Linklater, Mason, whose life we have watched develop from childhood to college student, is sitting on a rock with a new acquaintance Nicole. They are both 'freshers', out hiking in Big Bend Ranch State Park

© The Author(s) 2018   65
D. Atkinson, *Art, Disobedience, and Ethics*, Education, Psychoanalysis, and Social Transformation, DOI 10.1007/978-3-319-62639-0_5

with their friends Dalton and Barb. Whilst absorbing the amazing landscape and watching their friends silhouetted in the near-distance, Nicole turns to Mason and tells him that she has been ruminating on the notion that we are always encouraged to seize the moment, but that she is not so sure about this anymore. She believes, to the contrary, it's not that we seize the moment but that the moment seizes you. Mason agrees; 'yes' he says, 'you are always in the moment'.

Whitehead's philosophy of organism provides a complex theoretical discursus of what we might call moments of experience, actual occasions, that constitute human and non-human beings as well as organic and non-organic entities. He borrowed a phrase from William James to describe actual occasions as 'drops of experience'. Such moments are considered as producing novelty in the process of becoming. The idea of a pre-established subject 'seizing the moment' would run counter to Whitehead's ideas on becoming, because the subject is always a product of on-going relational processes that affect each other. Thus, the notion of 'becoming in the moment' is closer to Whitehead's ontology. He proposes a dual ontology, which embraces the endless process of becoming and the emergence of states of being. This complex ontology will be considered in more detail by discussing some of the conceptualisations he employs in building the theoretical framework for his philosophy of becoming. In this construction, Whitehead develops his own 'philosophical inversions' of Descartes and Kant.

Back to Mason in the film *Boyhood*: at various points in the movie, initially with his father (separated from his mother) and then later with his school girl friend, he questions the meaning of things. Why do things die? What's it all about...why do we have to go to school? Why do we have to chase after qualifications? And so on. Like many teenagers, he is seeking this elusive 'meaning of life'. In the final scene with Nicole, the emphasis shifts from the desire for meaning to acknowledging the importance of 'being (or better, becoming) in the moment'. This emphasis invokes an implicit recognition that becoming in the moment is not simply concerned with meaning but also, perhaps more importantly, with the notion of what Whitehead called feeling, or what we might today call affect. This idea is absolutely central to Whitehead and, in his book *Process and Reality*, he provides an elaborate theory of feelings. 'In the moment' for human beings constitutes an experiential phase involving a multiplicity of affects as well as a multiplicity of thoughts, envisionings, memories and so on. Becoming in the moment is a becoming in a world composed of other becomings (human and non-human) and their inherent affects/feelings, memories, etc., which suggests that human becoming is not to be taken as privileged, but as one amongst a multiplicity of processes that emerge, relate to other processes, change and pass on or pass away.

It tends to be the case, however, that rather than trying to work with 'being/becoming in the moment', whilst recognising that we can never grasp its full complexity, we try to 'seize the moment' according to our pre-established patterns of thought, categories of understanding, assimilated experiences, codes of conduct, fantasies or ideals. Such forms of categorisation circumscribe 'the moment'. It is not uncommon to find that in new or unfamiliar situations, when the moment seizes us, such predetermined frameworks fail to provide a satisfactory resolution to issues with which we are confronted. Take the case of student teachers in their initial and continuing struggles to learn how to teach where their ideals of 'the good teacher' or their ideological 'calling' to be a teacher tend to fall away or are shattered in the heat of experience, or they become obstructions to the very task of learning how to teach (Moore 2012). The notion of 'seizing the moment' might be prey to what Whitehead termed subject-predicate forms of thinking about experience, which captures experience according to pre-established categories and criteria. Such forms of thought constitute what current philosophers under the name of speculative realism critique as correlationist modes of thought/action that interpret experience according to established parameters of what it is to be human, to be a teacher, for example.

Whitehead's process philosophy encourages us not to be trapped by what he termed 'abstractions;' his idea of the purpose of philosophical enquiry is to see philosophy as a 'critic of abstractions' and 'to maintain an active novelty of fundamental ideas illuminating the social system' (1938, p. 174). For Whitehead, although 'the aim at philosophic understanding is the aim at piercing the blindness of activity in respect to its transcendent functions' (Ibid, p. 169), he also acknowledges, crucially, that 'Philosophy begins in wonder. And at the end, when philosophic thought has done its best, the wonder remains' (Ibid, p. 168). He is thus encouraging us not to allow the sedimented power of concepts (abstractions) or categories to totalise our understanding of experience so that the concepts *become* experience, but to allow the wonder of experience to challenge our thinking, to generate alternatives and opportunities and create new modes of thought and practice. This open stance towards experiencing has profound implications for pedagogical work.

Whitehead was a world famous mathematician and philosopher; he studied theoretical physics and also wrote about science and education. Among other philosophers, he was influenced by the empiricism of David Hume and Bergson's work on creative evolution; in particular, he admired the radical empiricism of William James and the importance James placed upon events of experience. Experience, for Whitehead, constitutes the ontological fulcrum of his philosophical work, which he termed a philosophy of organism. Along with James, Whitehead's process philosophy, in which the world is conceived as an-going flow of process and relation rather than a collection of discrete entities, has close affinities with the work of Charles Saunders Peirce and John Dewey. For many years, his philosophical work was largely ignored in Europe, though in recent years, there has been a renewed interest and recognition of the importance of his writings in philosophy and metaphysics, and commentators have drawn clear similarities between this work and the philosophical work of Gilles Deleuze (Stengers 2002; Massumi; Shaviro 2009; Halewood 2005; Robinson 2006). For Whitehead, the process of becoming along with the ideas of novelty and creativity are central to his metaphysics, which he presents in his difficult and complex book, *Process and Reality: An Essay in Cosmology* (1929b) followed by *Adventures of Ideas* (1933) and *Modes of Thought* (1938). Shaviro tells us (2009: ix) that Whitehead's great question was, 'How is it that there is always something new?' He was writing during a period of significant change that had already witnessed revolutions in fields of science, mathematics and technology, as well as art and philosophy, but also change and turmoil in social and political contexts. Rather than ignore the problems and difficulties that such changes bring, he urged that we face their challenge and work through them to negotiate their potentialities for new opportunities and becomings.

A very important philosophical position taken by Whitehead is his opposition to what he termed 'the bifurcation of nature'. Put simply, this bifurcation relates to the separation, stemming from the scientific developments of the seventeenth century, between a natural world of brute meaningless matter, so called objective reality, and the subjective world of human consciousness and knowledge. This establishes a division between a subject who knows and an objective world that is known; a division that is manifested in the Cartesian dualism of mind and body, the separation of a world of extension from a world of thought. In this ontology subjectivity is therefore excluded from the world of nature: 'Scientific reasoning is completely dominated by the presupposition that mental functionings are not properly part of nature' (Whitehead 1938, p. 156).

Whitehead combined his rejection of the bifurcation of nature with another concept, which he termed the *fallacy of misplaced concreteness*. The conception of nature as a brute meaningless reality that is aimless and value free is not a concrete reality but, as Stenner (2008) points out, 'a high-level abstraction of thought that turned out to be highly productive in limited domains'. The key point is that we frequently take abstractions as true reflections of reality without knowing that we do so. Therefore, an important challenge is to tackle such abstractions and to try to see how they function. An example of a high-level abstraction that was very influential in developmental psychology, for example, is the idea of developmental stages that emerged from the work of Jean Piaget and which influenced research in many aspects of child development.

We know from the developments of science and other fields since the nineteenth century that this bifurcation of nature is untenable; that when we investigate living organisms and their relations, issues of value and purpose cannot be ignored. In this spirit, Whitehead's philosophy is concerned with the complexity of relational processes and he employed the term *experience* not only to refer to human beings and their relations but to other organic and inorganic relational processes. For him, in differing degrees, all entities manifest some degree of experience and value: humans, animals, plants, mountains, planets, and so on. Moreover, all experience is constituted by an on-going series of relational processes. He therefore sought a conception of nature that incorporated all existence so that the division between, 'the nature apprehended in awareness and the nature which is the cause of awareness', made no sense to him (Whitehead 1964). A meshwork of inter-relating processes characterises the process of becoming, 'how an actual entity becomes constitutes what that actual entity is...Its being is constituted by its becoming' (1929a, p. 23), and this becoming is relational. So in contrast to the traditional subject-object dualism, the inter-relatedness of becoming implies that a subject does not confront an external world of objects beyond it because both 'actants' constitute a series of relational processes that affect each other in the world (Ibid, pp. 56–57). This process of affect is explicated through the notions of prehension, proposition and concrescence, which are discussed in more detail below. However, as I will tackle shortly, Whitehead does not dismiss subject-object relations, but treats these in relational terms through the notion of actual occasions and societies, the latter having a particular sense for Whitehead.

In passing, Halewood, (2005) following Whitehead, describes how historically the bifurcation of nature led to a kind of distorted comprehension of nature that produced 'discrete realms of academic inquiry' (Ibid, p. 59) whereby, in general terms, the natural world has become the province of scientific enquiry whilst subjectivity and the world of social relations including, for example, education, politics, ethics and aesthetics are studied by the social sciences. Science was deemed to deal with an objective world of facts, where nature is reduced to a realm 'devoid of feeling and value' whilst the social sciences addressed meaning, value and purpose in the world of human existence. Of course, today, the discreteness of such divisions is dissolving and more multi-modal forms of inquiry have developed across and between disciplines.

Whitehead refuses to accept this binary division and he employs the ideas of becoming, feeling and value to address all of existence, including molecules, plants, animals, humans, mountains, oceans, planets and universes. An important ontological term for Whitehead is 'event', which he later termed 'actual occasion': an event of experiencing in which there is a fusion between subject and object. He writes 'If we are to look for substance anywhere, I should find it in events which are in some sense the ultimate substance of nature' (1964, p. 19). Actual occasions do not only involve human experiences as we have seen but also include relations with and between non-human actants. Actual occasions and experiences are not of the same quality, but are different according to context; for example, actual occasions involving human consciousness are different from those in the context of lions, birds or mountains. Whitehead does not abandon subject-object relations but, as Stenner (2008) states, what is crucial is the relational *concern* emerging within actual occasions, put another way, the way in which subject and object are brought together as 'relative terms in the unity of an actual occasion of experience'. The notion of concern used by Whitehead is important in describing the fundamental structure of actual occasions, as Stenner expands,

> The occasion as subject has a "concern" for the object. And the "concern" at once places the object as a component in the experience of the subject, with an affective tone drawn from this object and directed towards it. With this interpretation, the subject-object relation is the fundamental structure of experience.

An actual occasion, or a nexus of such occasions, which is called a society by Whitehead, is a relation of concern whereby a subject has a concern (or perhaps a feeling of value) for its objects; its objects become components in the subjectivity of the actual occasion, but crucially, the subject becomes a subject through its objective concerns. Whitehead views actual occasions (and societies) as 'drops of experience, complex and interdependent' (1929a, p. 18), they introduce something new into the universe. These ideas paint a picture of a world of inter-relating processes that are continually becoming in spurts of becoming. They suggest a deep inter-relatedness that has the potential to produce new or novel occasions. Whitehead's principle of creativity embraces this idea of entities emerging from a multiplicity, and thus adding to it, and he describes this in an unusual phrase, 'the many become one and are increased by one' (Ibid, p. 21). Events of actual occasions can therefore be viewed as processes through which new or novel materialisations can emerge. They involve a realisation of potential in a particular concrete form that Whitehead calls a *concrescence*.

Up until now, I have been discussing the term 'actual occasion' as if it denotes something that endures when in fact, for Whitehead, this is not the case. An actual occasion is what we might call a brief temporal event that emerges and subsides. It is the nexus of actual occasions or what Whitehead calls 'societies' that constitute the things that endure. These points will be elaborated shortly. In terms of human becoming, Whitehead's philosophy of process, or organism, does not assume a prior subject who experiences a world, but a series of actual occasions (that form societies) in which there is a fusion between a kind of pre-subject-world cemented by a concern or an affect from which emerges a subject and a world. It is a process of becoming through experiencing. In contrast to essentialist philosophies, Whitehead writes:

> The philosophies of substance presuppose a subject which then encounters a datum, and then reacts to the datum. The philosophy of organism presupposes a datum which is met with feelings, and progressively attains the unity of a subject. But with this doctrine, "superject" would be a better term than "subject". (Ibid, p. 155)

For Whitehead, a subject does not exist prior to encounters in a world but rather emerges as a consequence of such encounters. The process of subjectivity, or more precisely, of subjectivation, denotes a process of becoming from a determinate past of a society of actual occasions towards a more indeterminate future, a process of adventure. Once 'subjects' are formed, then they perish and have to be created again, so speaking in terms of human subjectivity, it is not a case of a prior subject creating a thought, but of actual occasions of experiencing forcing thought and the temporary production of a subject. Inverting Descartes, Whitehead writes in *Process and Reality*:

> Descartes in his own philosophy conceives the thinker as creating the occasional thought. The philosophy of organism inverts the order, and conceives the thought as a constituent operation in the creation of the occasional thinker. The thinker is the final end whereby there is the thought. (p. 151)

ACTUAL OCCASIONS, SOCIETIES, PREHENSION AND CONCRESCENCE

In place of a world conceived through a dualism of objectivity and subjectivity, as reflected in the bifurcation of nature, Whitehead constructs his philosophy of organism on the process (becoming) of experience, or more precisely, *experiencing*, which is applicable to all forms of existence, organic and inorganic. He argues that the actual units from which the universe is composed are momentary occasions of experience (PR77), or events of experiencing. Put another way all existence is constituted by events, but in *Process and Reality* Whitehead breaks down the idea of event viewing it as constituted by a *nexus of actual occasions* that are 'inter-related in some determinate fashion' (PR 73). Such occasions in themselves are transient moments, but may form what he calls a *society* in which exists a common thread or characteristic. So in our everyday worlds, the things that endure, molecules, human minds, plants, and so on, are conceived as temporally ordered societies of events or what Whitehead sometimes refers to as enduring objects (1929a, pp. 34–35).

Actual occasions do not simply occur out of the blue, but emerge through a process of inheritance from previous occasions but this is achieved in a novel way so that each actual occasion brings something new into the world. So, in general terms, events that consist of a nexus (society) of actual occasions, relate to other events in the process of becoming. The process through which events relate or where an actual entity takes account of another actual entity is called *prehension*.

> The actual entity is composite and analyzable; and its 'ideas' express how, and in what sense, other things are components in its own constitution. . . .I have adopted the term 'prehension' to express the activity whereby an actual entity effects its own concretion of other things. (Ibid, pp. 51–52)

Every event is the prehension of other events (Shaviro 2009, p. 29). Actual entities appropriate various aspects of their environment out of which they emerge, each process of appropriation is called a prehension. The term 'positive prehension' is also equivalent to what Whitehead calls a *feeling* (1929a, p. 220). This appears to have some resonance with Spinoza's joyful affects discussed in Chap. 3.

The completed process of prehension whereby an actual entity takes account of another to constitute a phase of becoming is called *concrescence*. Concrescence thus refers to the actualisation of experience, and its constitution as a process of transition is summarised by Whitehead in terms of five factors, which as described appear to constitute separate entities, but which in fact refer to an overall relational process, the five factors are:

> The subject which feels, the 'initial data' (multiplicity) which are to be felt, the 'elimination' in virtue of negative prehensions, the 'objective data' which is felt and the 'subjective form' which is *how* that subject feels that objective datum. (Ibid, p. 221, my bracket)

We can interpret the term 'negative prehension' in terms of initial data that are eliminated, or not taken up, but which may have some effect upon the final concrescence. A successful or completed state of concrescence is described as a subject achieving a state of satisfaction, and each concrescence becomes the source for further new prehensions (events).

Applying these relational and transitional ideas to more practical contexts, we might consider a child painting. This practice should not be viewed as an independent subject interacting with the separate materials of painting, but as a practice in which a *concern* between different elements of the practice and their relations evolves; relations between a body, memories, prehensions, thoughts, paint, water, paintbrush, and paper. For the child, it is a matter of *how* (the subjective form) the 'experiencing' of these events or inter-weavings of the painting process *matters*. In this process, there is no 'pre-existing' subject who decides the course of action, rather the subject (the child in this case) constitutes a complex temporal process produced through the series of inter-weavings that constitute the practice.

To summarise what I have discussed so far, for Whitehead, the world is constituted by events, or what he terms actual occasions that prehend each other and come together in a process of concrescence, forming societies that denote processes of endurance and becoming. Actual occasions and their subsequent concrescence occur in all forms of life, organic and inorganic.

Not all prehensions and subsequent concrescences are positive or creative, but when they are they are likely to bring something new into the world. For Whitehead, there is no continuity of becoming because each process of becoming is unique and produces a new concrescence, so there is instead a *becoming of continuity*. The production of novelty produces a state of *satisfaction*. Whitehead's philosophy of organism presents a cosmology whereby the process of experiencing is applicable to all entities, organic or inorganic but in this chapter I am concerned with the field of human experiencing and, in particular, with human processes of learning and pedagogic relations.

In human terms, we can consider each process of perception as having the possibility of producing a new subject. This creative advance into novelty has implications for ontology and axiology in that becoming is not conceived in hylomorphic terms as constructing the world through a series of subjective predicates (categories of the mind imposed on the world), but as a series of encounters in the world through which subjects and values emerge. Whitehead is proposing a relational ontology and axiology in which subjectivity, or more precisely, subjectivation, is a production of and imma-nent to societies of actual occasions (events). Such occasions consist of positive and negative prehensions, and both of these are significant for becoming. In proposing a relational ontology and axiology, Whitehead places emphasis upon the relational *concern* emerging from actual occasions and the subsequent subject-object relations that emerge. Successful learning processes therefore consist of a series of prehensional events and their subsequent concrescence that acquire what Whitehead terms *subjective form* that emerges from a *subjective aim*, which determines how particular prehensions are prehended and actualised to achieve a specific satisfaction.

FEELING AND BECOMING

Whitehead argues that the basis of all experience is feeling and, in *Process and Reality*, he presents his theory of feelings. This term does not refer only to human experience, but to all life, organic or inorganic, from molecules to planetary formations, from single celled organisms to human beings. He suggests that feeling, or what in more recent times is called affect, (though they are not the same), constitutes a fundamental process of life, and he places aesthetics at the centre of philosophical enquiry rather than ontology or ethics (Shaviro, p. 47). Kant, on the other hand, gives precedence to concepts of understanding—that constitute a cognitive sieve (Shaviro,

p. 50)—through which we come to know the world and, in doing so, he maintains the importance of the *cogito* and its transcendence to the world it observes. As Shaviro states, Kant's subject 'monopolizes experience and exempts itself from immersion in that experience (50)'. This separation or dualism is rejected by Whitehead, who argues that as subjects we emerge *from* experience, *from* the world, we are not transcendent to it, even the concepts or categories proposed by Kant as prior to and formative of experience emerge from experience, they are immanent to experience.

> For Kant the world emerges from the subject; for the philosophy of organism, the subject emerges from the world – a 'superject' rather than a 'subject'. The word 'object' thus means an entity which is a potentiality for being a component in feeling; and the word 'subject' means the entity constituted by the process of feeling, and including this process. (PR 88)

The immanent process of feeling in occasions of experience is fundamental to Whitehead's metaphysics, and it seems very close to the notion of value. At the root of this immanence is a relational ontology and axiology, *how* entities take account of (prehend, feel or concern) each other. This *how* constitutes the subjective form of prehension in a particular actual occasion, a particular occasion of experience. It's not that difficult to pass from this theoretical exposition to the world of pedagogy and learning and to think about the subjective form of prehension or feeling that underpins each learner's and teacher's processes of learning, their local immanence. The subjective form of a particular occasion of experience determines the way in which a learner or teacher prehends experience, or the datum of learning. Shaviro (Ibid, p. 55) points to the importance of what he terms the *affective tone*, which constitutes the way in which an entity receives (feels and values) the datum; it is this process of affect that provides the potential for novelty and, for Whitehead, this process precedes cognition. The emphasis is placed therefore upon *how* a subject is affected; affect precedes knowledge. From such processes of affect emerge cognitive processes of ideas and concepts.

As Shaviro states, 'we respond to things in the first place by feeling them, it is only afterward that we identify and cognise what it is we are feeling' (Ibid, p. 58). We can conceive the process of feeling as an event, an encounter, which is irreducible to cognition but which forms the basis for other, supplemental feelings and for cognition to emerge. Whitehead distinguishes between 'conformal feelings' in which the datum is transformed into a subjective feeling, the initial process of 'taking account of', and

supplemental feelings which function reflexively upon this subjective appropriation, thus perhaps modifying the data or comparing it with other
remembered (or imagined) data (Ibid, p. 65).

The event of feeling holds an infinity of potential as it inherits a past and
projects towards a future. If feeling forms the basis of experience, then it
would be reasonable to suggest that its organisation or coherence has to be
immanent to its local or subjective form. This raises the notions of *interest*
and *aesthetic* in the sense that the extent and coherence of the way in which
things are felt and valued depend upon their interest to the subject-in-
process, the extent to which things become interesting (or not), and, as
Shaviro (Ibid, p. 66) comments, such interest and its coherence relate to the
notion of truth, not as adequation or verification, but as enjoyment and
purpose or what Whitehead terms 'satisfaction'. This is a pointer for effective pedagogic strategies: to arrange learning encounters through which
enjoyment and purpose lead to the satisfaction of successful ontogenesis.
This prioritises the aesthetic in relation to the situated nature of truth in
local processes of concrescence. Of course, the idea of arranging situations
for enjoyment and purpose does not automatically imply smooth consensual
environments. These are rather to be conceived as sites of struggle, of
challenge, of uncertainty, of risk, for as Whitehead states, 'It is the business
of the future to be dangerous' (see Shaviro, pp. 68–69).

Satisfaction does not refer to a state of contentment, but only to a
termination of a particular process of experiencing (concrescence) so that
this completed state in turn becomes a platform for new experiencings, new
prehensions. Shaviro (Ibid, p. 69) addresses this point, maintaining that 'the
same movement that transforms an affective encounter into an objectively
cognizable state of affairs also, and simultaneously, offers up that state of
affairs as an object for aesthetic contemplation'. In this process, we can
perhaps detect the ongoing dynamics between affect and cognition as well
as between the actual and the potential. For Whitehead, satisfaction, as an
outcome of experience, is an aesthetic process involving the production of
intensities of feeling and value that deepen experience. This depth is
enriched by the transformation of incompatible aspects of experience that
are integrated to form a greater but inconsistent or heterogeneous complexity, so that, in a sense, we might view satisfaction not as a permanent
state of fulfilment, but more in terms of a metastable state (Shaviro, p. 81).

POTENTIAL AND BECOMING

We can think of potential in terms of the force of intensity and quality. In a learning event potential relates to a phase of incipience where, for example, disparate elements create conditions for the emergence of novelty, a creative event leading to a particular concrescence. In an art practice such as painting the disparate elements of materials, brush, canvas, water, body, thoughts, feelings, and so on, participate in the event of learning, a fusion of human and non-human processes. This is not a reflective or a deductive process but an event in which something happens that generates a sense of discovery, 'ah now I see a way forward'. Here the force of active participation and concern precede conscious perception. It's an event that allows you to see new possibilities but the eventfulness of the event is a fusion of yourself and the other constituents in the situation.

So the term potential used by Whitehead refers to the quality of relations that form a particular concrescence, it denotes a feeling of intensity that emerges from an actual occasion of experience where something matters in some way to someone. This seems to be illustrated in the following anecdote told to me by a friend, when a disjunctive state is transformed into a positive conjunctive state. A young boy is adept at solving simple equations of the type $5 + 7 = ?$ However when confronted with a modification such as $5 + ? = 12$ he is baffled. He struggles for a time, but then approaches his father expressing his frustration. His father points to the '=' sign and says, 'this can also mean "the same as"'. Hearing these words the boy exclaims, 'ah now I see', and runs off to complete his work. It is the grasping event (a prehensional relation) that consists of the successful ingression of the potential of the abstract notion 'the same as' (equivalence) that seems to echo Whitehead's notion of potential. The father's expression of equivalence could be said to act as 'a lure for feeling' (1929a, p. 25, 184 passim), or a 'proposition' that captures the boy's attention through a fusion of the '=' sign and the potential 'equivalence', and this fusion opens up a new field of possibility.

Each actual entity is determined by what Whitehead calls the *ingression* of specific eternal objects (potential) into it. (Shaviro, p. 42, my brackets)
   The term ingression refers to the particular mode in which the potentiality of an eternal object (potential) is realized in a particular actual entity, contributing to the definiteness of that actual entity. (PR 23, my bracket)

Whitehead's notion of potential and its 'immediacy' is an important aspect of learning events in which a new quality and intensity emerges in practice that opens up new possibilities. The intensity transforms prior relations into new relations. How potential becomes manifest in a learning encounter, that is to say, how a particular learning encounter *matters* for a particular learner, seems to be a crucial aspect determining the efficacy (or not) of learning. How can we draw alongside, the way in which a learner constructs experience in such learning encounters in order to comprehend and extend the latter's understanding? If we acknowledge the importance of what Whitehead calls potential that constitutes the quality and intensity of actual occasions of learning encounters, then we might try to be sensitive to the myriad ways in which such processes of affect become enfolded into these encounters. Actual occasions of events of learning will enfold a range of qualities and intensities such as hope, desire, expectation, excitement, disappointment, failure, success, curiosity, and so on. How are the experiencings of such potentials for affecting learning translated into the materials and materialisations of art practice in the form of drawings, paintings, photographs, performance, digital images, 3D work? How do such materialisations 'give voice' to experiences of learning? And what methodological issues *vis a vis* pedagogic work are raised by this question in relation to generating effective responses to the different ways in which learning encounters are experienced and given flesh in their diverse materialisations?

PROPOSITIONS, BECOMING AND CREATIVITY

Whitehead's notion of propositions has, I believe, a more direct application to the task of pedagogic work of initiating and supporting learning. According to him (PR 184), historically, propositions broadly denote statements that 'have been handed over to logicians' and whose function is to be judged as true or false, they are material for judgements. For Whitehead, however, a proposition involves what he calls a 'lure for feeling'; propositions can be considered as 'theories' (1929a, p. 25, p. 184).

> The conception of propositions as merely material for judgements is fatal to any understanding of their role in the universe. In that purely logical aspect, non-conformal propositions are merely wrong, and therefore worse than useless. But in their primary role, they pave the way along which the world advances into novelty. Error is the price which we pay for progress. (Ibid, p. 187)

He suggests, 'a proposition is a hybrid between potentialities and actualities' (Ibid, pp. 185–186). A proposition can be understood in the active sense of 'being propositioned' in or by a particular occasion, where a penumbra of alternative propositional prehensions (potentials) may suggest themselves, and where some are admitted into feeling or are valued because they are germane to this particular experience, leading therefore to actualisation. Propositions 'constitute a source for the origination of feeling (Ibid, p. 186)' and they are realised when they are admitted into feeling. Propositions are composed of actual entities and potentials; that is to say, they combine a reference to things in the world and a series of potentialities germane to the latter. Whitehead advances the idea that propositions are 'tales that perhaps might be told about particular actualities' (Ibid, p. 256) from the particular perspective of a specific actual occasion. They can be conceived as suggesting possible lines for enquiry.

Whitehead distinguishes between two kinds of propositions in their relation to actuality: conformal propositions and non-conformal propositions. The former relate to propositions that generate a conformation of feeling to established facts, a resonance with existing states of affairs, similar to the idea of assimilation as discussed by Piaget. Non-conformal propositions relate to the production of novelty, when a new potentiality is actualised:

When a non-conformal proposition is admitted into feeling [...] A novelty has emerged into creation. The novelty may promote or destroy order; it may be good or bad. But it is new, a new type of individual, and not merely a new intensity of individual feeling. (Ibid, p. 187)

Non-conformal propositions 'pave the way in which the world advances into novelty' (Ibid, p. 187). Such propositions, as described by Whitehead in a positive sense, have some affinity with Badiou's (2001, 2005) relation between event and truth procedure, the process in which the grip of established forms of knowledge and practice is undone by the interruption of an event that leads to new or modified ways of seeing, thinking or doing. They also relate, I believe, to Deleuze and Guattari's (1988) work on probe-heads and abstract machines; the production of new conceptualisations or visual practices that disrupt existing forms of knowledge and practice. Many artists working at the edge or boundaries of practice can be viewed as dealing with non-conformal propositions. The term 'proposition' is not restricted to discursive practices, but can include visual and other forms of practice. Whereas conformal propositions perpetuate a stable, social order non-conformal propositions constitute an adventure, a wandering and a wondering, without clear sight of an outcome. In one sense, we might equate non-conformal propositions with the notion of disobedience, which will be discussed more fully in later chapters. We may not be the same person at the beginning of a learning encounter that we are at its end. As a propositional process, art practice has no essential meaning; it is a process of experimentation that can generate unanticipated new possibilities. We can witness this propositional sense of art practice in the practice of young children through to the work of adult practitioners. Recent events in contemporary practice come to mind, such as the propositional encounters organised by Tino Seghal and other artists working in the area of performance.

The 'primary mode of realization of a proposition in an actual entity is not by judgment, but by *entertainment* (Ibid, p. 188).' Whitehead maintained that it is more important that a proposition be interesting than be correct. We might view the idea of 'propositioning' as invoking a challenge: imaginative, speculative, logical, ethical, political, and so on; the challenge encountered by the students in *The Dead Poets' Society.* When we consider learning, bearing in mind Whitehead's notion of propositions, we can conceive one aspect of it as a process in which things *proposition us,* where we are drawn towards particular alternatives, possibilities, potentials, opportunities, accessibilities or viabilities, and so on. Such propositions may lead to expanded worlds of understanding and practice or, alternatively, they may be unproductive. In other words, they may involve positive as well as negative prehensions. In terms of human experience, it is important to recognise that this process of 'propositioning' does not assume a prior subject who is propositioned by something, some idea or somebody, but rather, it is through the propositional relation that subject and object emerge (in concrescence). When confronting contemporary art as an experience of being propositioned, some works inspire and project me into new modes of comprehension, they seem to invoke an ontological and epistemological displacement. Some leave me puzzled, and I struggle to resonate with what I am confronted. Others elicit a deep sense of wonder, but leave me lacking comprehension. The penumbra of 'propositional feelings' orbiting around these relational experiences lead into different actualisations in which subject and object emerge.

Propositions then, in their function as lures for feeling and value, are proposals about how things might be or become. In the context of pedagogical practice, we might view this process as one in which the notion of *being propositioned* constitutes an important pedagogical strategy that teachers might employ with learners when initiating a learning encounter; so that learners are challenged to envision, question and weigh up possible routes of action and thought. Can we therefore develop pedagogies grounded in the *adventure of propositions* that encourage learners to wander and wonder? An adventure that in terms of a learner's experiencing is epoch making? And how then, in the practice of assessment, can we at least draw alongside the ripples of such adventures?

In passing, there seems to be a resonance between Whitehead's notion of propositions in relation to learning (events of learning) and Deleuze's ideas on learning mentioned in *Difference and Repetition*. For Deleuze (2004), according to Williams (2013, pp. 146–147), learning is experimental, 'to learn is to learn how to be sensitive to and respond creatively to signs and problems, as things that necessarily go beyond what is known or what can be done in a given situation'. Here, Deleuze's notion of problem, close to the idea of encounter, has, I believe, some affinity with Whitehead's term proposition (in the sense of 'to be propositioned') or, to be more specific, non-conformal propositions. Encounters with problems may invoke learning that precipitates subsequent work in the form of conceptual, visual or other kinds of practice that respond to the problem or proposition without creating a sense of closure or resolution but rather, perhaps, a pause in an ongoing process of inquiry. A resolution can be viewed as a phase in which new facets of a problem emerge. So although we can learn facts, skills, practices and so on, in responding to problems or propositions, it is also important to 'learn how to learn', to maintain an eternal vigilance in the process of inquiry and to be open to new or modified problems, viewed as opportunities.

Whitehead's non-conformal propositions are events that mark a *disposition* and a *disclosure,* bringing into view a range of potentials for becoming that thereby signify a fracturing of the continuity of the status quo. Put in Ranciere's (1999) terminology, we might say that a non-conformal proposition disturbs the existing 'distribution of the sensible', or in everyday language, a proposition disrupts our existing frameworks of knowledge, ways of thinking, doing and seeing. Stengers (2011, p. 409) calls '"propositional efficacy" the capacity of a propositional feeling to make a path of occasions to bifurcate, to "mark an event"', that presumably may open up new opportunities or potentials.

The process of the actualising of propositions in a concrescence, which constitutes the subjective form of experience, is for Whitehead an aesthetic process. It is a combination of the actual and the potential, whereby each concrescence may bring something new into the world. Propositions might be viewed as catalysts for the creative advance of novelty where, according to Whitehead 'The many become one and are increased by one' (1929, p. 21), the enigmatic phrase that denotes his ultimate principle of creativity.

> Creativity...is that ultimate principle by which the many, which are the universe distinctively, become the one actual occasion, which is the universe conjunctively. It lies in the nature of things that the many enter into complex unity. (Ibid, p. 21)

It is worth quoting Whitehead at length in order to ascertain a fuller picture of his idea of creativity, which constitutes the fulcrum of his metaphysical adventure.

> 'Creativity' is the principle of novelty. An actual occasion is a novel entity in the 'many' which it unifies. Thus 'creativity' introduces novelty into the content of the many, which are the universe disjunctively. The 'creative advance' is the application of this ultimate principle of creativity to each novel situation which it originates.
>
> 'Together' is a generic term covering the various special ways in which various sorts of entities are 'together' in any one actual occasion. Thus, 'together' presupposes the notions 'creativity', 'many', 'one', 'identity' and 'diversity'. The ultimate metaphysical principle is the advance from disjunction to conjunction, creating a novel entity other than the entities given in disjunction. The novel entity is at once the togetherness of the 'many' which it finds, and also it is one among the disjunctive 'many' which it leaves; it is a novel entity, disjunctively among the many entities which it synthesises. The many become one, and are increased by one. In their natures, entities are disjunctively 'many' in process of passage into conjunctive unity. The category of the ultimate replaces Aristotle's category of 'primary substance'. Thus, the 'production of novel togetherness' is the ultimate notion embodied in the term 'concrescence'. (Ibid, p. 21)

The content of *Process and Reality* and later work provides a detailed, highly complex and original elaboration of the creation of novelty through the terminology already discussed above: actual occasions, societies, prehension, concrescence, potential, propositions, ingression and satisfaction. The world consists of 'the many', a disjunctive universe (multiplicity), and a new actual occasion or event (a one) introduces novelty into the world, into the content of the many, thus unifying, or bringing together, the many in terms of a 'creative advance' and adding to the many. The particular ways in which entities 'come together' constitutes an occasion's particular novelty. In terms of effective human learning, perhaps we can see this process as a creative advance whereby a learning encounter precipitated by a proposition constitutes a new event that forms a new kind of unity among the many facets of being. In the words of Felix Guattari (1995), it constitutes a reconfiguration of existential territories that form processes of becoming. Learning can be viewed as a process that is conditioned by the actual world, but also by the creative advance into novelty, which increases the world. In this advance, the conditions of the world are recreated and provide potential for further new occasions. For Whitehead, 'Creativity is the actualization of potentiality, and the process of actualization is an occasion of experience' (1933, p. 179).

In passing, this creative advance into novelty apropos of human learning does not seem to take account of psychic states such as desires, fantasies, fears and ideals, which can have a serious impact upon learning. I am not suggesting that Whitehead is unaware of this problem; he insists, for example, that the 'how of our present experience must conform to the what of the past in us' (1927, p. 58), but I am not certain about how much Whitehead deals with 'what is in us' in psychic terms. I am uncertain about how he conceives his ideas of prehension and concrescence—in relation to desires and fantasies—that frequently affect our processes of psychic becoming. Having made this point, this does not detract from the power of Whitehead's thought for establishing ontological and axiological grounds for exploring processes of learning and teaching. It can be argued that no philosophical work can formulate a solution to all issues and some may be more effective than others depending upon the nature of inquiry and its specific focus.

WHITEHEAD AND EDUCATION

Whitehead stressed the value of education above other social practices and, more particularly, he stressed the importance of education, teaching and learning as an *adventure*, not as a practice controlled by measurement or the 'professionalisation' of teachers; an attitude that dominates educational policies in many countries today. Stengers informs us:

> When a teacher feels that what she is doing is important, that it is not only a transmission of useful knowledge, Whitehead's metaphysics tell us that she

indeed participates to what may be called a cosmic adventure, because the manner the children will experience new possibilities, feelings and ideas, or stubbornly keep to their abstractions, to their judgement about what matters and what does not, is indeed a cosmic stake. (Stengers paper: Whitehead and science: from philosophy of nature to speculative cosmology, p. 15)

In *The Aims of Education* (1929a/1966) in the chapter entitled *The Rhythm of Education*, Whitehead proposes a theory of intellectual growth that he conceives in terms of three stages, 'the stage of romance, the stage of precision and the stage of generalization'. (p. 28) The stage of romance concerns 'the vividness of novelty', it refers to those moments of affect, of excitement, puzzlement, fear, curiosity and so on, when we encounter new experiences; where a penumbra of possibilities half appear and where knowledge is not systematic but more contingent and piecemeal in its construction. (A little like Spinoza's first kind of knowledge.) It's a matter of encounters with new entities that involve a search and a curiosity for comprehension of their unexplored relations. This is quite close to Dewey's exploratory approach to learning advocating the importance of direct experience of phenomena. The stage of precision relates to a stage of 'exactness of formulation' where a learner begins to systematise the more vague apprehensions of subject matter in the stage of romance that is nevertheless crucial for the stage of precision to become effective. The stage of generalisation refers to a successful phase of learning where the initial excitement of encounter is coupled with the systematic analysis and ordering of precision leads to a sense of achievement. Both The stages of precision and generalisation seem close to Spinoza's second kind of knowledge. Whitehead views effective learning as the continued repetition of the cycle of these stages in the ongoing dynamic of experiencing. We might link these three stages of learning identified by Whitehead with his three processes of becoming: prehension, concrescence and satisfaction, so that each stage is constituted by these three phases. Reading his text today suggests a distance from the educational world that Whitehead was writing and speaking about; a world, I suspect, characterised by the English Grammar School and its traditional curriculum, even though many children in his day would not have attended such schools, and, of course, he was well aware of this and was very active in the process of teacher education in London. But the main point on which I wish to dwell, which still has significance today, is the notion of rhythm and its cyclic structure, since this seems to me to be an essential characteristic of the process of becoming qua learning. The idea of rhythm, as discussed in the previous chapter and in Chap. 8, provides an interesting way of thinking about individual processes of mattering in learning encounters.

Whitehead discusses the cycle of early learning processes in which children succeed in the most difficult challenges concerned with coordination and perception, the acquisition of language and the development of emotional relations, followed by the use of language to classify thought and deepen the level of perception. He compares this with institutional learning in which the extent of early success is generally not repeated, not because subsequent tasks are too hard, but because they follow an unnatural route, 'without rhythm and without the stimulus of intermediate successes and without concentration' (Ibid, p. 32). Ranciere, many years later, makes a similar point, particularly in relation to concentration, when discussing the achievement of early learning and the failings for many students of programmes in institutional learning (See Biesta and Bingham 2010).

In the following chapter, Whitehead elaborates his idea of the rhythm of education by adding to his cycle the important notion of *interest*, making the point that without an initial surge of interest and its continued periodic refreshment, learning will inevitably run dry or be reduced to a mechanical or stagnant process. Effective learning involves a constant interrelation of the principles of freedom and discipline, the opportunity to explore and experiment coupled with the endeavour to formulate an ordering of knowledge and practice. Interest followed through the dynamic interplay of freedom and discipline will take different pathways according to each learner's processes of prehension and concrescence. Nevertheless, the important aspect of learning and the acquisition of knowledge for Whitehead concerns the way in which knowledge is used so as to transform experience. The equation of knowledge or practice with effective use is identified as wisdom.

ASSESSMENT IN EDUCATION

Whitehead's theory of creativity involves feelings, value, prehensions, concrescence and satisfaction emerging on a local level and leading in some cases to the production of novelty. As we contemplate the idea and practice of assessment in relation to these local processes, it would seem that if we are not to prejudice their 'individual' nature by reading them according to established parameters, then we have to approach them almost *without criteria*, because each production of novelty is grounded in its own *thisness*, constituted through local processes of concrescence which are particular to its becoming in a world. Thus, to predicate such concrescence according to established criteria may distort its novel particularity. It seems important therefore not to allow established abstractions in the form of assessment criteria that are not 'relevant' to a learner's practice to distort it, and so exaggerate their power. Put in other terms, sometimes assessment criteria may be irrelevant to the relevance of how something matters to a learner in a learning encounter. In his last book, *Modes of Thought* (1938, 1966, p. 116), Whitehead gave us a gentle but profound piece of advice that we can use in pedagogic work when we are trying to consider the relevance of a learning encounter for a learner, he writes, 'have a care, here is something that matters!' The pedagogical imperative driving the pedagogical adventure stemming from having a care is to ask, 'how is this 'here' constituted for a learner and how can we support and extend a learner's capacities there?'

This is a very difficult issue. Assessment criteria are essentially abstractions from particular forms of practice that identify particular generic skills and their respective forms and qualities. They function as established transcendent and valued parameters. Though such algorithms are important, their constant and prolific employment in education has created a situation in which they often predicate or totalise learning and teaching. In England, the USA and other countries, the current domination of educational practices in schools and in teacher education by a powerful audit culture of assessment and its algorithms has precipitated a situation in which criteria for assessment actually constitute what teaching and learning are. These cultures of audit illustrate the functioning of Whitehead's fallacy of misplaced concreteness. However, the factors and values (prehensions, concrescence) that generate local processes of learning, potential and actual, are immanent to their emergence and they may not necessarily correspond with the way in which such processes are constructed by established algorithms of assessment. If, on the other hand, learning *is* viewed solely as a process of the acquisition of established knowledge, of facts or particular skills where success can be measured through testing the degree of acquisition, then such difficulty may not be so apparent. The important point to stress though is that if learning is viewed more as a process of heuristic exploration, of noticing and weighing up possibilities, of experimentation, seeing what happens, envisaging possible routes, then there is every chance of learners following localised pathways of learning that may diverge from those 'abstract' routes predicated by established criteria.

We need therefore to be careful not to let the weight of assessment criteria, their abstract terminologies, create a 'fallacy of misplaced concreteness' where the criteria 'define' what learning is and thereby fore-close the significance for a learner of local concrescences of experience; *how* something affects somebody, *how* something matters for someone. The generalising nature and repeatability of assessment criteria may foreclose the singularities and the diversity of learning processes.

Having registered a health warning against abstractions, it is also the case that Whitehead was not against abstraction, far from it; he was against the abuse of abstraction within domains for which it was not relevant. His message was to be a critic of abstractions, which he saw as the purpose of philosophy, and to produce more relevant and useful abstractions. In *Science and the Modern World* he wrote:

> You cannot think without abstractions; accordingly it is of the utmost impor-tance to be vigilant in critically revising your modes of abstraction. It is here that philosophy finds its niche as essential to the healthy progress of society. It is the critic of abstractions. [...] An active school of philosophy is quite as important for the locomotion of ideas, as is an active school of railways engineers for the locomotion of fuel. (1967, p. 59)

Isabelle Stengers writes:

> Whitehead embarked upon the philosophical adventure because he felt mod-ern thought needed new abstractions. The abstractions he produced are meant to activate resistance against the power of generalization, the power to eliminate away what does not fit our explanations, (www.mcgill.ca/hpsc/files/hpsc/Whitmontreal.pdf, p. 15)

Thus, abstractions are important tools for helping us to expand our comprehension of the world but they should not be 'taken for granted'. Deleuze and Guattari argue that the central task of philosophy is the creation of concepts, and I think it is in this light that Whitehead's philo-sophical approach to abstractions should be seen. Abstractions can be considered as encouraging 'leaps of imagination' they act as lures for 'feeling something that matters'. It is not only the task of the philosopher, but of other practitioners, to pay due attention to our modes of abstraction and to try to create new more relevant modes of abstraction when things begin to go awry.

Perhaps we can appreciate this task when we consider the failure of economic capitalism in recent years and the pressing need to construct new ways of thinking about and practising economic relations. In our current epoch, there is a pressing need to invent new ways through which humans can relate to their environments. The proliferation of war, of human catastrophes and cruelty suggests we need urgently to develop new ways of living together. The world of educational practices in schools may also be confronting a time that calls for new ways of conceiving the purpose of education and the nature of learning.

Teachers and educators may need to engage in extending narratives of understanding, as they learn from different encounters with learning, when faced with *how something matters* for a learner, here the question of relevance and value becomes significant. The recent obsession with algorithms of audit and assessment in many educational contexts has invoked normative assessment and audit practices that define learning (and teaching), that prescribe what learning and teaching are, with the consequence that practices that do not fit within such algorithms, that manifest other qualities, other values, are ignored or pathologised. Different or divergent forms of learning (or teaching) are 'explained away'. Thus, such algorithms *condition* experiences of learning and teaching and so constitute a pedagogic screen through which other forms of learning and teaching are occluded.

If learning encounters are conceived as the taking up of propositions in Whitehead's sense of this term, where it is a case of how a proposition is *entertained* by a learner, the way it is taken up in particular experiences, then what would be required in terms of assessment of learning would not be a fixed set of criteria that already prescribe learning, but a more flexible *concern*. This important term, already mentioned above, refers to the nature of actual occasions and concrescences of learning, the primary relational process from which emerge subjects and object (learners and things learnt). Thus, *concern* relates to how the fusion between subject and object is formed, it relates to specific forms of coherence and relevance that emerge from actual occasions of learning, it relates to how a learning encounter is given concrescence (relevance and meaning) by a learner. Such an approach to assessment would therefore entail, on the one hand, a circumspect stance towards established assessment criteria and, on the other, an openness towards each learner's pragmatic *concern,* asking where *this* particular practice of learning is leading and its consequences for the continuance of learning. In a general sense then, this approach to assessment does not *prescribe* learning but approaches learning processes from a more open perspective, we might say *beyond knowledge and without criteria* and, in doing so, has the potential to generate new 'abstractions' with the power to overcome irrelevant prescriptions or predications and create new or modified understandings and narratives of learning.

I think that this is where Whiteheads view of becoming as being fundamentally an aesthetic process has direct relevance for learning and assessment, where each process of learning is conceived as an aesthetic process. Where, in the context of each learner's experiencing, a combination of the actual and the potential might bring something new into the world, a creation of novelty. Such combinations emerge from each learner's background influences and circumstances and their respective patterns of sensibility and understanding combined with the *propositions* of a new learning encounter. Isabel Stengers tells us that the reason she loves Whitehead is that, 'the wonder that remains after he did his best is combined with a sense of adventure, and protected against any temptation to bow down in front of powerful, reductive explanations (Ibid, p. 15).'

Following on from Spinoza's practical philosophy and his inspirational suggestion in the *Ethics* that we do not know what a body is capable of nor what thoughts are capable of being thought, Whitehead's process philosophy adds the crucial notion of the creative advance into novelty whereby 'the many become one and are increased by one'. And Whitehead's gentle but invaluable advice to 'have a care' provides pedagogic work with a clear imperative. Both men offer a view of existence that celebrates the incipience of creative events of becoming and both warn against being seduced by established ways and forms of understanding that may occlude such incipience. For them, it seems that what I call events of learning constitutes an adventure, an experiment, out of which new ways of acting, thinking, feeling may emerge. Equally, pedagogic work that aims to support and extend such learning is also an adventure in which we may expand our understanding of what it is to learn and to engage in teaching. In the next chapter, I focus upon some of the writings of Gilles Deleuze and Felix Guattari that relate to and extend the ideas of Spinoza and Whitehead that I have drawn upon and that further extend my concern with learning and pedagogic work into domains of ethics and politics. A further discussion of Whitehead's ethics of creativity will follow in Chap. 10.

REFERENCES

Badiou, A. (2001). *Ethics: An essay on the understanding of evil.* London: Verso.

Badiou, A. (2005). *Handbook of inaesthetics.* Stanford: Stanford University Press.

Bingham, C., & Biesta, G. (2010). *Jacques Ranciere: Education, truth, emancipation.* London/New York: Continuum.

Deleuze, G. (2004). *Difference and repetition.* London/New York: Continuum.

Deleuze, G., & Guattari, F. (1988). *A thousand plateaus.* London: Athlone Press.

Guattari, F. (1995). *Chaosmosis: An ethico-aesthetic paradigm.* Sydney: Power Publications.

Halewood, M. (2005). On Whitehead and Deleuze: The process of materiality. *Configurations, 13*(1), 57–76.

Moore, A. (2012). *Teaching and learning: Pedagogy, curriculum and culture.* London/New York: Routledge.

Ranciere, J. (1999). *Disagreement: Politics and philosophy.* Minneapolis: University of Minnesota Press.

Robinson, K. (2006). The new Whitehead?: An ontology of the virtual in Whitehead's metaphysics. *Symposium, 10,* 69–80.

Shaviro, S. (2009). *Without criteria Whitehead, Deleuze and aesthetics.* Cambridge, MA/London: MIT Press.

Stengers, I. (2002). www.mcgill.ca/hpsc/files/hpsc/Whitmontreal.pdf

Stengers, I. (2011). *Thinking with Whitehead.* Cambridge, MA/London: Harvard University Press.

Stenner, P. (2008). A.N. Whitehead and subjectivity. *Subjectivity, 22,* 90–109.

Williams, J. (2013). *Gilles Deleuze's difference and repetition: A critical introduction and guide.* Edinburgh: Edinburgh University Press.

Whitehead, A. N. (1927/1985). Symbolism: Its meaning and effect. New York: Fordham University Press.

Whitehead, A. N. (1929a/1966). The aims of education and other essays. New York: Free Press.

Whitehead, A. N. (1929b/1978). Process and reality: An essay in cosmology. New York: Free Press.

Whitehead, A. N. (1933/1967). Adventures of ideas. New York: Free Press.

Whitehead, A. N. (1938/1968). Modes of thought. New York: Free Press.

Whitehead, A. N. (1964). *The concept of nature.* Cambridge: Cambridge University Press.

Whitehead, A. N. (1967). *Science and the modern world.* New York: Free Press.

CHAPTER 6

Ethics and Politics in Pedagogic Work

Event and Encounter

The notion of event persists throughout this book, which is specifically concerned with local events of learning and their situated commitments and the sensibilities that might allow teachers to respond to them in the context of art education. In an earlier book, (Atkinson 2011) I used the work of Alain Badiou on the event as the primary philosophical source for exploring events in pedagogic work. For Badiou, an event is that which occurs in a situation but whose effect is 'a profound transformation of the logic of a situation' (2005, p. 130). We can view thinking as an event, an idea supported by Deleuze who conceived thought in terms of trespass and violence (1994, p. 175). Badiou views an event as something that opens a space for a truth procedure manifested in terms of being faithful to a new idea, a way of thinking or acting. It involves a disruption of knowledge through the truth of an event, and the subsequent perseverance with this truth and its transformative potential.

> To be faithful to an event is to move within the situation that this event has supplemented by thinking...the situation 'according to' the event. And this, of course – since the event was excluded by all the regular laws of the situation – compels the subject to invent a new way of being and acting in the situation. (2001, p. 41)

D. Atkinson, *Art, Disobedience, and Ethics*, Education, Psychoanalysis, and Social Transformation, DOI 10.1007/978-3-319-62639-0_6

Many years ago, my doctoral supervisor Bill Brookes often discussed the idea of disturbance in teaching experiences when a teacher is confronted with something mysterious that disturbs his or her mode of functioning. This could be, for example, a particular piece of work produced by a child or student, or a student's response to a question. So, for me, event relates to a disturbance, a rupture of ways of understanding or acting which has the potential to precipitate new modes of becoming. I am using the term *events of learning* to refer to learning as a risky process of encounter with that which lies beyond established frameworks of knowledge and whose affects may transport us into new ontological and epistemological territory and a reconfiguration of being. The term applies equally to teachers/educators and learners/students.

The idea of truth then is related to the notion of *being truthful to something*, and this truth process denotes a process of subjectivation which can be viewed as a 'commitment to' an idea, an affect, a new practice, a new way of seeing, a new way of making sense, and so on, which involves a struggle where we can be carried beyond our normal range of responses.

For Badiou, subjectivation arises as a consequence of an event whereby a subject *becomes* a subject through persevering with a truth, of being truthful to something. Ranciere takes a similar view on subjectivation:

> By *subjectification* (subjectivation) I mean the production through a series of actions of a body and a capacity for enunciation not previously identifiable within a given field of experience, whose identification is thus part of the reconfiguration of the field of experience. (1999, p. 35, my bracket)

Irit Rogoff (2008) clearly expresses this sentiment in her discussion of Foucault's (2001) lectures of *parrhesia* in his text *Fearless Speech*. I quote:

> I think "education" and the "educational turn" might be just that: the moment when we attend to the production and articulation of truths – not truths as correct or provable, as fact, but truth as that which collects around its subjectivities that are neither gathered nor reflected by other utterances. Stating truths in relation to the great arguments, issues and great institutions of the day is relatively easy, for these dictate (and govern) the terms by which truths are arrived at and articulated. Telling truth in the marginal and barely-formed spaces in which the curious gather – this is another project altogether: one's personal relation to truth. (Rogoff, e-flux 11/2008, my bracket)

For me, this quote advocates a *concern* for local processes of learning and a subjectivation to the on-going truths of such learning. That is to say, it is arguing for a need to 'have a care' for the emergence and perseverance of truths of learning within local or even marginalised or obscure (from the dominant traditions and forms of knowledge) positions; forms of learning that may easily be overlooked by established frameworks and norms, but which have a personal legitimacy and, which when allowed to appear, expand our comprehension of what learning is. I always remember occasions when I was puzzled and then surprised by the sense children deploy in their drawings, which was not immediately apparent but which when revealed expanded my comprehension of drawing practice. These were local pedagogical events, if you like, which, for me, had transformative affects and effects. The disruption of established ways of knowing, through learning events, means that learners need to be able to handle states of uncertainty as new ways of knowing and new competences begin to emerge. This suggests a rather curious almost contradictory ontological relation of learning to states of not knowing and the experience of affect, mystery and wonder.

Peter Hallward (2003, p. xxvi) sums up the relation between event, truth and subject:

> Truth, subject and event are all aspects of a single process: a truth comes into being through the subjects who proclaim it, and in doing so, constitute themselves as subjects in their fidelity to the event.

The event itself comes and disappears. It seems to subsist in a strange temporality between being and becoming: that which exists and that which-is-yet-to-come. Such temporality seems close to the Greek term *kairos* explored by Antonio Negri, Agamben and others, which I discuss in Chap. 8.

Martin Savransky (2016, p. 155) influenced by the cosmology and process philosophy of Alfred North Whitehead states simply that an event is a 'transformation induced by an occurrence', something that happens and, as a result of which, a transformation occurs in a particular situation. The event is not what happens or how it is experienced, but is to be viewed, as Deleuze (1994, p. 7) put it, as an 'incorporeal effect' upon bodies and their practices. For Deleuze, events are not 'substantives or adjectives but verbs' (Ibid, p. 7). The event is not to be thought of as what happens, but more in terms of the injection or occurrence of novelty in what happens that opens a potential for something new to emerge, a new way of thinking, seeing, acting, feeling. For Deleuze (2007, p. 233), events are spatio-temporal bifurcations, 'a deviation with respect to laws, an unstable field which opens up a new field of the possible'. Thus, for Deleuze, as with Whitehead and others, events seem to be inherent to all processes of becoming in all entities, organic, inorganic, human or non-human. They can be conceived as constituting the vibration or pulsation of the world.

Savransky (Ibid, p. 156) also points to the temporality of events, to the outcomes of events that have happened and the potential for what might happen. This has particular relevance for events of learning in each singular context. From the perspective of pedagogic work, it introduces a question of ethics because it raises the issue of the teacher's obligation towards the relevance (truth) of how something matters for a learner in a particular learning encounter; it concerns how this demand of obligation is inherited by a teacher, and then how the obligation pertains in working with a learner's exposure of the learning event towards potentials for becoming—the coming to matter of a new way of thinking, seeing, acting, feeling. In this scenario, pedagogic work can be conceived as a becoming-with and a making-with, what Donna Harraway (2016) terms *sympoiesis*.

It is this situated nature of events of learning (teaching) with which this book is concerned and the kinds of pedagogic sensibilities that emerge towards learning events and their different local matterings and outcomes; the different obligations that such matterings call upon which are conceived by teachers and which may expand or 'constrain' pedagogic work. White-head's statement in *Modes of Thought* (p. 116), 'Have a care, here is something that matters', suggests both an ethics and a pragmatics of an event and its relevance, a pragmatics that involves both a past and a future in the present captured by Susan Buck-Morss's phrase *the pragmatics of the suddenly possible*. Such pragmatics relating to pedagogical work have a concern for the way events of learning matter for a learner, the problems they pose, the anxieties, frustrations, illuminations, breakthroughs that emerge, how they are inherited and precipitate new ways of thinking, seeing, making and feeling. How does a teacher become obligated to these matterings in each local context of learning and how do such oblig-atory dispositions expand (or not) the horizons of teaching and the practice of pedagogical work?

Speculatively, we might consider events of learning as producing the possibility for what I call *disobedient potentials*. Paul Klee made the point that art does not represent the visible, but *makes visible*; in a sense, it disrupts and is disobedient towards established ways of seeing and thinking.

Savransky (Ibid, p. 166) makes a similar disruptive claim by stating that, 'an event is not what *is made* possible but what *makes* the possible'. I am using the notion of disobedience, then, in relation to events that precipitate disruptions to established parameters of being and coexistence and expose learners to new potentials for becoming, the event of disobedience.

Within a process-oriented approach to becoming and becoming-with, we can say that events happen all the time; some may perpetuate existing forms of coexistence and their patterns or habits of functioning whilst others may disrupt established patterns, habits and boundaries, thus opening up new possibilities for becoming. This applies to all entities and their relations, including molecules, cells, bodies, plants, animals, ideas and feelings. In the worlds of human coexistence with other humans and non-humans, events in the form of *encounters* may disrupt established ways of functioning and as a consequence create new or modified ways of thinking, seeing, acting and feeling. It is when we are confronted with the event of an encounter that we may be forced to reconstruct the way we think or act, as Deleuze (1994, p. 139) states, '[s]omething in the world forces us to think. This something is an object not of recognition but of a fundamental *encounter*'. An encounter with a challenging artwork or practice does not summon established ways of thinking *about* art, for this would negate the idea of encounter, but rather challenges thought to think. That is to say, it disrupts any previous ways of thinking and speaking about art so that we are placed in a position where, referencing Deleuze, we have to think without image. Such encounters may lead to the invention of propositions or questions that transform habits of functioning and thus make available new modes of becoming. In a strange way, such art objects or practices *object,* they constitute a recalcitrant force that may precipitate the invention of questions or propositions that in turn may generate new and unpredictable ways of thinking, seeing and acting. Savransky (Ibid, pp. 175–176) provides a concise statement concerning the lure and *disclosure* of an event and subsequent creation of novelty in contrast to the *closure* of the possible according to existent worlds and bodies of knowledge; it is of direct relevance to the heart of pedagogic work that this book advocates.

> ...to be lured by the possibility of an event, to work with a view towards a possible invention requires, first and foremost, that one encounters situations and objects of inquiry without a predefined conception of what is naturally or culturally possible. Indeed, insofar as the event is that which, by introducing a novelty in the world, makes a difference that transforms the possible, to

encounter a situation with a predefined sense of what that situation is capable of is to mobilise the notion of 'the possible' as that which sets the ultimate limits to what might become relevant in that situation. It is, in other words, to reduce the possible to the known and to silently prophesy the death of the event. This is precisely what the question of relevance seeks to resist. Indeed, to orient an inquiry not towards the production of a solution to a pre-existent problem but towards the question of 'how is it, here, that things matter?' is to expose such a mode of inquiry to an unknown, and thus, to be lured by the emergence of a different order of the possible.

Nearly a century ago, in his text *Reconstruction in Philosophy* (1920), John Dewey wrote about the demands of the world with which people were confronted and the need to acquire what he called 'intellectual instrumentalities' that would facilitate creative and pragmatic responses (Savransky pp. 8–9). It was a call for a new relevance of practice, a pragmatics of thinking probably inherited from Charles Saunders Peirce and William James that might facilitate appropriate forms of action. The notion of reconstruction as employed by Dewey to meet the demands of a changing world, of reconstructing the ways in which we come to terms with our worlds, is deeply resonant with a call for engaging with the notions of relevance and encounter in pedagogic work.

Relevance and Obligation

We know that in recent decades in England, the United States and elsewhere, the word relevance, as employed by government policies for education, connotes a concern for relevance of action towards prescribed and valued outcomes that meet the agenda for economic ambition and competition. This book opposes this prescriptive inflection of relevance by contrasting it with situations in which pedagogic work attempts to respond effectively to the not-yet-known; the different ways in which learners engage with the process of learning in their local learning encounters, and how these different learning experiences come to matter for them. Here, Whitehead's deceptively simple warning, 'Have a care...' denotes a different but crucial use of relevance from the notion of prescription. So, rather than working from a prescribed agenda for learning and specified outcomes that are judged accordingly, the approach to relevance taken here in pedagogic work is viewed as an adventure (Atkinson 2017) in which a teacher needs to respond to the immanence of local events of learning and their specific situated values that may lie beyond the parameters of a teacher's judgement informed by her established pedagogical knowledge. To work with how a learning encounter matters for a learner is therefore to engage in a pedagogical adventure, that does not adopt a pre-figured scenario set by a teacher of a problem and its respective solutions, but to view the relevance of an encounter for a learner, as Savransky (p. 9) puts it, 'inhering in the situated specificity' of his or her becoming, which is really a becoming-with the encounter and its human and non-human components.

One consequence of attending to this situated specificity of a learner's practice is that it may force teachers to examine or interrogate their habits and frameworks of pedagogic practice in order to test out or to invent propositions for how this might be achieved. Whitehead's profound warning 'have a care, here is something that matters' captures the notion of relevance emerging in a learner's practice and Savransky's modification into the question, 'how is it, here, that things matter?' sets in motion the pedagogical adventure of trying to ascertain the mode of relevance in a learner's practice. An important pedagogical question therefore is asking what this 'here' is for a learner and how things matter 'there'. Following this, the question arises as to how this mattering for a learner becomes inherited by a teacher, which in turn raises ethical, political and aesthetic challenges towards providing effective responses to each learner's mode of learning and their specific modes of mattering in relation to a learning encounter. In trying to draw alongside or negotiate how a learning encounter matters for a learner (and here we need to speak of an ecology of mattering), pedagogic work seems to require an *invention* itself; that is to say, such work constitutes an inquiry that demands an invention of forms of negotiation towards how things matter for a learner. The relation between a pedagogic object (a learner's mode of practice, way of thinking, acting), and the invention of propositions and questions towards such objects has to be considered carefully, this entails an ecology of questions stemming from 'have a care...'.

In *Adventures of Ideas* (1933/1967), Whitehead pursues what we might call an ethics of concern. The term concern is taken in the Quaker sense of obligation in the structure of experience. Whitehead (p. 176) asserts that 'the basis of experience is emotional' by this, he is referring to what he calls an 'affective tone' that emerges in a relation of relevance between things.

> The occasion as subject has a 'concern' for the object. And the 'concern' at once places the object as a component in the experience of the subject, with an affective tone drawn from this object and directed towards it. (p. 176)

In his discussion of his concept *prehension,* Whitehead (1929, 1933) provides a more elaborate description of this relational notion of concern, of how things take account of each other:

> The subject and object are relative terms. An occasion is a subject in respect to its special activity concerning an object; and anything is an object in respect to its provocation of some special activity within a subject. Such a mode of activity is termed a 'prehension'. (p. 176)

An experience, such as a learning encounter, consists of a prehended object or objects, and a subjective form that is the affective tone that determines the quality and effectiveness of a prehension for a learner in the learning encounter. The pedagogical task is to try to ascertain the relevance for the learner of the object that provokes the learner's prehension of the object and the subjective form of the prehension: how it matters for a learner. The negotiation of relevance in pedagogic work thus involves the teacher's inheritance of the event of the student's learning encounter, and the teacher's invention of possible openings, questions and propositions for the student's learning; this inheritance and this future constitutes the adventure of pedagogy. As Savransky (Ibid, p. 51) states:

> Thus, an adventure of relevance (pedagogy) does not endow an (pedagogical) inquiry with the right to demand compliance of those to whom its questions are posed. If it is to learn something, an inquiry must *first* learn to deal with how, in a situation that it inherits and in which it partakes, things matter, and to take those senses of relevance as constraints upon its own inventive activity. (my insertions in brackets)

Such negotiations of relevance of what matters for a learner and the constraints of such mattering that affect a teacher's inventive responses are not infrequent in pedagogic work. In my experience of working with young children and older students engaged in art practices, such negotiations were always present but, I suspect, that rather than trying to work with the immanence of relevance for a learner, I tended to respond by addressing what a child or student produced from a series of established prepositional relations that allowed me to speak *about* outcomes *from* acquired perspectives, bodies of knowledge and prescribed identities. Such moments raise the contrast between responses determined by the *closure of knowledge* and those that remain open to the *disclosure of knowing*. To try to think from the immanence of how something matters for a learner is likely to confound one's mode of thought and understanding; it's a tricky exercise, full of pitfalls, which demands treading carefully and a speculative disposition.

Savransky (Ibid, p. 79) makes a crucial point about dispositions towards problematic encounters, such as when we are confronted with learning practices and their outcomes that are perplexing, and the need for inventing creative responses:

> ...the event of invention could be characterised by the risky process of devising a creative, choreographic process that might invent a manner of attending to the obligations generated by the recalcitrance of the object of inquiry.

The recalcitrance of a learner's practice and outcomes to a teacher's mode of understanding introduces an interesting take on the idea of objectivity discussed by Savransky (pp. 79–85). Such recalcitrance or, as I call it, *disobedience*, raises the fundamental issue of the possible irrelevance of a teacher's questions to the learner's mode of practice, but also how such irrelevance may have the power to (mis)construe a learner's achievement or lack of achievement. By submitting to the irrelevance of a teacher's questions that impose the latter's sense of how things matter or do not for a learner, pedagogic work may easily occlude the relevance of how something matters for a learner in his or her specific mode of inquiry. The task therefore is to consider how a learner's practice or outcomes may 'object' to the questions asked by a teacher so that the latter has to reconfigure his or her inquiry according to the obligations interposed by this 'objection' and move towards the learner's experience of how something matters in a specific learning encounter. In other words, such reconfigurings 'have a care', they have a concern, they try to cultivate and develop an ethics of concern. Drawing upon Andrew Pickering's (1995) notion of a 'dance of agency', which Pickering uses to describe the on-going relations with the material world in which humans and non-humans participate alternately influencing events, Savransky proposes a notion of *becoming with* through the event and relevance of an encounter, which for me relates very much to a becoming-with, a thinking-with, a seeing-with, or a making-with of pedagogic encounters.

> A dance in which actors are neither all-powerful nor created *ex nihilo*, but reciprocally transformed through the patterns of their often joined, often

different, senses of relevance, as they become together in an *encounter*. The task is thus not to enforce a normative ethics of reality that be imposed upon the habits of thought and practice of a future social inquiry, but to create some of the tools required for an ethics that can be cultivated *in* the process of learning how to think and know in an encounter. To that extent, what is at stake is the production of an image of inquiry that—as Deleuze (1994: 167) would put it—be ultimately an inquiry without image. (p. 79)

However, Tim Ingold (2013, pp. 98–102) provides a useful response to Pickering's notion of a dance of agency between participants in the process of becoming-together in an encounter. He argues that the notion of agency be replaced by a *dance of animacy,* where the emphasis is placed not so much on interacting agents but on an evolving process of *correspondence* in which the participants, human and/or non-human respond to one another in counterpoint. He gives the examples of flying kites and making pots on a wheel and states:

> As with any dance, this should be read not laterally, back and forth, but longitudinally as a movement in which partners (human and non-human) take it in turns to lead and be led. (p. 101. My bracket)

The dance of animacy is thus a contrapuntal interweaving of bodies, minds and materials in an 'encompassing, morphogenetic field of forces' which, in the case of kite flying, is composed of wind force and, in the case of throwing pots, the force of the turning wheel.

The different dimensions of becoming-together in pedagogic work, emanating through events of encounter, involves a becoming-together of different pathways of inheritance towards horizons of future potentials, or disappointments. Becoming-together, as Deleuze and Guattari state (1988, p. 293), is always 'in the middle', involving previous pathways of inheritance, the obligations and relevance of the present encounter moving towards the potentials of a future of not yet known possibilities or the disappointments of failure. The process of becoming-with is open to disclosures of experience; to inventions of knowing, seeing, thinking and acting. The formation of knowledge often precipitates the openness of experiencing towards a closure of experience. Whitehead (1938) comments with feeling:

The history of thought is a tragic mixture of vibrant disclosure and of dead-ening closure. The sense of penetration is lost in the certainty of completed knowledge. This dogmatism is the antichrist of learning. (p. 58)

How might we take on board these ideas of event, encounter, obligation and relevance when considering the notions of politics and aesthetics of learning in pedagogic work? I have already mentioned the need to develop ethical sensibilities in relation to 'having a care', of trying to develop an ethics of concern emerging from the immanence of how something matters for a learner during and after a learning encounter, which by implication, if we are not to resort to an established or normative ethics, means, in the spirit of Deleuze and Guattari, that we have to cultivate an ethics without image. What, though, are the further implications for a politics and aes-thetics without image for pedagogical work that 'has a concern' for the different ways in which things matter for learners in their pursuit of learning? In the next section I will attempt to consider the issue of politics.

ETHICS AND POLITICS OF LEARNING WITHOUT IMAGE: PEDAGOGY OF IMMANENCE

It goes without saying that here I am not concerned with politics in terms of party politics. Badiou and Ranciere hold similar ideas on politics that are helpful. They both reject the use of politics to refer to the manoeuvres of political parties and insist upon it as a term that refers to processes of thinking and acting that strike out from normative or dominant ideological forces that perpetuate social injustices in order to invent new, more eman-cipatory possibilities for coexistence. With some modification, in the con-text of pedagogical work, a politics of learning therefore relates to those learning encounters through which learning becomes a political act when the stubborn 'objection' of a learner's practice, its recalcitrant force, invokes an obligation for the teacher to have a concern and where the consequences of such concern may transform pedagogic work in its comprehension of both teaching and learning; a transformed pedagogical coexistence through which unknown or unrecognised modes of learning are valued. So here, it is important to contemplate a politics that emerges from ways of thinking and acting that may be excluded from a teacher's parameters of pedagogic work; ways of thinking and acting that are disobedient to such parameters and which in turn shed light upon the latter's 'irrelevance' to a learner's mode of practice. Here, politics relates to the transforming of modes of coexistence in pedagogical work through a becoming-with that can be characterised as an ethico-political adventure.

An issue of politics perhaps arises when the irrelevance of a teacher's questions or advances, an irrelevance arriving perhaps from a prescribed agenda for learning, meets the relevance of a learning encounter for a learner. The event of politics thus requires a refusal of the subordination of learning to teaching and engaging in a reciprocal dance of animacy or correspondence that invents new modes of thinking and acting in the pedagogical context. To engage in such an on-going reciprocal dance in pedagogic work, the transcendence of prescribed knowledge, teaching methodologies or mode of assessment have to be relaxed in order to allow the immanence of a learner's mode of practice to appear.

In Chap. 2, I referred to the transcendence of established forms of practice and bodies of knowledge that constitute curriculum content in school art education and which pedagogise teachers and learners as pedagogic subjects. I am using the term transcendence to refer to that (forms of knowledge, values, systems of belief, etc.) according to which practice (teaching and learning) is conceived, explained and evaluated or assessed. I mentioned a series of important genres in art education, which in their respective terms have influenced and advanced curriculum content and its aims, thus expanding our understanding of art education and its practice. I contrasted this transcendence of knowledge with the immanence of local learning processes; the particular way in which a learner engages with the content of learning through learning encounters, the way something matters for a learner, how a learner makes sense of this mattering. These local flows of immanence produce what I termed a *necessary transcendence*, that is to say forms of transcendence that are inherent to and emerge from the immanence of practice in contrast to the external transcendence or the hylomorphism of established forms of knowledge and practice that are frequently employed to assess the quality of this immanence. Immanence thus refers to an intrinsic creative process that proceeds, if encouraged, by means of experimentation and invention or what Daniel Smith (2012, p. 221) calls 'unforeseen becomings'. The act of assessing such processes according to established knowledge and practice involves an external control that may occlude the inherent vitality of practice that extends and affirms the creative act of becoming.

In an essay discussing transcendence and immanence in the philosophies of Derrida and Deleuze, Smith (Ibid, p. 284) comes down on the side of Deleuze in that he believes that 'the "philosophy of the future" needs to move in the direction of immanence' as advocated by Deleuze, most importantly because of the practical ramifications of philosophical work that engage with ethics and politics. But, as Smith points out, whilst Deleuze and Guattari in *What is Philosophy?* (p. 45) recognise the 'natural' place of immanence in philosophical work, they also notice that it has not always been welcome, and that opposition to giving priority to immanence is usually set in moral terms along the lines that without the guiding hand of transcendence, we would descend into subjectivism or relativism. We can witness a particular manifestation of this moral position in those approaches to pedagogical work that prioritise knowledge over learning, where knowledge is viewed in terms of packets of information that are held by teachers whose task is to deliver them to learners. Such approaches seem to pay little regard to the complex syntheses and correspondences of experience that form human beings on many levels, nor do they acknowledge the importance of trying to comprehend how something matters for a learner (a new concept, a new practice, a new value, a new affect) and how this mattering is crucial for effective learning.

In acknowledging the notion of immanence in Spinoza's *Ethics*, Deleuze considers the immanence of being in terms of intensity or 'degree of power' (Smith, p. 285). For Spinoza, ontology *is* ethics (Thiele 2008), and the fundamental question therefore is not a moral one as in 'What must I do?' but a practical one, 'What can I do?' in a particular situation or encounter. What *are* my capacities or capabilities to act or to think in *this* situation? How can I extend my capacity to act or think more effectively? Such questions raise a critique of transcendence in an ethico-political sense. Do the transcendent forms of knowledge and practice that are deemed important for learners to acquire—and their respective forms of assessment—actually separate or detach some learners from their capacity to act and to learn? In other words, from the perspective of a pedagogy of immanence, does a pedagogy grounded in transcendence reduce learners to a form of servitude and some to marginalisation? In the practical domains of teaching and learning, the ethical and political issues of immanence and transcendence become acute. Do we conceive teaching and learning in the transcendent terms of what might be called the transmission view of pedagogy, where learning is subordinated to teaching (the power of knowledge transmitted by a teacher to a learner, see Cattegno 1972), or do we conceive pedagogic work in terms of trying to respond to the particular immanence and intensity of a learner's experience (existence) and their particular capacities to think and act? If we take the former position then pedagogy presupposes a transcendence that guides the moral/political compass of pedagogy, it is grounded in a hylomorphic principle—the imposition of form on matter—whereas if we take the latter position, this transcendence could obscure and prevent a pedagogical ethics and politics grounded in the capacities of a learner's existence, through which form emerges from within local process of mattering.

I was once asked after giving a presentation on the event in pedagogic work, 'how do we recognise an event?' At the time, I did not see the implicit transcendence in the use of the term 'recognition', which would deny the novelty of an event, its rupturing of any framework of recognition. Pedagogies of recognition function on the basis of a presumed transcendence that determines the 'recognised' object—the practice and outcome of learning—according, for example, to a teacher's expectations that constitute his or her framework of recognition. Learning encounters as events can transform thinking and acting, whether this be a teacher encountering a learner's practice that is unexpected or mysterious, or a learner being confronted with a new learning challenge. This latter approach to pedagogic work may be conceived in terms of pedagogies of the event or a pedagogy of immanence. Artists that push the boundaries of art practice frequently produce work that generates encounters whose fundamental dimension is one of affect that forces thought to think rather than following established routes of thought. Encounters with such work can expand both what it is to be human as well as our understanding of what art is.

Deleuze made a clear distinction between ethics and morality, regarding the latter generally to refer to established rules such as moral codes that are employed by independent subjects to judge actions according to the transcendent values of the code (religious, normative criteria, etc.). Ethics, on the other hand, for Deleuze, does not flow from a transcendent position of judgement held by an independent subject, but is rather to be viewed in terms of a process of production, the building of a life from the immanence of its becoming. The important point here is that the ethical emerges from the immanence of a particular mode of existence, Smith (Ibid, p. 147) writes:

> Rather than judging actions and thoughts by appealing to transcendent or universal values, one evaluates them by determining the mode of existence that serves as their principle. A pluralist method of explanation by immanent modes of existence is in this way made to replace the recourse to transcendent values; an immanent ethical difference is substituted for the transcendent moral opposition.

But does adopting this pluralist position open it to the criticism of 'anything goes'? Surely we require some normative criteria by which to judge our actions and thoughts, for if we simply employ intrinsic criteria immanent to modes of existence and their particular ways of acting and thinking, how can we compare and evaluate them? Deleuze's response to this conundrum is to argue that we can evaluate modes of existence by the *immanence of their power*, that is to say by considering if a particular mode of existence has pushed its capacity to act as far as it is able. Alternatively we might ask, has a particular mode been prevented from deploying its power to act?

These points need to be qualified in relation to the idea of subjectivity. Deleuze is not assuming a prior independent subject experiencing the world, but a subject who emerges from experience in a world. In other words, he is not assuming a transcendent subject who synthesises experience, but a subject who emerges from the immanence of a series of syntheses that constitute experience. Therefore, for Deleuze, ethics is not grounded in the notion of a transcendent subject or a transcendent set of rules but emerges from the specificity of modes of existence and their particular affects.

The notion of ethics with which I am concerned apropos learning and pedagogic work is that which relates to the intensity of immanence in particular modes of existence (learning, teaching). It is the notion that occupied Deleuze (1988, 1990) and his philosophical forerunners, Spinoza and Nietzsche. Modes of existence are not judged according to some external set of rules, principles or criteria but they are evaluated according to the degree to which they can fulfil their capacity to act effectively. How can I actively and fully deploy my capacities to act effectively? An ethics of immanence will therefore be critical of that which obscures and prevents my capacity to act.

Daniel Smith (Ibid, p. 153) formulates three questions concerning ethics and modes of existence based upon Spinoza's three formulations of the ethical question suggested above:

1. How is a mode of existence determined?
2. How are modes of existence to be evaluated?
3. What are the conditions for the creation of new modes of existence?

These questions have important implications for pedagogical work as viewed from the notion of modes of existence rather than, for example, abstract classifications of ability or standards. Here I am thinking of the particular modes of existence that constitute a learner in a specific learning encounter or modes of existence that compose a teacher in specific phases of pedagogical work. Taking Smith's first question from the standpoint of an immanent ethics; a mode of existence is not determined by transcendent forms external to it, such as assessment criteria in educational contexts. It also rejects the notion of a transcendent subject existing prior to a particular experience. Modes of existence consist of degrees of power to act and relations of affectivity, or alternatively, a curtailing of such power. Spinoza's theory of affections refers to the idea that a body is composed of a multiplicity of parts and relations and that a body is defined intensively by degrees of power—or a capacity to affect and be affected by other bodies (Smith, p. 154). In his text, *Spinoza, Practical Philosophy*, Deleuze (1988) writes:

> An individual is first of all a singular essence, which is to say, a degree of power. A characteristic relation corresponds to this essence, and a certain capacity for being affected corresponds to this degree of power. (p. 27)

Extensively, a body is composed of a complex series of relations in a world whilst intensively a body is composed of a certain capacity to affect or be affected by other bodies. A mode of existence is therefore defined in terms of its capacity to affect or be affected. So we might ask what in a particular context affects a person? How is a person affected? What has no affect? What affects threaten its cohesion and thus lowers its capacity to act effectively? What can a person's body achieve or mind think? How does a person enter into composition with other bodies (ideas, concepts, ways of seeing)? These questions are difficult to conceive from a neutral perspective in that bodies and their modes of existence are frequently subject to transcendent forms of subjection in social formations, what Foucault terms *dispositifs*. The issue of politics is therefore inevitably part of an immanent ethics that seeks to release lives from capture by transcendent forms or formations. It entails acts of resistance or disobedience to such formations and introduces Foucault's notion of a life becoming a form of resistance, of inventing new ways of life and relations with others.

Smith's second question, 'how do we evaluate particular modes of existence?' raises the issue already mentioned: how can we achieve such evaluation without norms of judgement or normative criteria, without image? Do we need to develop, as Deleuze suggests, a pedagogy of the image? Can we employ purely immanent criteria? How do we arrive at these? Such issues are inextricable from social forces and frameworks that may facilitate but also constrain the capacity to act effectively. Evaluation of a mode of existence that attempts to address its immanence cannot be determined by external principles, but according to the extent to which and the manner in which a person is able to act in line with his or her capacity for acting.

The third question asks how we might create or invent new modes of existence that are not determined by external social forces, even though we are never free of these, but which emerge from an intrinsic acting upon the self in order to bring about a self-transformation. It is in relation to this question that some interesting notions emerge from Deleuze and Guattari, including, for example, their idea of the minoritarian, discussed in Chap. 7. Minor practices are those that arise within the majoritarian or dominant practices, and which make the latter *stammer*. They challenge transcendent and normative social formations. It is also in relation to the issue of minor practices that we can consider *events of learning* as shifts into new or modified ontological and epistemological phases.

If we prioritise a pedagogy of immanence, then the pedagogical imperative is to try to understand learning from the perspective of the learner's capacities to learn and not to judge such capacities from external criteria. This form of pedagogical ethics demands that pedagogical work engages with the intrinsic capacities of learners, it requests that we try to understand *how* something matters for a learner in a particular learning encounter. It is this 'how', or more specifically, *the relations and correspondences that compose this 'how'*, that constitutes the immanent criteria from which forms of *necessary transcendence* emerge, the latter acting as transient stepping stones that may or may not facilitate further learning.

Ranciere, Emancipation and Learning

The relation between ethics and immanence apropos teaching and learning can be considered through a reading of Ranciere's writings on learning and emancipation, which raise both ethical and political issues. For Ranciere, of paramount importance in emancipatory education is the act of revealing 'an intelligence to itself' (1991, p. 28). This involves encouraging and supporting the immanence of a learner's intrinsic capacity to learn and although Biesta, following Ranciere, states that the route students will take to use their intelligence is unknown, it is, I suggest, possible to work with the responses that students make along these routes in their learning encounters.

Ranciere formulates his ideas on emancipatory education not for the purpose of developing a more effective pedagogy but as a political position in the context of education. His intense discussions of the nineteenth century pedagogue Joseph Jacotot in the book, *The Ignorant Schoolmaster: Five Lessons in Intellectual Emancipation,* are now widely discussed and they have generated a growing body of literature dedicated to exploring Ranciere's work and its relevance to education. It is helpful to consider the key ideas that Ranciere develops in this book towards an emancipatory education and to ascertain what this term means.

Biesta (2010) identifies one approach to emancipatory education that has grown over recent decades, and this is characterised by what he calls 'the new language of learning' where emphasis is placed upon the terms learner and learning. Generally the intention is to move away from didactic models of teaching, assessment and the delivery of curriculum content towards giving priority to the learner and the different ways in which learners learn. This approach has not been taken up in schools in England and elsewhere (apart from the child-centred pedagogies from the mid-1960s to the mid-1970s), and recent decades have seen an unrelenting emphasis in state schools in many countries upon the delivery, monitoring and assessment of subject knowledge. However, variations of a more learner-centred approach to learning have taken effect in places such as gallery and museum education or 'alternative' schools, which are not subject to government or state educational policy. In a sense, this approach to education can be viewed as a liberation of learners from imposed knowledge and institutional structures. Biesta argues, however, that the term 'learner' in its common usage, rather than being liberatory, actually constructs the learner in terms of lack. This is because the general conception of a learner is of someone who is required or wishes to learn something, whether that might be a skill, a body of knowledge, a set of values, a competence, critical awareness, a series of procedures and so on. In other words, this common conception of learners constructs them in the mode of 'not-yet' competent, skilful or learned.

Of course, this is quite a natural state, for in order to operate a piece of machinery or a computer, to learn a second language or how to conduct a chemical experiment, to build a brick wall and so on, we have to learn the sets of skills and techniques required. But the problem that Ranciere and Biesta contend is endemic to schools and other institutions, is that the transition from the state of not knowing to knowing requires an intervention by a teacher because the learner is viewed as incapable of learning by herself or himself. There is therefore a double lack: a lack of skill or knowledge and a perceived lack relating to a self-capacity to learn.

According to Ranciere and Biesta, the teacher-learner relationship is based on a fundamental inequality between those who possess knowledge (teachers) and those who lack knowledge and the capacity to learn by themselves (learners). The chief mode of overcoming these two lacks is through *explanation*. But Biesta retorts, 'Is it?' Explanation may appear to reduce this inequality such as when something is explained to somebody but the latter has to makes sense of the explanation, *it has to matter*, this *mattering* is not simply transferred from teacher to learner. So explanation does not provide a pure conduit of communication between a teacher and a learner. What it does communicate however, according to Ranciere, is the idea that a learner is unable to understand without explanation.

> . . .to explain something to someone is first of all to show him he cannot understand it by himself (Ranciere 1991, p. 6)
>
> To explain something to one who is ignorant is, first and foremost, to explain that which would not be understood if it were not explained. It is to demonstrate an incapacity. Explanation offers itself as a means to reduce the situation of inequality where those who know nothing are in relation with those who know. But, this reduction is, rather, a confirmation (Ranciere 2010a p. 3).

The explicative order of most institutionalised education confirms a fundamental inequality between teacher and learner, which for Ranciere, constitutes the myth of pedagogy that institutes a logic of inequality as axiomatic. The terms 'learner' and 'learning' in many educational institutions and practices are saturated by this axiom of inequality.

However, is it possible to conceive learners and learning from another place that rejects this axiom; a place informed by an assumption of equality and a demand for its verification in practice? A further question emerges, 'is it possible to teach without an explicative order?' These issues lead Ranciere (2010a) into a wider debate that conceives the explicative order not only in educational contexts but also as a kind of universal model that structures society; it constitutes a social logic. This has ramifications for the questions just posed: is it indeed possible to proceed from an axiom of equality in a social structure grounded in inequality and is it therefore possible to teach beyond the controlling devices of an explicative order that perpetuates inequality?

A conception of learners beyond what Ranciere terms the explicative order entails a rejection of the terms learner and learning that assume a fundamental inequality between teachers and learners, between the intelligence of the teacher and the intelligence of the learner. A different kind of pedagogical relationship has to emerge, not based upon an inequality of intelligence but one in which learning encounters, initiated by a teacher, demand a response from learners through which their intelligence, that is to say, their capacity to learn, is revealed to them. Ranciere describes this demand by the teacher as a demand for 'speech' on the part of the student, but he is using the term 'speech' in a specific way that introduces a political dimension to the practices of teaching and learning. The purpose of the teacher's demand is not to lead the student to the established knowledge of the teacher; this may result in learning, but not to emancipation whereby an intelligence is revealed to itself. The pedagogical imperative of the teacher is to initiate learning encounters and to demand that students 'pay attention' (or have a care) and develop a critical disposition to what confronts them and how they see it, think about it, evaluate it, and so on. This critical disposition engages with the subject matter of an encounter but also, crucially, with the student's capacity to learn. If we are using the terms learner and learning therefore with a view towards advocating this pedagogical imperative then such terms must necessarily abandon the subordination of one intelligence to another, they must reject any assumption of lack. Biesta (2010) suggests that in being called to *study* by the teacher, the learner can 'in the most literal sense' be conceived as a student. Thus in what follows the terms learner and student become synonymous.

The demand by the teacher for the student to 'speak', that is to say, to engage in practices that reveal its intelligence to itself, its capacity to learn by itself, is not simply aimed at a student's *ability* to speak but, more significantly, at who is allowed to 'speak', or in other words, who is allowed to develop this immanent capacity to learn. Being allowed to speak in Ranciere's terms is not about someone having the power to allow others to speak or for others to feel the need to be recognised as speakers by such power. Such situations only repeat the inequality of the explicative order. The term 'being allowed to speak' relates to Ranciere's (1999) notion of 'the distribution of the sensible', which designates a social space in which certain ways of speaking, acting or being are recognised and others are not. In relation to the focus of this chapter, it concerns those learners whose modes of learning are recognised according to specific pedagogical orders and those that are not. Such distributions are held in place by what Ranciere terms a police order (Ibid, p. 29) that determines which bodies and group-ings are visible or invisible. The policing of a particular distribution of the sensible does not entail a purely disciplinary structure, but is more reflective of hegemonic relations whereby particular rules or codes allow particular bodies, ways of speaking, seeing and acting to appear and others to be marginalised. It is an inclusive structuring in which every body is identified, where some are able to speak and participate but others have no say or approval to act. In educational contexts, we might view examination or assessment processes as forms of police order that oversee particular distri-butions of the sensible, where some learners appear positively and where others do not.

The police order affirming and perpetuating a particular distribution of the sensible is therefore a form of transcendence, as discussed above, that exerts an external force upon processes of becoming in social spaces. It is reasonable to assume that such transcendence, as already argued, is likely to occlude or ignore the immanence of learning processes inherent to those learners whose ways of learning are 'invisible' to the transcendent order. This does not mean that all transcendent orders are bad, they are not, and some may be well intentioned. The key issue concerns those points or situations when a particular transcendence privileges certain ways of speak-ing, seeing or acting whilst others are deemed illegitimate, or are completely overlooked, so that some learners are dispossessed, thus denying the axiom of equality. It is at such points of dispossession or invisibility that for Ranciere the practice of politics emerges in order to challenge the authority of transcendence imparted by a particular distribution of the sensible and its respective police order. It is at this point, where the police order meets the force of politics in the form of a particular issue of equality and where the notion of an ethics of immanence, of building a life, where ontology and ethics function reciprocally as inventive processes, that all seem to converge.

Ranciere argues that politics invokes a challenge to the police order. Politics does not refer to the manoeuvrings and bickering of political parties, which is to say politics as conventionally understood. This is not politics for Ranciere (1999, 2004, 2006). Politics emerges as an event when someone or a body of people *appear* in a social setting when, previous to their appearance, they were devalued or ignored. Such appearance creates a stuttering or a break within the existing police order so that a re-distribution of the sensible, ways of seeing, speaking and acting arise. There are some similarities here with Deleuze and Guattari's (1994) ideas on minoritarian and majoritarian practices. The driving force behind such appearances is equality. Politics in the words of Ranciere, 'makes visible what had no business being seen, and makes heard a discourse where once there was only place for noise (1999, p. 30)'. Politics is therefore an event where the force of the police order meets the force of politics in the name of equality and this meeting process is given the name *dissensus* (Ranciere 2010b). Dissensus does not refer to acts of disagreement but rather to a break within existing systems of representation and identity created by new appearances and the force of equality. We might consider how dissensus functioned in the struggle to gain voting rights by black people in the state of Alabama. Bodies of people and individuals took action through marches and other forms of protest. Their persistent appearance in the name of equality and the violent resistance of state authorities eventually led to a hiatus whereby the authorities had to accede to the protestors' demands. These events of dissensus produced a new form of existence for black people which, previous to their protests, had no place, or more specifically a place of no part, in the existing police order, though the situation today still remains problematic and intolerable for many.

The difference between the consensus of the police order and the dissensus of politics rests on a difference between the notion of *subjectification* and *subjectivation*. Within an existing police order and its distribution of the sensible, people achieve forms of subjectification, identities that are consistent with particular ways of speaking, seeing and acting. We might view current systems of schooling and their curriculum, examination and assessment systems as forming a distribution of the sensible with its respective police order in which teachers and students achieve their pedagogised identities. Subjectivation is a process of passing beyond existing forms of subjectification, it is:

> ...the production through a series of actions of a body and a capacity for enunciation not previously identifiable within a given field of experience, whose identification is thus part of the reconfiguration of the field of experience. (Ranciere 1999, p. 35)

The process of subjectivation therefore adds to the existing distribution of the sensible but, in adding to it, the sensible is reconfigured. Thus, as Biesta comments, we can speak from and perpetuate a place of subjectification by existing orders or, alternatively, and perhaps rarely, we can speak from a place of subjectivation in the name of equality and thereby challenge the existing frameworks of subjectification. The process of speaking as subjectivation echoes my earlier point about the relationship between the immanence of local practice and transcendent structures. Is it possible within our current frameworks of education for the immanence of local practices and their forms of necessary transcendence that are sometimes given little credence in existing pedagogical structures to add to and change the transcendent order of such structures, thereby changing how learning is understood? Such immanent processes relate to what Ranciere terms a personal orbit of practice: when a student embarks upon an orbit of learning entirely his or her own (Ranciere 1991, p. 59).

To repeat a point made earlier, it is not a case of viewing transcendent structures or police orders as necessarily bad and the immanence of local learning processes as good. It is possible for institutional frameworks to respond favourably to the forces of equality as might be seen in the establishment of comprehensive schools in the UK in the 1960s or the movements to institute forms of teaching that responded to cultural legitimacy and diversity in the USA and UK from the 1970s. Such institutional changes were by no means universally effective but they were attempts to respond to forces of equality in the Rancierian sense of this term. Equally, the immanence of local learning processes does not necessarily lead to more effective learning; such processes may simply subscribe to established frameworks and patterns of learning and prevent expansion. In other words, they perpetuate local normative processes of learning in contrast to what I have termed events of learning when a learner is projected into new ontological and epistemological phases.

The key issue regarding being a student or learner is that the systems in which such being and becoming occur do not impose explicate orders to the effect that the student's 'speech' is not their own. Such systems become effective in promoting emancipatory education when learning happens without the controlling effects of a teacher's explanations and where teachers demand that learners deploy rigorously their own capacities to learn. However, having made this point it is important to consider Ranciere's words about the dissonance between structures or systems of education and more local acts of teaching and learning. Earlier, I raised some questions about the possibility of conceiving learners and learning beyond the axiom of inequality that is perpetuated in institutional contexts of education. Is it possible to teach beyond the controlling frameworks of an explicative order that perpetuates inequality? Such questions raise the notion of dissonance that Ranciere (2010a, p. 15) discusses.

This dissonance consists of the difference between institutional structures in which knowledge and teaching come together to promote social programmes that work towards achieving equality but begin from an axiom of inequality, and acts of teaching that are grounded in an axiom of equality. Institutional programmes tend to operate from established values, bodies of knowledge and frameworks of identification, whereas teaching grounded in an axiom of equality attempts to function by putting such frameworks on one side and acts, as it were, without such criteria and beyond the closure of knowledge, waiting for the learner to emerge as learner through the disclosure of his or her own 'speech'. The idea of equality is not something that can be aimed at, as it often is in institutional contexts, but it is something that can only be assumed as a starting point and then verified in the acts of individuals or groups. Within institutional contexts such as schools pedagogic work that is grounded in the notion of emancipation is frequently if not always subject to an inherent paradox, whereby such work in pursuing emancipatory intentions is underpinned by the assumption of an inequality of intelligence, a dissonance between intention and practice. Biesta and Bingham write:

> The greatest conceit in education, then, is the one that is constantly embraced by so many who try to improve schools, programmes and pedagogies. It is the conceit that there is some institutional means by which to improve education in order to emancipate students (2010, p. 24)

Emancipation can only happen when a learner sets out on his or her own 'orbit' of learning (Ranciere 1991, p. 59). The notion of events of learning that project a learner into new or modified ontological and epistemological phases proceed from such orbits. Teaching in this mode of emancipatory education can therefore be viewed as a political and transformative act, in the sense that it proceeds from an assumption of equality so that in responding to the different orbits of learning formed by learners, a teacher is constantly involved in expanding his or her pedagogical frameworks. The teacher is continually asked to expand his or her understanding of what learning and teaching are. The central idea of politics for Ranciere is that it involves dissensus, a process whereby in a particular world something is produced which is heterogeneous to this world but exists in this world; it involves a conflict between a logic of equality and a police logic from which emerges the *appearance* of that which had no existence beforehand, it occupied a place of no-place. To repeat again a point running through this book, it is not uncommon in the world of pedagogical relations for students to produce responses to learning encounters that lie beyond the frameworks of a teacher's understanding. Such responses may reveal ways of learning that expand the teacher's understanding of what it is to learn. Ranciere (2010b) writes in a rather Spinozan vein:

> Engaging in critique of the instituted divisions, then, paves the way for renewing our interrogations into what we are able to think and do. (Dissensus, p. 218)

Such interrogation of the frameworks and categorisations of practice and the distribution of practices and identities within educational contexts is important if we are to keep an open approach to the ontogenesis of learning and learners. The notion of dissensus in which something is produced or appears in a world, which is in some way heterogeneous to its existing patterns so as to open up new possibilities and transformations of a world, can be applied to local practices of learning and teaching. It is in these processes of dissensus that new subjectivations emerge, where established patterns (a learner's or teacher's own 'police' order) are expanded through events of learning.

Perhaps we can see that the notion of dissensus identifies an important process for an emancipatory education in contrast to the notion of consensus on which institutionalised forms of education rely. I have used the term disobedience in a rather similar way to Ranciere's term dissensus. The idea of emancipatory education (for both learners and teachers) in which an intelligence is revealed to itself as it pursues its own orbit of learning involves a political and ethico-aesthetic process. Events of learning are political when established patterns or frameworks are confronted with forms of practice that seem illegitimate, but which demand acceptance and they are ethico-aesthetic in that such practices introduce new ontological capacities for thinking, seeing, making and feeling.

> There are two major ways of symbolizing the community: one represents it as the sum of its parts, the other defines it as the division of its whole. One conceives it as the accomplishment of a common way of being, the other as a polemic over the common. I call the first police, the second politics. Consensus is the form by which politics is transformed into the police. In this form the community can be symbolized exclusively as the composition of the interests of the groups and individuals that make it up. (Dissensus, pp. 100–101)

Learning or teaching assume political (in Ranciere's sense of politics) force when they open up worlds of experience not recognised by common orders of experience that constitute established pedagogic work so that a process of dissensus emerges in which our understanding of learning and teaching may be expanded. In England, the USA and other countries, recent decades have witnessed increased government policing of education grounded in the pursuit of economic ambition and competition.

REFERENCES

Atkinson, D. (2011). *Art, equality and learning: Pedagogies against the state.* Rotterdam/Boston/Taipei: Sense Publishers.

Atkinson, D. (2017). Without criteria: Art, learning and the adventure of pedagogy. *The International Journal of Art and Design Education, 36*(2), 141–152.

Badiou, A. (2001). *Ethics: An essay on the understanding of evil.* London/New York: Verso.

Badiou, A. (2005). *Being and event.* London/New York: Continuum.

Biesta, G. (2010). Learner, student, speaker: Why it matters how we call those we teach. *Educational Philosophy and Theory, 42,* 5–6.

Bingham, C., & Biesta, G. (2010). *Jacques Ranciere: Education, truth emancipation.* London/New York: Continuum.

Cattegno, C. (1972). *What we owe our children.* London: Routledge Kegan Paul.

Deleuze, G. (1988). *Spinoza, practical philosophy.* San Francisco: City Lights Books.

Deleuze, G. (1994/2004). *Difference and repetition.* London/New York: Continuum.

Deleuze, G., & Guattari, F. (1988). *A thousand plateaus.* London: Athlone Press.

Deleuze, G., & Guattari, F. (1994). *What is philosophy?* London: Verso.

Deleuze, G., & Parnet, C. (2007). *Dialogues II.* New York: Columbia University Press.

Dewey, J. (1920). *Reconstruction in philosophy.* New York: Dover Publications.

Foucault, M. (2001). *Fearless speech.* Los Angeles: Semiotext(e).

Hallward, P. (2003). *Badiou a subject to truth.* Minneapolis/London: University of Minnesota Press.

Harraway, D. (2016). *Staying with the trouble: Making kin in the chthulucene.* Durham/London: Duke University Press.

Ingold, T. (2013). *Making: Anthropology, archaeology, architecture and art.* London/New York: Routledge.

Pickering, A. (1995). *The mangle of practice: Time, agency and science.* Chicago: University of Chicago Press.

Ranciere, J. (1991). *The ignorant schoolmaster: Five lessons in intellectual emancipation.* Stanford: Stanford University Press.

Ranciere, J. (1999). *Disagreement: Politics and philosophy*. Minneapolis: University of Minnesota Press.

Ranciere, J. (2010a). On ignorant schoolmasters. In C. Bingham & G. Biesta (Eds.), *Jacques Ranciere: Education, truth emancipation*. London/New York: Continuum.

Ranciere, J. (2010b). *Dissensus: On politics and aesthetics*. London/New York: Continuum.

Rogoff, I. (2008). Turning. *Eflux Journal, 11*, 32–46.

Savransky, M. (2016). *The adventure of relevance*. London/New York: Palgrave Macmillan.

Smith, D. (2012). *Essays on Deleuze*. Edinburgh: Edinburgh University Press.

Thiele, K. (2008). *The thought of becoming*. Zurich/Berlin: Diaphanes.

Whitehead, A. N. (1929). *Process and reality: An essay in cosmology*. New York: Free Press.

Whitehead, A. N. (1933/1937). *Adventures of ideas*. New York: Free Press.

Whitehead, A. N. (1938/1966). *Modes of thought*. New York: Free Press.

CHAPTER 7

Becoming in the Middle

A line of becoming has neither beginning or end, origin or destination, a line of becoming has only a middle. A becoming is always in the middle: one can only get at it by the middle….a becoming is the in-between the border or the line of flight (Deleuze and Guattari 1988, p. 293)

Swarms of molecules, streams of wind disturb particles of sand that scramble along a shoreline whipping the water into creamy foam. Keratin and molar bodies become wind machines. Nitrogen, oxygen, and carbon, rays of light, a young blue iris catches the flight paths, the spray, the yellow; retinal images and aspirations. A vision machine. Digital patterns and aural receptors, silences, a sound machine mingles with movements, seeing, memories, anticipations and excitations. Multiplicities of becomings but never a genesis; always a becoming in the middle. Connections and more connections into unknown openings without plans, precipitating inventions.

A much older eye looks out at the ocean, the foam, the gulls, from this yellow sand but it sees other images. There are more children; cold, wet and frightened huddled together with carers on rubber boats. Memories of home, of friends, of a lost life. What will happen? Where are we going? A complex multiplicity beginning again and again and again in the middle of fear.

The young girl picks up a shell and marks the sand, a shell-girl-drawing machine, extending imagination and potential for becoming. The older woman contemplates the struggle for life, a politics not-yet-arrived, a people yet-to-come.

Just off the coast a wreck lies south of the cockleshell landings in the light of Cardouan and a river mist. An opening, a chance, the terror of courage.

© The Author(s) 2018

D. Atkinson, *Art, Disobedience, and Ethics*, Education, Psychoanalysis, and Social Transformation, DOI 10.1007/978-3-319-62639-0_7

Flying kites on the shoreline, soccer on the sand, building barricades against the ocean. Molar compositions, segmentations, corporeal and incorporeal intensities. A leather satchel passing connects a memory chain: letters, maps, music, old miners boots, Orgreave, Harrison's V, roads not taken, the lights of Blackbush, intensities of teaching, infinities. Half-winged but half restrained.

In this chapter, my intention is to examine some concepts developed by Deleuze and Guattari that have direct implications for pedagogic work and its relations of learning and teaching. The idea of events of learning will be explored through some of these concepts. In particular, the concepts of multiplicity, deterritorialisation, virtuality, actuality, transcendence and immanence will be addressed to show how they can be useful tools for conceiving processes of learning and teaching and the practice of pedagogic work. Though this use of concepts perhaps runs counter to Deleuze and Guattari's insistence that we should not simply apply *their* concepts to *our* problems but try to invent our own, in order to expand our comprehension in the task of building a life, I have found them very helpful in the pursuit of this endeavour. This chapter attempts to show how.

For Deleuze, to think is to experiment, to explore beyond existing frameworks or connections and to consider or invent new ones. In *Difference and Repetition* he writes, 'thought is primarily trespass and violence (1994, p. 175)'; it is that which is precipitated as a consequence of an encounter, an encounter that forces thinking.

> Something in the world forces us to think. This something is an object not of recognition but of a fundamental *encounter*. (ibid, 176)

We might think of this notion of thinking as a mode of disobedience that breaks through existing modes of thought. Rajchman (2000, p. 7) holds that we need to be 'attentive to the unknown knocking at the door'. and then invent ways of coping with any ensuing problems, which of course lead into other problems. Thought, therefore, is a kind of experimentation precipitated by encounters with what we cannot yet determine. Equally, when we consider the notion of subjectivity, this should be viewed not in terms of an established or pre-given state or natural disposition, but as a process of making and transforming; in other words, subjectivity should also be conceived as an experiment, a journey with no clearly determined end-point. Perhaps a better term is subjectivation. The journey, in reference to the quote heading this chapter, is always 'in the middle', developing new ways of thinking, feeling and acting in relation to events and encounters as they occur. Conceiving pedagogical work as an on-going journey in the middle seems important. It is not to be conceived as a pedagogy aiming towards the production of presupposed identities of learners or teachers, but a pedagogy of events and multiplicities, a rhizomatic process, a process of deterritorialisation and reterritorialisation whereby learning and teaching are experiments that evolve through particular encounters and their outcomes. A multiplicity can be conceived as a becoming in the middle, in the sense that becoming emerges from a concrescence of numerous kinds of relations. At this early point, we might see that the contingent notions of self or subject as experiments raise some interesting implications concerning how we might comprehend ethics and politics; these matters will be discussed in due course.

For Deleuze, the force or the trespass of thought can expose the power of transcendence and representation, that is to say it can reveal those established forms of thinking, seeing and doing that predicate the way we think see and practice. In chapter three of *Difference and Repetition*, he refers to the *dogmatic image of thought* to describe such forms of transcendence that infiltrate and control our ways of thinking. For example, the idea of the unified conscious individual emanating from Descartes, signified by the term 'I', is still a powerful image of thought that determines the way we think and talk about our selves. In the domain of art education in schools and elsewhere, the notion of 'self-expression' is still employed to argue for the value of art practice; it presupposes an already formed self that facilitates expression. This notion of a prior individual is contested by the idea that it is in the very process or act of expression that what we call a self becomes materialised, whilst others would argue further that the notion of self is a transcendent fiction and that what we really should be concerned with are a series of on-going relations and events with other people or things that form and dissolve in the process of building a life. This latter notion relates back to the notion of becoming in the middle: not points but relations of becoming.

The force of thought is a disobedient force that questions established ways of thinking, seeing and acting and their respective methodologies. The force of thinking can emerge during encounters in which something does not fit with habitual forces of practice; events or encounters during which prior knowledge seems redundant and this generates a desire to experiment and explore beyond established parameters of knowledge and its transcendent forms. Here, thinking and learning are grounded in the *immanence of experiencing*, an immanence through which knowing may proceed to develop new or modified forms of comprehension or practice.

Perhaps the idea of a fundamental encounter proposed by Deleuze as the trigger for thought can be considered through the intense experience of standing inside a waterfall in contrast to standing outside and observing it. Standing inside the waterfall, you have to cope with the tumult and intensities of the torrent crashing over your body. For many, this would be a disturbing, unpredictable and very testing experience; for others, it may be intense, exciting and exhilarating as the water cascades over and affects the body sensorium. Looking at the waterfall from outside is not the same kind of experiencing and it is likely, though not necessarily, to be influenced or informed by other similar kinds of experience or predicates of experience. This experiential contrast, when applied to pedagogic contexts and relations, has implications for ethics and politics as well as aesthetics. . .inside the waterfall (a specific learning encounter) in contrast to looking at it. The immanence of being inside an encounter is not the same as the immanence or transcendence of observation. Both experiences are in the middle, but they have different kinds of intensities. The disturbing experience of being inside the event of an encounter amplifies the notion of multiplicity that occupied Deleuze and Guattari throughout their collaborations. For to attempt to embrace the experiencing of being in the middle of, or the multiplicity which we call an encounter, requires a way of thinking not governed by established identities, representations or predications (such a logic would tend to apply to the experience of observation that draws upon established categorisations), but by a logic of sense and event or of what Deleuze terms singularities.

> In all my books I have sought the nature of the event, it is a philosophical concept, the only one capable of destituting the verb to be and the attribute. (Pourparler 1990: 194)

Encounters are initially experienced through 'affective tones' (1994, p. 176); they are initially *sensed* and not *recognised* in this 'being of the sensible,. . . that by which the given is given (Ibid)'. So the encounter is 'imperceptible' from the 'point of view of [established forms of] recognition (Ibid, my bracket)'. Thus, it is from this initial experiencing of the affects of an encounter and of being imperceptible that we try to make sense or to comprehend our relation in the encounter.

Multiplicity

A multiplicity is a complex relational structure; it does not denote a set or aggregate of separate entities, but is more like a disparation that produces relational potential for becoming. Deleuze was influenced by the mathematician Bernhard Reiman and the philosopher Henri Bergson as he developed his work on the concept of multiplicity. From Reiman, he took the idea that all situations are composed of different multiplicities that form a kind of infinite collage without becoming a totality (Roffe, p. 176 in Parr 2005). For example, a body can be conceived as an ensemble of different cells, organs, limbs, actions, affects, thoughts, memories, and so on, but there is no final essence of the body that we can determine. This notion of multiplicity provides an opportunity to abandon the idea of a unified and self-contained self, or essentialised individual, and to view what we call an individual as a constantly evolving series of processes that occur on many levels. It helps us to see that learning itself, as a vital process, is composed of a series of multiplicities.

In his book *Bergsonism*, Deleuze (1988) discusses two kinds of multiplicities proposed by Bergson—extensive multiplicities and intensive multiplicities—which Deleuze links respectively with his notions of the actual and the virtual. An actual multiplicity relates to events, relations and beings in a world. A molecule, a brain, a body, a thought, a concept, a river, a desert, anger, joy, disappointment, disgust, elation are all multiplicities of differing orders. A virtual multiplicity is real, without actually existing in an objective sense in a world. It can be conceived as a source of infinite potential that lies within particular situations and relations. However, the changes that are brought about by actual multiplicities impact upon and effect changes in virtual multiplicities. Put another way, we might see existence as a folding and re-folding of both actual multiplicities, actions and outcomes in the world, and virtual multiplicities that consist of intensive affects and potentials that may precipitate change.

The notion of events of learning that involve encounters with the unfamiliar, that which is-not-yet-known, or what Deleuze describes as the *imperceptible*, when considered through the notion of multiplicity, is quite complex. When faced with that which is unfamiliar, a learner may experiment, test things out; actions and thoughts that are composed by evolving actualisations and the intensities of virtual potential as these unfold in a particular situation. We might see events of learning as an iteration of multiplicities in which components of the process are not clear-cut or clearly distinguished, and as components change, then, so does the general process. The process of a learning event is not linear and predictable, but is a constantly differentiating process beginning again and again in the middle.

So events of learning viewed as a multiplicity can be conceived as an on-going series of foldings, unfoldings and refoldings precipitated by a learning encounter. This is not a hylomorphic process where form—established knowledge, for example—is imposed upon matter, where predicates or transcendent operators inform thought and practice. Events of learning lie in contrast to normative learning that is *informed* by established knowledge or practice. Events of learning as a complex of multiplicities are grounded in the not-known (the imperceptible) and, emerging through the process of experimentation, could be the affirming of new ways of thinking, seeing, feeling, doing and their potentials, though not always. The actual and virtual of learning events emerge as a process of invention and can perhaps be viewed as a kind of disobedience to established ways of thinking, seeing and acting. Through the force of the combination of actual and virtual multiplicities in encounters of learning, we can become something new. In such encounters, our ways of thinking, seeing, feeling and acting may be uprooted and transformed. Encounters with art or encounters in the making of art sometimes generate the force to disrupt or challenge established ways of seeing, forms of representation or established modes of affect and precipitate new sensibilities and ways of seeing and thinking.

Taking on board these ideas about multiplicity, the actual and the virtual, it is necessary to change or sometimes abandon concepts that have informed the ways in which we think and act: concepts such as 'individual', 'self' and 'self-expression', which are grounded in the idea of identity. This is important, particularly when we encounter situations when habitual responses no longer work or when such habits or predicates do not exist and we need to figure things out. In such situations where established knowledge or ways of acting seem inadequate, the notions of ethics and politics grounded in established codes or modes of identity need to move towards an experimental format in which there is no clear or concise idea of subjectivity or consensus for prescribed action. Here, as Rajchman states,

> the lines of our lives are more complex than the segmentary identifications imposed by society and so they can precipitate 'diagrams' of other spaces and times for living. (p. 83)

So the problem of multiplicity in human terms is a problem of building a life: a life beyond the human or, in pedagogical terms, learning beyond the human. Life is a confusion of multiplicities, processes of invention and experimentation, but also ossification, stagnancy, subservience or failure. Life is not the life of an individual, but a virtuality that surpasses the individual and opens up a potential for new connections and relations. This is the force of life and of transformative learning. The pedagogical task is to work with the singularities of learning encounters (haecceities, phases that don't fit existing conceptions), to release vital differences when, at the same time, teachers are constantly faced with the power of institutional segmentation. Here, we are faced with two kinds of violence, the violence of institutional segmentation through which teachers and learners become categorised and pedagogised, and the violence or disobedience of learning events whose force precipitates new onto-epistemic phases.

The flow of life, of learning, is always in the middle, in that it always rests upon what has happened, what has been felt, what has been thought or seen as well as what is being encountered. Thus it is perhaps more appropriate not to speak of individuals, but of *dividual becoming*. This middle, or this flow of life, is dividual (Raunig 2016, p. 11). And this notion of the dividual gives us some sense of the different multiplicities, relations and connections that compose the flow of life, not as a series of identities but more in terms of a concatenation of intensities and actualisations. Of course the dividual also refers to the way that our lives are now subject to endless division in the world of 'big data', a world in which digital technologies, social media, machinic capitalism operate on molecular levels to control and simultaneously proliferate human sensibilities and desires through new markets that are seemingly without limits. These issues form the focus of one of Deleuze's last articles entitled *Postscript on the Societies of Control* (*October*, Vol. 59, 1992, pp. 3–7).

TRANSCENDENCE AND IMMANENCE

In general, the notions of transcendence and immanence are used by Deleuze to denote different kinds of relations. Transcendence concerns relations in which something is viewed in accordance with something such as an identity, a principle or a set of criteria used to judge or to recognise phenomena, whereas immanence denotes relations that emerge within phenomena. We might say that transcendence is grounded on a principle or a logic of an already constituted identity, whilst immanence is grounded in a logic of difference where there are no transcendent relations. Difference is not difference according to a prior identity or resemblance, for that would introduce a form of transcendence; it is concerned with a genetic production of the new, the singular. What is important is to try to grasp the singular nature of experiencing that is 'internal' to this process or this event; to try to grasp this becoming in its complex relationalities, however difficult this may be. Because to put aside our habits of thinking, seeing and acting in order to invoke such grasping is not easy. Thus, the task of deploying a pedagogy of immanence is to try to grasp the singular nature of a learner's particular learning encounter or, in the words of Whitehead, to consider how something matters for a learner in a learning encounter.

Daniel Smith (2012, p. 284), in an essay mentioned earlier (which I repeat here) comparing transcendence and immanence in the philosophies of Derrida and Deleuze, comes down on the side of the latter in that he (Smith) believes that 'the "philosophy of the future" needs to move in the direction of immanence', most importantly, because of the practical ramifications of philosophical work that engage with ethics and politics. But, as Smith points out, whilst Deleuze and Guattari in *What is Philosophy?* (1994, p. 45) recognise the 'natural' place of immanence in philosophical work, they also notice that it has not always been welcome and that opposition to giving priority to immanence is usually set in moral terms, along the lines that without the guiding hand of transcendence (rules or principles to follow), we would descend into subjectivism or relativism. We can witness a particular manifestation of this moral position in those current educational policies that advocate specific methods of teaching, curriculum content and assessment, coupled with a tenacious regime of inspection. Such policies seem to pay little regard to the complex syntheses, the multiplicities of experiencing, that form human beings on many levels nor do they acknowledge the importance of trying to comprehend how something matters for a learner (a new concept, a new practice, a new value, a new affect) and how this mattering effects what I call real learning.

In acknowledging the importance of the idea of immanence in Spinoza's *Ethics*, Deleuze considers the immanence of becoming in terms of intensity or 'degree of power' (Smith 2012, p. 285). For Spinoza ontology *is* ethics (Thiele 2008) and the fundamental question therefore is not a moral one, 'What must I do'? but a practical one, 'What can I do?', in a particular situation or encounter. What *are* my capacities or capabilities to act or to think in *this* situation? How can I extend my capacity to act or think more effectively? Such questions raise a critique of transcendence in a more political sense. Do the transcendent forms of knowledge and practice that are deemed important for learners to acquire, and their respective forms of assessment, actually separate some learners from their capacity to act, to learn? Put another way, from the perspective of a philosophy of immanence, does a pedagogy grounded in a philosophy of transcendence reduce most learners to a form of servitude and some to marginalisation? In the practical domains of teaching and learning, the ethical issues of immanence and transcendence become acute. Do we conceive teaching and learning in transcendent terms according to what might be called the transmission view of pedagogy, where learning is subordinated to teaching (the power of knowledge transmitted by a teacher to a learner, see Gattegno 1972), or do we conceive pedagogic work in terms of trying to respond to the particular immanence and intensity of a learner's experiencing and their particular capacity to think and act? If we take the former position, then pedagogy presupposes a transcendence that guides the moral compass of pedagogy; it is grounded in a hylomorphic principle—the imposition of form on matter—whereas if we take the latter position, this transcendence could obscure and prevent a pedagogical ethics grounded in the capacities of a learner's existence through which form and expression emerge from local processes of relevance and mattering.

Nevertheless, does adopting this emphasis upon immanence open it to the criticism of 'anything goes'? Surely we require some normative transcendent criteria by which to judge our actions and thoughts, for if we simply employ intrinsic criteria immanent to modes of existence and their particular ways of acting and thinking, how can we compare and evaluate them? Deleuze's response to this conundrum follows Spinoza, and argues that we can evaluate modes of existence by the *immanent criteria of their power*, that is to say, by considering if a particular mode of existence has pushed its capacity to act as far as it is able. Alternatively, we might ask, has a particular mode been prevented from deploying its power to act?

These points need to be qualified in relation to the idea of subjectivity. Deleuze is not assuming a prior determined subject experiencing the world, but a subject who emerges from experiencing in a world. In other words, he is not assuming a transcendent subject who synthesises experience, but a subject who emerges from the immanence of a series of multiplicities and their relations that constitute experience. So, for Deleuze, ethics is not grounded in the notion of a transcendent subject or a transcendent set of rules, but emerges from the specificity of modes of existence and their particular relations and affects.

If we prioritise the notion of immanence in pedagogical work, an ethics of immanence in such work means that a pedagogical imperative is to try to understand learning from the perspective of the learner's capacities to learn and not to judge such capacities from external (transcendent) criteria. This form of pedagogical ethics demands that pedagogical work engages with the intrinsic capacities of learners, it requests that we try to understand *how* something matters for a learner in a particular learning encounter. It is this 'how', or more specifically, *the relations that compose this 'how'*, that constitutes the immanent criteria from which forms of *necessary transcendence* emerge, the latter acting as transient stepping stones that may or may not facilitate further learning.

These points about immanence have further ramifications for the notion of learner and how a learner is conceived. Gert Biesta (2006, 2010a, b) has approached this issue in his work on equality and education, which is influenced by Ranciere's writings on education. Biesta explores the terms, learner, student and speaker, and his explorations have direct links with the relations between immanence and politics and to the notion of modes of existence, to which I have briefly alluded above.

Learning and the New

What is the status of the new in teaching and learning? This is a tricky question when we reflect upon these processes in schools where emphasis, generally speaking, is placed upon a reproduction of culture, valued practices and bodies of knowledge. These occupy an understandable transcendent position, according to which teaching and learning subscribe. We might say that teaching and learning become pedagogised (Atkinson 2003) according to these practices and bodies of knowledge. The latter seem to occupy an atemporal reality, in that the teaching of art or other subjects consists of an established and repeatable set of practices and forms of knowledge. In some ways, we might think that there is nothing new in such curriculum content apart from when new content is added or existing content is modified. Nevertheless, the actual practices of teaching and learning are riven through with the new in the sense that each phase of teaching and learning involves an incessant process of becoming, a differentiation inherent to all life. A learner's encounter with established practices or forms of knowledge is likely to produce something new in terms of how a particular practice or knowledge content *matters* for that learner. Moreover, how this matters for a learner, if this mattering is allowed to follow its own pathway and not be pushed along a prescribed route, has the potential to creatively effect the pedagogical work of a teacher. In other words, the materiality of pedagogical action *is* the new in relation to each learner's ontogenesis of learning and each teacher's ontogenesis of pedagogical work. Such materiality 'cracks open' a subject.

We can contrast the transcendence of established forms of knowledge and practice that constitute the art curriculum with the immanence of local learning processes that constitute the particular way in which each learner engages with the content of a learning encounter. In a previous chapter devoted to the philosophy of Whitehead, human beings are viewed in terms of relational processes, not as beings with a unified self or identity. Life for Whitehead, in all its manifestations, human and non-human, is an on-going process of becoming involving a creative advance into novelty (which may have good or bad outcomes). Becoming is proposed as a dynamic series of prehensional relations through which beings try to take account of each other, and such relations are underpinned by a composition of feelings and conceptual processes. The philosophical work of Deleuze is equally keen to avoid the capture of identity and representation, and to view human beings as a synthesis of multiplicities and their relations, of different forces and intensities including affect and cognition, conscious and unconscious processes. He does not discount identity and representation, but rather, views these in terms of phases of stability, which in time become subject to change and transformation. For Deleuze, identity and representation are to be viewed as illusions that often have the power to totalise thought (transcendental illusions) and care needs to be taken to resist such totalisation. He places emphasis not upon identity, but upon difference and its repetition, which is close to Whitehead's idea of the production of novelty.

Events of learning project a learner into new or modified ontological and epistemological phases. In chapter three of *Difference and Repetition*, Deleuze discusses learning as an experimental process. Williams (2013) writes that for Deleuze, 'to learn is to learn how to be sensitive to and respond creatively to signs and problems, as things that necessarily go beyond what is known or what can be done in a given situation (146–147)'. Deleuze thinks of signs beyond systems of signification and the relations between a signifier and signified; for him, a sign denotes an *encounter* with a problematical or perplexing experience that is initially 'felt' rather than conceived. Thus, whilst a recognised object can be felt, it can also be conceived, memorised or imagined, but an encountered sign is beyond this realm of recognition. The affective experience of a sign is located subjectively in terms of a limit experience; it cannot be grasped by the common sense of recognition, but it points towards a realm of potentialities beyond. An initial affective encounter with a sign then has the potential for opening up new worlds of thinking, speaking and doing. Learning is an experimental process; its priority is a kind of apprenticeship in learning how to learn rather than the acquisition of knowledge or skill. Deleuze gives the example of learning how to swim as an illustration of apprenticeship to signs. On the one hand, this will involve skills that are developed but more importantly it involves a series of 'unconscious' relations, becomings and intensities of body and water that facilitate learning and skills, and such relations do not involve recognition but rather a passing beyond established faculties. Similar relations occur whenever we learn something new—learning how to paint or to draw, for example; such learning encounters, viewed in terms of the Deleuzian sign, are intensive events that have the potential to expand or transform our capacities to see, to think and to act.

For Deleuze, though we are able to learn facts or skills the important point is to develop capacities that facilitate creative responses to experience that are problematic or challenging and which 'lie beyond' existing knowledge/skill frameworks or frameworks of recognition. The challenge is learning how to do something new or to think in new modes and the way this happens is likely to be different in each individual. Deleuze holds that learning is not simply concerned with conscious processes, but also with processes of which we are unaware when we enter into new experiences and their relations. This last point raises the relation between the actual and the virtual, already discussed, and its importance for events of learning.

According to Daniel Smith (2012, p. 235), 'Deleuze frequently said that the question of the conditions for the production of *novelty* (Bergson) or *creativity* (Whitehead) was one of the fundamental questions of contemporary thought'. It involved a shift from the universal to the singular and that, in general terms, 'the conditions of the new can be found only in a principle of difference (Ibid)'. The main reason for this appeal to difference is that if identity were conceived as pre-given or presupposed, then this would automatically deny the production of the new because there would always be a pre-given ground. Steven Shaviro (2009, pp. ix–x) contrasts Heidegger's question of Being—'Why is there something rather than nothing?'—with Whitehead's question, 'How is it that there is always something new?' He suggests that Whitehead's question, in our contemporary world, is the 'truly urgent one'. In the world of education and learning, I argue that Whitehead's question is imperative for developing effective pedagogical practices that try to respond effectively to the ontogenesis of local learning processes.

Smith's chapter on Deleuze's conception of the *new* in his book *Essays on Deleuze*, raises for me a number of issues relating to learning or, to be more precise, the genetic conditions of learning, which have implications for pedagogical practices and also how we might conceive the pedagogical force of learning. Here, I am making a distinction between pedagogical strategies and relations that arise between teachers and learners, and the point that learning itself as a vital force is pedagogical in its capacity of disclosure. The idea of transformative disclosure constitutes understanding for Whitehead; understanding is not primarily the acquisition of knowledge, facts or definitions. As an experience of transformative disclosure, learning includes a realisation of actual outcomes as well as potentialities that lie beyond such realisation. In Deleuzian terminology learning involves both actual and virtual dimensions.

The philosophical exploration of the conditions of *real experience* by Smith/Deleuze has deep implications, if we agree with their outcomes, for conceiving pedagogical relations and practices. Events of learning as already mentioned involve a movement into new ontological relations, expanded and affirmative relations that in *each learner* will take different relational pathways, which are unpredictable at the inception of a learning encounter. Though some learners will respond to established and valued pedagogical strategies, others will not and, as a consequence, may perhaps be viewed as 'lacking in ability'. Such pathways include a learner's relation to pedagogical objects such as those constituting a mathematical problem, a scientific experiment or the production of a visual form in art practice. Learning in Deleuzian terminology, then, is the production of difference, and such production will vary from learner to learner. Pedagogical work therefore is charged with responding effectively to these different productions of difference, or put another way responding effectively to the different signs (encounters) of difference. Deleuze (1994) writes:

> The new – in other words, difference – calls forth forces in thought that are not the forces of recognition, today or tomorrow, but the powers of a completely other model, from an unrecognized and unrecognizable *terra incognita*. (p. 136)

For Deleuze, following Whitehead and Bergson, the new is a 'fundamental ontological concept: Becoming = Difference = the New' (Smith 2012, pp. 236–237), and he concentrates on the conditions of *real experience* in contrast to conditions of possible experience or what is logically possible. The conditions of real experience can be equated with the conditions of learning events. So what are the conditions of real experience for Deleuze? He provides a number of requirements summarised by Smith (Ibid, pp. 239–241). Firstly, there must be 'an intrinsic genesis not an extrinsic conditioning' (DR 154) this places emphasis upon the immanence of real experience/real learning. Second, each process of actualisation is a production of the new, the production of a new difference. Third, the conditions of real experience/real learning must be determined '*along with* what they condition and thus must change as the conditioned changes (240)'. Fourth, that as well as a foundation and ground of experience (for example, present experience emerging from the ground of past experience), there has to be an ungrounded (unconditioned) element or dimension which is the future or the condition of the new. There is an immanence to learning events that produces a new difference and the conditions of such events are changed as what is produced changes (reciprocal determinism), but for the new to be realised, there has to be an opening towards future (unknown) potential. This unknown refers to the virtual multiplicity of learning.

ETHICS AND LEARNING EVENTS

We can conceive processes of learning on two general levels: one constituted by preconscious or virtual processes (which will be discussed below) and one constituted by actual outcomes. In pedagogical relations, teachers and learners work with what is 'actualised' through the actions of teaching and learning, the on-going productions and outcomes of practices that are composed on a number of levels including cognition and affect. An important aspect of such relations is that teachers restrain from totalising what learners actualise from the teacher's perspective of understanding, and try to locate the outcomes of learning within the ontological relations, the real experience and conditions of the learner, how things matter for a learner, even though these cannot be fully grasped.

Such issues precipitate the notion of the other and processes of expression. We cannot 'know' the other in the sense that teachers cannot know learners in-themselves, but they can respond to the intensities and ideas that a learner *expresses* through practice in processes of learning. Pedagogical encounters in which a teacher is confronted with a learner's form of expression that the former finds mysterious can make the teacher's world strange or adventurous. Towards the very end of chapter five of *Difference and Repetition*, Deleuze discusses the relations between individuals[1] not in terms of 'subject to subject' relations, but in terms of dynamic processes that function on different levels. In such processes, individuals are viewed as a series of multiplicities; intensities, actualisations and virtual ideas that arise in relation to other individuals (multiplicities). In a learning encounter, a learner expresses particular fusions of intensities and ideas that may be obscure from the teacher's perspective and vice versa. Such intensities/ideas may produce outcomes (actualisations) such as a drawing or a response to a mathematical problem whose emergent form may be difficult for the teacher to comprehend. Such occasions precipitate what might be termed a pedagogical ethics, and it is useful, I believe, to consider briefly what this involves.

Deleuze (1994, pp. 323–324) recommends that in relation to the other that we adopt a critical view upon our knowledge of the other in order to undermine illusions of identity of the other. He advises not to totalise the other in terms of your identification, but to try to see the other 'as the expression of a possible world' (Ibid, p. 324). This point has important ramifications for practices of assessment in education where, for assessors, it is almost inevitable not to be seduced by established (transcendent) criteria that identify, position and regulate learners. What Deleuze (and others such as Foucault) is requesting is that we take a critical perspective upon how such forms of identification emerge, in other words, how such assessment criteria 'pedagogise' both learners and teachers. This was a central theme of earlier work (Atkinson 1993, 1995, 2003) in which I considered how students' drawing ability is constructed pedagogically within specific assessment discourses. Deleuze asks us to consider therefore what ideas and intensities of experience our transcendent framing of the other's power of learning occlude. Thus, in general terms, an important ethical principle for Deleuze as summarised by Williams (Ibid, p. 253) is, 'Do not impose identity on the other. Do not impose an identity on yourself for the other'. The task is therefore to encourage the other (learner) to express its intensities and ideas as experienced in a learning encounter and try to understand how these are significant, how they matter for the learner. Thus, for a teacher, the pedagogical process involves a critical accountancy of his or her pedagogical and subject knowledge as well as a creative and open project towards helping the learner to expand his or her world.

Learning, in the Deleuzian sense, is not to remain within established ideas or practices but to try to connect with changes and potentials brought about by new experiences, or encounters that create new kinds of intensities and ideas in relation to actual entities that expand our capacities of becoming. So, effective learning encounters involve trying to connect with the virtual potential arising from relations with the actual content of the encounter. Such encounters include actual objects, but also the different intensities/ideas that are potentially available for expression; these are what Deleuze refers to as the virtual. Reality is a dynamic reciprocal relation between actual and virtual processes. The character of such relations will be different for each individual.

Example: You can teach perspective (or other methodologies) as an established drawing system and form of representation, or you can initiate a learning encounter in which learners are challenged to respond to the problem/s that the drawing system we know as perspective attempted to resolve. The latter approach opens up an infinitude involving the reciprocity between actual entities (materials, bodies, emerging drawing, etc.) and virtual potential (intensities, ideas, experimenting). The latter infinitude comes to form the significance of the actual outcomes of the drawing for the learner. Such actual-virtual events and their significance are unique to each individual. . .they denote how something matters to each learner. Yet it is impossible for the teacher to acquire comprehensive knowledge of this virtual aspect of a learner's experience.

IDEAS AND PROBLEMS

An Idea for Deleuze is closely associated with the notion of a problem in the sense that Ideas are problematic (1994, p. 214). Ideas have both virtual and actual dimensions, which means that they are never fully resolved but are likely to evolve, so that a problem is viewed in new ways. There are *actual* 'partial solutions' to Ideas, but also *potential* (virtual) for as yet unknown solutions, this is linked to the notion of an asymptotic ideal. Deleuze, according to Williams (p. 152), seeks to show how an Idea can be simultaneously, 'undetermined, determinable and determined according to an ideal of infinite determination'. For example, the idea of a perfect lesson is 'undetermined' as regards our understanding because it does not have a commensurate experience (though we might think it has!). Rather, it is problematic in the sense that many, perhaps contradictory, factors intervene; too much focus upon a particular way of attaining a learning objective may fail to acknowledge different ways of learning. Planning and organising a lesson according to a particular structure may prevent creative pedagogical responses to the spontaneity of events, and so on. However, we can take steps towards this somewhat abstract idea of a perfect lesson in the form of an on-going process of *experimentation* that moves a teacher further towards the ideal. Therefore, the Idea in the form of an ideal is never fully resolvable in actuality; in other words, the problem of the perfect lesson is 'determinable but never finally determined (Williams, p. 153)'. We can have an ideal vision, but this will not tell us *how* we are to proceed from one procedure to the next. An Idea can generate both actual objects as 'part solutions' to its problematical character, 'it conditions and gives rise to actual objects of experience (Ibid, p. 154)', but also virtual idealisations to aim for, some of which become actualised in future practice.

This process of experimentation is crucial for the Deleuzian thought-action complex and, of course, in relation to pedagogical work, it demonstrates the creative adventure of pedagogy, a series of on-going practices driven by an ideal determination to perform effectively, but whose functioning reality consists of a reciprocal determination—an experimentation—between actual outcomes and potential futures as pedagogical work proceeds.

EVENTS OF LEARNING AND RELATIONS

In this section, I return to the conditions of real experience already mentioned above, but with the notion of events of learning as my focus. Such learning events, as described above, involve a spark that interrupts established patterns of learning. They are events of becoming that shake up 'normal' functioning; they can be viewed as singularities in contrast to more regular forms of learning established in conventional relations of existence. Smith (Ibid, p. 247) suggests that individuals can be conceived as amalgams of 'the singular and the ordinary, remarkable and regular', and perhaps we can apply this contrast to that between transformative learning and normative learning. He provides both physical and psychical exemplifications of singularities: water boiling or freezing or someone breaking down or erupting with anger. The important point in these exemplifications is the transformation of relations where in one phase—for example, in the case of water—one series of relations between its constituents and its ambient milieu exist but, in another phase, these relations are transformed as ambient temperature falls and water turns to ice. In the case of someone losing their temper or becoming angry, a series of stable relations are suddenly transformed or punctured by an unacceptable act or statement. In these exemplifications, we might see that what we are dealing with on an ontological level is not a collection of things, objects or individuals, but rather, a series of relations, or multiplicities, that are constantly changing (becoming). In the case of learning events, established ways of learning are jolted by a disclosure of new insights, new ways of doing or thinking. Such transformations involve a change in the conditions of relation that constitute events of learning. In pedagogical contexts, the conditions of relation that spark the singularities of learning events amidst the patterns of normative learning are difficult, if not impossible, to detect in the 'thisness' of the sparking.

The conditions of real experience for Deleuze are grounded in the concepts of relation and difference (event), and their fundamental temporality is the future. He turns to Leibniz, Spinoza and Bergson, among others, to articulate the complexity of these conditions. I will refer briefly to Leibniz as discussed by Deleuze and Smith to give some indication of the complexity of the conditions of real experience that can be translated to the conditions of events of learning.

Leibniz's theory of perception provides an investigation into the genesis of conscious perception that emerges from a multiplicity of minute unconscious perceptions. For example, though we hear the sound of the wind rushing through the dense foliage of trees, we cannot hear the sound of every leaf being disturbed or one leaf clashing with another. From a distance, we can hear the noise made by a crowd at a soccer match, but not individual voices. Leibniz therefore attributes the conditions of real experience to an obscure 'unconscious' zone, to a virtual multiplicity, which is incomprehensible to conscious perception but out of which emerge, or actualise, finite conscious perception constituted by a series of differential relations. Smith writes:

> A conscious perception is produced when at least two of these minute and virtual perceptions [...] enter into a differential relation that determines a singularity which 'excels' over the others and becomes conscious. (p. 248)

The differential relation, Smith informs us is 'the psychic mechanism that extracts from this multiplicity my 'finite zone of clarity on the world (Ibid,

p. 248)'. Put more simply, we might view consciousness as a process in which certain things stand out or achieve clarity, whilst others, though present, fade into the background. This suggests that conscious perception is actualised from an infinite obscure zone, 'an unconscious within finite thought' (Ibid, p. 248). We can conceive this differential unconscious as a chaotic multiplicity, where multiplicity is understood in temporal (not logical) terms, thus indicating a potential of that-which-is-yet-to-come. This has further temporal implications, in that perception is not a process that consists of the perception of an already existing object or pre-given conditions of space and time, by a pre-given subject, but is a process which is constituted by a series of differential relations through which objects, subjects, time and space become actualised, they are, as it were, folded into each other in the on-going process of perception.

In more concrete and practical terms, and particularly in relation to learning, in our everyday lives, we will notice certain things and events as we function in different circumstances, but there are things and events we do not notice, but which nevertheless are part of the situation or surrounding milieu. In other words, we *will* perceive these things/events, but we will not be consciously aware of them. I remember observing students confronted with the demanding and emotional task of learning how to teach and, as their tutor, noticing particular things they did: how they related to their pupils, how they presented the learning task or encounter, how they organised and conducted their lessons, the kind of questions they asked their students, and so on. At the end of the lesson, during the 'reflective feedback session' with the student, it was always interesting to find that there were situations we both noticed but there were also others that the student noticed, usually infused with a deep affective intensity, that I did not, and there were things I noticed which were off the student's radar. In some ways, this seems to illustrate in practical terms how perception is constituted through an unconscious chaotic multiplicity out of which emerge conscious perceptions of real experience according to what and how something matters for a particular individual—its relevance. Furthermore it suggests that 'classroom experience' is not a matter of a pre-given teacher and pre-given learners coming together in pre-given conditions of space and time, but is constituted from a series of differential relations and their conditions (unconscious and conscious multiplicities) out of which emerge 'teacher' and 'learners' and the different space times of their real experience.

The complexity of such experience can be glimpsed when we consider that a teacher cannot predict in advance how learners will *actually* respond to his or her pedagogical strategies, nor how he or she will *actually* respond to their responses. In moving from learner to learner, the *intensity* of relations varies. A teacher responds to a student asking for help, whilst responding, the teacher's attention shifts to someone else making a disturbance, which he or she feels must be dealt with. After dealing with 'both' situations, he or she notices another student struggling and offers help, but the teacher is not 'welcomed' and is pushed away. Then the teacher feels a need to talk to the whole class to comment on the students' work. After this 'group feedback' period, the teacher continues to respond to individual students...and so on. Each of these relations is composed of different intensities or affective relations, and they contain different potentials; they can be viewed as transformations of the space of the classroom which effect transformations in the whole (time or duration) of the classroom. The teacher's relations move from one difference of potential (virtual) to another, and so the classroom as a functioning system is metastable, changing from one moment to the next. The temporal 'whole' of the classroom consists of sub-durations and their different affective intensities and relations. Smith writes:

> Thus, at every moment, my existence [...] is objectively problematic, which means that it has the structure of a problem, constituted by virtual elements and divergent series, and the exact trajectory that 'I' will follow is not predictable in advance. In a moment from now I will have actualized certain of those virtualities; I will have, say, spoken or gestured in a certain manner. In doing so I will not have 'realized a possibility' (in which the real resembles an already-conceptualised possibility) but will have 'actualized a virtuality' – that is, I will have produced something new, a difference. (Ibid, p. 253)

DIFFERENT/CIATION AND THE CONDITIONS OF REAL LEARNING

A virtual multiplicity is endlessly *differentiated* but in becoming actualised it is *differenciated*, which is to say that a new difference emerges and adds something new. A learning encounter can be conceived as endlessly differentiated in the sense that it consists of numerous relationalities on a variety of levels stemming from previous and present experiences as well as numerous potentials for future action. A decision to act in a particular way, to produce a particular outcome, constitutes a specific actualisation, or differenciation, which in turn changes the space of potential (differentiation).

The creative effect of events of learning is twofold, to rupture existing forms of practice and associated ways of seeing and understanding and also to produce new forms of practice, new ways of seeing and understanding. In practices of painting, sculpture, performance or drawing, for example, such learning is characterised by the affect of risk, in the sense that at each moment of experiencing practice, the artist (learner) is exposed to a sense of betrayal, particularly if he or she believes they can decide upon the path ahead rather than responding step by step to the thisness of experiencing and the questions that are posed by the work in these moments of experiencing. Therefore, risk taking has to be followed by a wait for what will answer.

In a recent edition of the television programme *Imagine* (BBC 1, November 18, 2014), Anselm Kiefer speaks about the importance of waiting for the work to answer after making a decision from a multitude of potential decisions. This problematic dynamic suggests therefore that the force of art effecting events of learning is deeply relational, involving human and non-human 'actants': body, affects, thought, materials (paint, paper, ink, digital media, clay, wood, stone, etc.), memories, and so on. These relational dynamics indicate that, in the flow of experiencing, there is an unpredictable virtual power of becoming, a that-which-is-not-yet, which becomes, in unforeseen or unanticipated ways, something that happens beyond established conceptions of practice and which has the potential to create new worlds of practice. The multitude of potential decisions seems analogous to the virtual domain of differentiation and waiting for an answer and making a decision analogous to the domain of actualisation.

So a learning event is a problematic process constituted by a virtual domain of potentialities and a domain of actualisations that produce something new, a new relation. Actualisations do not remove the problematic nature of experiencing because its temporal existence means that new experiencings will contain different problematic occasions. If we think about the process of art practice, for example, the on-going dynamic of this process consists of smooth and problematic phases. During the latter, when the process comes to a halt, when there is uncertainty about how to proceed, numerous potential directions come in and out of focus. If you're lucky, a direction emerges which you decide to take that resolves this particular problem but, in taking it, the process of practice changes, the relation between practice, materials, body, thoughts, feelings and so on changes, and the process throws up new problems. It is in these problematic phases that, perhaps, we can grasp the realities of the virtual and actual and the dynamics of different/ciation that Deleuze employs to discuss the production of the new (new relations) that is indicative of events of learning.

EXPERIENCE

Multiplicity characterises the nature of experience. Experience has no ground of transcendence, in the sense of a subject who proceeds to experience the world. There are only flows of experiencing, concatenations of experiencing, which may become crystallised or accumulated into personal or social productions: concepts, habits, values, customs, ways of thinking and seeing. Flows of experiencing may open up potential for further experiencings. The pedagogical point here is that learners considered as flows of experiencings each have the potential to invent in their different flows or rhythms specific capacities for becoming. Thoughts are experiencings connecting to other experiencings, and to potential experiencings. An idea employed to explain an experience is itself an event of experience, and has the potential to expand our capacity to think, to see, to make.

In his work on empiricism, Deleuze stresses the notion of immanence. Empiricism for him is not consistent with the traditional idea that all knowledge is derived from sensory experience because, basically, this idea involves the assumption of a transcendent subject who experiences. For Deleuze, experience is not an experience of a human being, an animal or a plant, rather it is a flow or multiplicity of experiencings; there is no transcendent ground of experience but simply experiencing. In his idea of transcendental empiricism, life is a combination of actual and virtual multiplicities. It is not a case of human beings having thoughts about the world, but of experiencing events, some of which we call thoughts that come to form human beings. The error of thought for Deleuze is to begin with the illusion of transcendence, where we presuppose an already established ground for experience. For example, if we hold fast to a particular notion of the purpose of education or to particular ideas about what constitutes good teaching, it is likely that such transcendent forms come to prescribe these practices and so legislate over experiencings of teaching and learning, thereby occluding or marginalising ways of experiencing that differ from the prescription, and which may have the potential to expand capacities to teach and learn.

Colebrook (2002, p. 88) suggests that the political implications of Deleuze's transcendental empiricism raise some difficulties, for if we are to reject or hold in abeyance any ground or set of principles to inform practice, then established ideas or principles for education, democracy, ethics, teaching, learning, cannot be the site of appeal for political or other forms of debate. In the book, *A Thousand Plateaus*, Deleuze and Guattari place great emphasis upon the notion of a *people to come*, in contrast to existing social relations. They encourage us to challenge the boundaries of discourses and practices that inform human experience in all its manifestations in order to think and act beyond these in order to extend our capacities for thought and action. It is not that we should disregard established forms of thought or practice, but that we should not allow them to totalise how we think, see and act, and thus remain open to other possibilities that extend these in as yet unimagined ways. Thus, in one sense, the idea of holding fast to a political position in relation to specific social issues would seem to be problematic for Deleuze and Guattari, because the notion of a political 'issue' is itself problematic and is likely to be a reduction of a complex series of multiplicities. In another sense, holding fast may delimit the productive potential of a people to come.

For them life is a multiplicity composed of actual and virtual flows in which the power of the virtual is a power to become other, to become in unforeseen ways beyond established ways of thinking, seeing and acting (Colebrook 2002, p. 96). Returning to Spinoza's notion of the power of the body, human beings are composed of actual and virtual powers, powers of being and of becoming.

MINOR, SENSE AND MACHINIC

I want to pick up on the point made by Colebrook and others regarding the implications of putting aside transcendent principles, methodologies or ideologies when dealing with political, ethical, aesthetic or pedagogical matters. This seems to be a crucial but extremely difficult task if we are to remain open to the complexities of becoming and avoid pigeonholing these in established practices, ideas, representations or identities. In the context of pedagogic work, it is not unusual to be confronted by things that learners produce or what they say, that appear mysterious. It is probably impossible to comprehend all the different ways in which students learn. The consequence may be inadvertently to brush such mysteries or some modes of learning aside. Another response is to try, however difficult, to comprehend such modes of existence and production. In Chapter 10 of *A Thousand Plateaus*, Deleuze and Guattari discuss the concept of the *minoritarian* in relation to minor languages, but which can be applied to other forms of expression and practice. We can employ this concept to think about these moments of mystery and their modes of production. The concept of the minor relates closely to the idea of sense formulated by Deleuze and Guattari and, later in this section, I want to link these notions, minoritarian and sense, to the concept of machinic processes as discussed by Guattari (1995) and developed by Deleuze and Guattari in *Anti-Oedipus* (1984) and *A Thousand Plateaus* (1988) and also by Gerald Raunig (2010) in his book, *A Thousand Machines*. The intention is to use these concepts to explore pedagogic work, learning and teaching practices, not in terms of subjects (learners, teachers) who experience the world, but in terms of a flow of corporeal and incorporeal events; or not in terms of a series of identities that inter-act but as a series of on-going connections and relations. If we consider pedagogic work from the point of view of 'subjects who experience', we tend to presuppose an already existing subject and a world that is experienced. In contrast, if we view pedagogic work in terms of a flow of corporeal and incorporeal events that constitute experiencing, then we are more concerned with relations and connections and how these emerge to precipitate what we call subjects (teachers, learners) and world.

Such events consist, for Deleuze and Guattari, as a series of emergent multiplicities; a fusion of virtual and actual processes that combine states of actualisation with inherent potential for new modes of becoming, new capacities to act, think, see or feel. Events of becoming in which such new capacities may emerge can be considered in terms of deterritorialisations and reterritorialisations as worked on by Deleuze and Guattari throughout much of their work. Something of the infinitude of the virtual-actual relation implicit to deterritorialisation and the event is captured, as Deleuze states (Deleuze and Parnet 2002, p. 73), by Blanchot's phrase, alluding to this infinitude 'to release the part of the event which its accomplishment cannot realise'.

A drawing consists of actual and virtual becomings, a production of actions, resistances, accommodations, marks, forms, as well as ideas, reviews, potentials, transformations, disappointments; corporeal and incorporeal materialisations that matter or do not; corporeal and incorporeal matterings. We tend to think along the lines that an 'I' makes a drawing, 'I' employ a pencil, brush, pen, charcoal, and so on, to make marks on a surface. A subject who makes predicates the drawing. Can we put such transcendent thinking aside? Can we think in other ways? Can we take a nudge from Deleuze and Guattari and begin in the middle from the notions that the action and sense of drawing produces both drawing and drawer (a particular drawing-drawer machine). Beginning in the middle, there is no subject or object, but a series of actual and virtual events that precipitate marks, forms and images. It is our traditional investment in particular molar forms of production (forms of representation and practice) that produce modes of identification and their social machines (a good drawing, a competent drawer, assessment). Such investments dominate what and how we see a drawing, and thus may occlude more immanent molecular (minoritarian) strivings of drawing.

A material practice of learning through making a drawing enables particular material (re) configurations of the world whose boundaries, properties and meaning are constantly shifting (stabilising and destabilising), thus enabling specific material changes in what it means to make a drawing. The process of mattering through making a drawing is a continual iterative performance. So here, agency is not something which is attributable to subjects or objects, but to a series of on-going relational processes that (re) configure boundaries and meaning, that in turn can, 'contest and rework what matters and what is excluded from mattering' (Barad 2003, p. 827), in particular contexts of practice.

Such strivings can be viewed in terms of minor processes in contrast to majoritarian investments that act as transcendent enunciators determining the quality and value of learning or teaching. In educational contexts, such investments become pedagogical machines that create pedagogical identities. Minoritarian processes of learning denote those ways and modes of learning that do not subscribe to majoritarian values. We might say that events of learning' or art events are therefore minoritarian, in that such processes refer to events that leap beyond established frameworks of practice in order to transform practice. The emergence of the minoritarian within a particular field is equivalent to the emergence of *sense*. Here sense refers to the force of the untimely out of which new lines of becoming may emerge. The emergence of sense is a deterritorialisation, it is an event, it does not denote what something is but rather its power to become. Colebrook (Ibid, p. 60) describes how words allow us to place things in virtual connections and the same can be done with images, thus she states that 'sense is the power of *incorporeal transformation,*' whereby how a thing is conceived in language or image 'will alter what it is in its incorporeal or virtual being'. For example, we might witness an *actual situation* in which a body is hit by a rock but then read it as an accident or, on the other hand, a violent assault; how we read the actual event will change it in its incorporeal being. We might witness an actual learning encounter and then conceive it in a number of ways. As Colebrook states, 'sense expresses not what something actually is but its power to become', and further, 'sense allows certain powers of becoming to be given being; it is sense that produces [...] identities (Ibid, p. 60)'. However, although sense produces identities, it is important not to allow these to become transcendent operators that prevent the emergence of new forms of sense and their deterritorialisations.

The crucial point here is how the force of sense, coupled with the force of affect, produces individuation, in other words, how it expands capacities for becoming. We can view the process of sense producing blocks of becoming not leading to the production of individuals, but to the emergence of *dividuals* (see Raunig 2016). The idea of the dividual is important viewed in terms of a force of becoming in contrast to the idea of an individual as a production of power. The dividual can be linked to the idea of the *machinic* developed by Deleuze and Guattari. Machinic assemblages are essentially concerned with flows of connections and relations, not with representations or identities. Thus, rather than viewing people as individuals, we might see them as a flow of continually dividuating connections and relations. In his book *Dividuum: Machinic Capitalism and Molecular Revolution* (2016), Gerald Raunig explores the genealogy of the concept of dividuality, showing how, in our contemporary world in which we are constantly being divided, dispersed and produced by capitalist forms of production which operate rhizomic powers of control and regulation, dividuality can also function *disobediently*, through the cracks as it were, to produce forms of resistance or alternative potentials for creative action and thought. The implications for how we conceive politics and ethics, if we take on board the notion of the dividual, are important to consider.

Raunig's (2010) book *A Thousand Machines* provides a clear and concise presentation of the concept of the machine as it developed historically, and I think it is helpful to look at some of Raunig's discussion of this conceptual development in the writings of Marx up to the work of Deleuze and Guattari. Marx views the machine not in terms of easing labour, but as a means of extracting surplus value by optimising the exploitation of labour. Machines are not to be viewed like a tool that is used to effect more effective action, but more in terms of a fusion of the knowledge and skills of workers as well as scholars. Machines bring about subjectivation and socialisation so that humans become components of the machine. The workers who operate machines are as much part of them as the intellectual work of inventors and others who constitute the social context such as economists, planners, engineers and so on. Human action is therefore subjected to the order of the machine, and not the reverse. Raunig writes:

> Even the immaterial, intellectual, cognitive work that consisted in developing the machine, due to its enclosure in the technical apparatus, becomes an alien, extra-human power of the machine on the human components acting in the machine. (Ibid, p. 23)

Machines are not therefore constrained to technical matters but are in fact mechanical, intellectual and social assemblages. They coordinate and regulate workers modes of existence and thus bring about social subjection and machinic enslavement (Ibid, p. 24). I remember from my childhood in the north of England visiting my father and other relatives who worked in heavy woollen and cotton mills. These factories of machines consisting of looms, mules, tentering machines and other devices governed the daily existence of workers; their sleeping, eating, socialising habits, their holidays and recreation, and so on. Such machinic assemblages produced an entire mode of existence for thousands of workers and their families. But also some of these workers through association brought about by these assemblages were able to form groups and societies that debated and questioned their mode of existence in more overt and resistant forms. Such forms of resistance link with what Marx termed the *general intellect*, whereby ways of overcoming subjection, enslavement and exploitation could be imagined towards a more emancipated existence. Such forms of social cooperation and communication therefore had the potential to bring about social change.

Jumping forward to Deleuze and Guattari's work on machines in the second half of the twentieth century, we find a much more extended notion of the machine concept, as Raunig writes, referring to Paolo Virno's idea of an overlap between Marx and Guattari:

> ...it is necessary to understand the machine not as a mere structure that striates the workers, socially subjects them and encloses social knowledge within itself. Going beyond the Marxian notion of knowledge absorbed in the fixed capital of the machine, Virno thus posits his thesis of the social quality of the intellect: in postfordism the raw material and means of production of living labour is the capacity for thinking, learning, communicating, imagining and inventing, which is expressed through language *(and I would argue other forms of expression)*. The general intellect no longer presents itself only in the knowledge contained and enclosed in the system of technical

machines, but rather in the immeasurable and boundless cooperation of cognitive and affective workers. (Ibid, p. 115, my bracket and italics)

Deleuze and Guattari employ the notion of machines not in our everyday sense denoting prosthetic extensions for human action and capacities. They use it in a more unusual way to refer to processes of connection, relation, exchange and concatenation. Raunig writes, 'For Deleuze and Guattari, becoming a piece with something else means something fundamentally different from extending oneself, projecting oneself or being replaced by a technical apparatus' (Ibid, p. 31). The key focus for Deleuze and Guattari is summed up by Raunig:

> The narrative of man's becoming machine as a purely technical alteration misses the machinic, both in its civilization-critical development and in its euphoric tendency. It is no longer a matter of confronting man and machine to estimate possible or impossible correspondences, extensions and substitutions of the one or the other, of ever new relationships of similarity and metaphorical relations between humans and machines, but rather of concatenations of how man becomes a piece with the machine or with other things in order to constitute a machine. The 'other things' may be animals, tools, other people, statements, signs or desires, but they only become machine in a process of exchange, not in the paradigm of substitution. (Ibid, p. 32)

There is a tentative link here, I would suggest, between the notion of the machinic as becoming a piece with something else and Whitehead's notion of prehension, discussed in the previous chapter, that refers to how something takes account of something else.

For Guattari (1995), machines are always connected to other machines in circuits of production, for example, cell machines are connected to other cell machines and to larger organ and body machines. A machine can involve the connection of a body with something: a camera, a sound system, a concept, a soccer ball, that produces a machine. Colebrook (Ibid, p. 56) gives the example of a bicycle machine; it only works as a machine when attached or connected to another machine, a human body. But of course, when the bicycle becomes attached to other kinds of machines, an art gallery or museum, then new or different connections and relations emerge. It is the centrality of connection, exchange and relation that is important to the notion of machinic connections or assemblages. Whilst molar state machines, in education for example, striate and regulate and impose forms of closure, machinic production is not limited to such forms, but is an immanent flow open to other perhaps alternative connections and exchanges. We can consider the process of painting or other forms of art practice through established discourses in which practice is constructed as such; this would be to apply the power of striation. Alternatively, we might consider practice as a series of on-going connections, exchanges and communications between bodies, materials, surfaces, ideas and affects, without imposing prior predications of practice.

We can conceive life processes as machinic and molecular in contrast to 'forms of life', identity machines that are molar and striating. There are multiple molar machines (aesthetic machines, pedagogical machines, subject machines, social machines, technical machines, animal machines, virus machines, and so on). Therefore, we need to make a distinction between molar machines that exert forces of subjection and striation, such as assessment machines in education and elsewhere, and machinic processes that occur on a molecular or pre-molecular level before striation occurs. On this latter level, when we think about processes of learning, we are dealing with immanent molecular flows and intensities, of relations, connections and attachments, dislocations and ruptures, modes of mattering. Such flows are prior to more molar connections, relations and striations between learner or teacher or art.

The term machinic, when used to describe molecular forces (rather than molar striations), therefore relates to potentialities and intensities before forms of stratification or segmentation begin to emerge either on molecular or molar levels, that is to say, personal or social levels. Machinic becomings involve machinic connections, couplings, dislocations, bifurcations, driven by a machinic desire for connection and relation. For Guattari, the world is conceived as a series of machinic assemblages that function on molecular and molar levels. However, the aforementioned distinction between molar machines and their forces of subjection and molecular machinic processes of connection, relation and exchange, needs to be qualified because the machinic subservience in machinic capitalism operates precisely on the molecular level. An important task therefore, on the level of molar institutions, such as schools and other educational sites, is to try to develop new molar forms, new reterritorialised forms, new forms of instituting, that do not subjugate but accommodate local machinic becomings. The importance of machinic thinking is that it abandons more traditional ways of thinking in terms of subjects and objects and reconceives these as phases in an on-going flow of connections, relations and communications between different kinds of machinic assemblages.

Raunig stresses the importance of the context of Guattari's early writings on machines. He was concerned about the rigidity of left wing politics post 1968 in relation to and in contrast with the different micro-politics of experience and therefore sought a kind of continuity of revolutionary praxis that would not be strangled by the closure of state apparatuses or identitarian forces of community. Guattari was thus seeking ways in which difference and its potential for becoming could be enhanced to produce new and different forms of sociality. This quest involves a notion of power not concerned with domination or striation but rather with Spinoza's notion of power relating to the potential of a body's capacity to act or a mind's capacity to think.

The force of art, as will be discussed in the next chapter, invokes a force of disruption to established machinic flows of connection. It is as though this force initiates points of rupture. Alongside the notion of *lines of flight*, Deleuze and Guattari employ the idea of the *diagram* or the *abstract machine* to discuss such moments of rupture and a turning towards that which is not yet known. Put another way, the force of art passes beyond established striations of practice, ways of seeing, thinking and feeling and enters a smoother space, from territorialisation into deterritorialisation towards reterritorialisation. The force of art is always in the middle between the virtual and the actual. The abstract machine, which seems synonymous with the notion of the virtual, is therefore orientated towards a world not yet known, a people yet to come (learners and teachers yet to come).

> Defined diagrammatically [...] an abstract machine is neither an infrastructure that is determining in the last instance nor a transcendental Idea that is determining in the supreme instance. Rather it is always a piloting role. The diagrammatic or abstract machine does not function to represent, even something real, but rather constructs a real that is yet to come, a new type of reality. (1988, p. 142, my underline)

The idea of the abstract, as Raunig (Ibid, p. 106) tells us, does not denote detachment or 'distancing from the real':

> Instead of actualising abstraction as detachment, as separation, I understand abstract machines as transversal concatenations that cross multiple fields of

immanence, enabling and multiplying the connections in this field of immanence. (p. 106)

We might say that in machinic terms events of learning involve abstract machines that pilot across experienced and experiencing connections that construct a world yet to come; phases of deterritorialisation or new lines of flight that offer a potential to precipitate new ways of thinking, making, seeing, feeling. Abstract machines then lie at the heart of experimentation in the struggles to build a life.

We can relate these ideas on machines and machinic flows to the three lines of becoming that are formulated by Deleuze and Guattari and discussed by Deleuze in dialogue with Claire Parnet (2002, pp. 124–147). These are rigid molar lines of segmentation such as those constituting family, jobs, school, university, factory, retirement (molar machines), then more subtle molecular lines of segmentation running through individuals, groups and societies in which different or deviant pathways that contrast with more normalising paths are taken and compose what might be termed micro-becomings (molecular machines). Then there are lines of flight that constitute a third kind of line, lines that deterritorialise and rupture established lines of becoming and which point to an as yet unknown future (abstract machines). These lines continually overlap and interweave, though they are not present in equal degrees and, indeed, some people may only experience the first or the first two kinds of lines.

These extended ideas of machines and machinic assemblages can be applied to different aspects of education and pedagogical work. On one hand, the social machine of education striates and regulates both learners and teachers. Machinic assemblages of assessment and examination as well as curriculum methodologies invoke forms of subjection that in today's context are deepened and made more invasive through panoptic practices of measurement to which all participants generally accede. On the other hand, more molecular machinic processes of connection, exchange and communication offer a way of viewing learning and teaching as practices in which bodies, materials, actions, concepts and affects have potential for expanding the power, in Spinoza's sense, of becoming beyond the hegemonic power of established striations. Perhaps we might apply these ideas of connection, communication and exchange to combat the harder segmentations of state striations of education and their respective pedagogised identities in order to consider the micro-politics of pedagogic work in terms of Spinoza's notion of power and potencies.

The distinction between the established striations of state education controlled by forces of measurement and singular flows of learning practices, singular flows of mattering, has some, but perhaps not absolute, resonance with Deleuze and Guattari's discussion, in chapter ten of *A Thousand Plateaus*, entitled *A Treatise on Nomadology: The War Machine*. State apparatuses that impose and regulate forms of identity in science, war, thought and other domains are contrasted with what are called war machines that, rather like the notion of minoritarian practices and abstract machines already discussed, create a militant kind of development that may change the normalising forces of established striations of practice and knowledge and their values. The difference between what we might call established striated processes and smoother rhizomatic or nomad spaces can be ascertained if we consider the notion of hylomorphism discussed by Deleuze and Guattari (1988, p. 369). Essentially, hylomorphism denotes the imposition of form upon matter; human ideas impose their form upon natural or other entities. Such forms (ideas, concepts, practices) organise matter and 'matter is prepared for the form' (Ibid, p. 369). We can see hylomorphism at work, for example, in psychology, psychiatry, clinical medical practice, education and other domains when human conditions or behaviours are read through existing forms of identification (criteria, rules, laws, theories, diagnoses). Rather than a relation of form imposing itself on matter, nomadic or rhizomatic processes are concerned with the relations and connections between singularities and their different 'traits of expression' (Ibid, p. 369). We might say that whereas hylomorphic processes tend towards homogeneity, rhizomatic or nomad processes deal with heterogeneity or, put another way, the striations of hylomorphism produce arborescent multiplicities whereas the smooth space of nomadic processes produces rhizomatic multiplicities. Deleuze and Guattari write:

> Smooth space is a field without conduits or channels. A field, a heterogeneous smooth space, is wedded to a very particular type of multiplicity: nonmetric, acentered, rhizomatic multiplicities that occupy space without "counting" it and can "be explored only by legwork." They do not meet the visual condition of being observable from a point in space external to them; an example of this is the system of sounds, or even colours, as opposed to Euclidean space. (Ibid, p. 371)

For me, this quotation is full of resonance with events of learning and pedagogic work. A studio, classroom or other contexts populated by learners and educators/teachers can be viewed as a rhizomatic multiplicity that needs 'legwork' in order to explore its differences, and this legwork constitutes what I call *the adventure of pedagogy*, an adventure that has political, ethical and aesthetic dimensions. This rhizomatic multiplicity, which is not accessible through observation from a point in space external to it, reminds me again of the waterfall experience I have mentioned earlier. Standing inside a waterfall is to occupy a smooth space that is not striated, but which is full of intensities and connections. It cannot be counted or measured. Standing outside and observing the waterfall involves a different, striated multiplicity that is subject to a viewing position, and how this is constituted, external to the waterfall.

Contexts of learning and teaching are more complex. The complexities, intensities, connections, and exchanges that occur inside a learning context between learners and teachers create a smooth rhizomatic space, but this will be segmented according to the forms of 'counting' and 'measuring' (theories, assumptions, presuppositions, methodologies, values) that a teacher employs from his or her observational perspective on what is happening and which subsequently informs his or her response.

Deleuze and Guattari distinguish between two kinds of procedures, which they relate to scientific practice but which I use for pedagogic work. These are *reproducing* and *following* (Ibid, p. 372). Reproducing relates to a reiteration of established forms of knowledge and practice: ways of thinking, seeing, feeling and making. Reproduction 'implies the permanence of a fixed point of view that is external to what is reproduced (Ibid, p. 372)'. Following is not the same in that it does not involve reproduction. 'One is obliged to follow when one is in search of the "singularities" of a matter, or rather of a material, and not out to discover a form...' (Ibid, p. 372) when, for example, one engages in a pedagogical relation to find out how something matters for a learner. Reproducing always tends to reterritorialise knowing, making and seeing around established points of view, practices, values and established relations; it imposes what we might call the closure of knowledge. Following extends capacities through the force of disclosure, through deterritorialisations, developing new connections and exchanges, constituting new assemblages of knowing, thinking, seeing, making and feeling.

Is it too fanciful or misguided to consider those processes of events of learning, in art practice, for example, that do not seem to fit with the evaluative criteria employed by teachers and others, as little war machines that compose different kinds of connections and exchanges that can be recognised by established striations of learning? This is not too difficult to accept when we consider the radical 'difference' of some contemporary art practices. We are concerned here with established modes of thought and practice in contrast to those that are external to them. Thought and that which is exterior to it.

> A "method" is the striated space of the cogitation universalis and draws a path that must be followed from one point to another. But the form of exteriority situates thought in a smooth space that it must occupy without counting, and for which there is no possible method, no conceivable reproduction, but only relays, intermezzos, resurgences. (Ibid, p. 377)

Can we extend our understanding of learning and art practice by 'following' (as discussed above) these seemingly aberrant or disobedient practices and connections rather than simply 'reproducing' them through established lenses? Deleuze and Guattari state that 'Learning to undo things, and to undo oneself, is proper to the war machine (Ibid, p. 400)'. These disobedient practices, which I have equated loosely with Deleuze and Guattari's notion of war machines, may effect what we might term, in reference to Jacques Ranciere (2004, p. 266), a process of *pedagogical dissensus*, which involves the production or appearance in a world of something (subject, practice, thinking, making) that is heterogeneous to it.

NOTE

1. Deleuze does not think of individuals as clearly defined entities, but in terms of an ongoing series of processes that connect thoughts, things, sensations to the pure intensities and ideas implied by them (Williams p. 6). An individual is not a self-sufficient or self-conscious 'I', but a series of ongoing (conscious and unconscious) syntheses of thoughts and intensities arising in relation to whatever is confronted.

REFERENCES

Atkinson, D. (1993). Representation and practice in children's drawing. *Journal of Art and design Education, 12*(1), 85–104.

Atkinson, D. (1995). Discourse and practice in the art curriculum and the production of the pupil as a subject. *Journal of Art and Design Education, 14*(3), 259–270.

Atkinson, D. (2003). *Art in education: Identity and practice.* Dordrecht/London/ Boston: Kluwer Academic Publishers.

Barad, K. (2003). Posthumanist performativity: Toward an understanding of how matter comes to matter. *Signs: Journal of Women in Culture and Society, 28*(3), 801–829.

Biesta, G. (2006). *Beyond learning; Democratic education for a human future.* Boulder: Paradigm.

Biesta, G. (2010a). A new 'logic' of emancipation: The methodology of Jacques Ranciere. *Educational Theory, 60*(1), 39–59.

Biesta, G. (2010b). *Good education in an age of measurement: Ethics, politics democracy.* Boulder: Paradigm.

Colebrook, C. (2002). *Gilles Deleuze.* London/New York: Routledge.

Deleuze, G. (1988). *Bergsonism.* New York: Zone Books.

Deleuze, G. (1990). *Pourparler 1972–1990.* Paris: Editions Minuit.

Deleuze, G. (1992). Postscript on the societies of control. *October, 59,* 3–7.

Deleuze, G. (1994/2004). *Difference and repetition.* London/New York: Continuum.

Deleuze, G., & Guattari, F. (1984). *Anti-Oedipus: Capitalism and schizophrenia.* London: Athlone Press.

Deleuze, G., & Guattari, F. (1988). *A thousand plateaus.* London: Athlone Press.

Deleuze, G., & Guattari, F. (1994). *What is philosophy?* London: Verso.

Deleuze, G., & Parnet, C. (2002). *Dialogues.* New York: Columbia University Press.

Gattegno, C. (1972). *What we owe our children.* London: Routledge Kegan Paul.

Guattari, F. (1995). On machines. In A. Benjamin (Ed.), *Complexity: Architecture/ art/philosophy* (pp. 8–12). London: Academy Editions.

Rajchman, J. (2000). *The Deleuze connections.* Cambridge, MA/London: MIT Press.

Ranciere, J. (2004). *The politics of aesthetics.* London/New York: Continuum.

Raunig, G. (2010). *A thousand machines.* Cambridge, MA/London: MIT Press.

Raunig, G. (2016). *Dividuum: Machinic capitalism and molecular revolution.* Cambridge, MA/London: MIT Press.

Roffe, J. (2005). In A. Parr (Ed.), *The Deleuze dictionary.* Edinburgh: Edinburgh University Press.

Shaviro, S. (2009). *Without Criteria: Whitehead, Deleuze and aesthetics.* Cambridge, MA/London: MIT Press.

Smith, D. (2012). *Essays of Deleuze.* Edinburgh: Edinburgh University Press.

Thiele, K. (2008). *The thought of becoming.* Zurich/Berlin: Diaphanes.

Williams. (2013). *Gilles Deleuze's difference and repetition: A critical introduction and guide.* Edinburgh: Edinburgh University Press.

CHAPTER 8

The Force of Art

Part One

Previous chapters were concerned with the notion of subjectivity as a process of becoming involving finite and infinite processes. Emphasis was placed upon the virtual and actual creative power of becoming; upon the immanent process of building a life; upon that which is yet to arrive. Chapter 3 focussed upon Spinoza and his future-oriented and immanent notion of power (*puissance*) formulated in his contention that we don't know what a body is capable of doing, nor what a mind is capable of thinking. Chapter 5 considered the process philosophy of Whitehead and the importance he placed upon the creative adventure of the emergence of the new in processes of becoming. Chapter 7 considered some aspects of the work of Deleuze and Deleuze and Guattari which, through concepts such as difference, multiplicities, rhizomatic assemblages, intensities, the virtual and the event, the subject and its established boundaries of knowledge, practices and values become undone so that rather than thinking of the subject in terms of an individual, we are encouraged to think of it as dividual—as constantly individuating according to contexts and circumstances. In a nutshell, this image of dividual becomings is captured by the notion of the rhizome that opens Deleuze and Guattari's great book, *A Thousand Plateaus*, where a rhizome is described as a series of machinic connections, continuously spreading and open to making further connections, or closing those established. We can view the rhizome as existing on a plane of consistency made up of

© The Author(s) 2018

D. Atkinson, *Art, Disobedience, and Ethics*, Education, Psychoanalysis, and Social Transformation, DOI 10.1007/978-3-319-62639-0_8

intensive flows, unformed matter, but also on a plane of organisation or composition on which singularities, forms and assemblages appear. Of course, whilst the idea of a subject composed of a flow of different intensities, of affects and sedimentations may facilitate new or mutant forms of becoming and an expansion of capacities to act and think, it is also open to exploitation by capitalist forces and their specific constraints on thinking, acting and production of desire. Such forces precipitate particular forms of capture, regulation and over-coding.

In this chapter, I want to discuss the force of art as a force of invention; an event of becoming, a virtual/actual creative force of transformation beyond the capture of representation, identity, established knowledge or established aesthetic parameters. This transformative force consists of a vital force of appearing and a force of rupture; a force of appearing that disrupts established forms of reproduction, a force of experimentation and not judgement; it displaces relations of power, production and regulation. The force of art cannot be captured by language; it is in excess of such capture. The force of art is a virtual multiplicity in excess of established forms and outcomes of practice. The force of art relates to its 'work' that transforms existing forms of representation and aesthetic formations. Krzysztof Ziarek (2004), in his book entitled *The Force of Art,* which I have borrowed for the title of this chapter, calls such work *forcework* where the notion of force relates to an on-going undercurrent, a flow of forces, that is pre-linguistic and pre-cognitive, but out of which emerge phases of transformation and rupture (p. 33) that work against accepted aesthetic, social and political forms of thought and relations. This undercurrent is a molecular unformed potential array of relations that seems close to Deleuze's notion of the virtual, to Spinoza's notion of immanence and power and Whitehead's notion of creativity (p. 34).

Ziarek states the 'the single most important problem raised in [his] book concerns arts relations to power (Ibid, p. 3)'. Here, the term 'power' refers in a similar way to what Deleuze and Guattari refer to as arborescent structures that capture, regulate and overcode ways of thinking, seeing, making and feeling. The power to which Ziarek refers is the power of capitalist production and its multiple relations; it is the power of commerce, control, regulation, normalisation, globalisation or identity that pervades western and other societies. In contrast, the force of art, according to Ziarek, is an event that ruptures such economies of power and production in order to disrupt such relations and to conceive alternative relational ways of thinking, seeing, making and feeling. To focus upon art's forcework, therefore, is to try to understand the transformative momentum of art practice, both in terms of making art and responding to it, rather than to view art works as objects or commodities within or beyond institutional sites. Thus, in Spinoza's sense of power and immanence, the forcework of art is that which enables a body, a mind, to extend capacities for acting and thinking.

Placing emphasis upon the forcework of art is simultaneously to question the notions of object and production of aesthetics in its traditional sense of formed content. Or put another way, giving priority to the forcework of art is to reject the traditional hylomorphism of aesthetic or other forms of judgement in which art objects are read and appraised through notions of established form and value. Forcework exceeds such aesthetic parameters and for Ziarek—referencing the aesthetic and other writings of Heidegger and Adorno—this excess is enabled in a space, not conditioned by the power of production captured by the term *macht*, but by the release from power indicated by the term *lassen* (Ibid, p. 11). This notion of release is also suggested by the Greek term *aphesis*, which denotes a releasing or a letting be in a deliberative and enabling sense. Thus, the aphetic character of forcework suggests that art practice is released from the regulatory power of habits of practice and representation and of established knowledge and values whilst simultaneously inaugurating different kinds of relations beyond regulatory power. To some extent, we might view this aphetic nature of practice in the painting practice of Jackson Pollock as it ruptured established parameters and values of painting and established new relational experiences of painting. Such painting is a productive practice, but it is a production not governed in itself by established forms and values of production but, as Ziarek might contend, it enters a different space and economy of production, one determined by the release from the power of established parameters of practice and the emergence of a new relational space of painting. Of course, the subsequent 'capture' of Pollock's paintings by the art market and the world of commerce reintegrates this work into the power of capitalist values. We might want to consider the immanence of the painting and drawing practices of young children—before they become subject to the transcendent gaze of established ideas and forms of representation—as functioning beyond the power and logic of such gazes, in a space of aphesis, a space of enabling and release.

We can view this aphetic nature of the force of art as a *disobedient* force in the context of art education, a force that, through the enabling of release and letting be, may fracture the parameters of instruction and pedagogic work and by doing so, effect a transformative dynamic that extends our capacity to comprehend art practice, learning and teaching. This fracturing process raises both political and ethical aspects of learning and pedagogical work. The aphetic nature of the event of art suggests a different kind of political relations to those established by the power of established forms of practice and regulation. Here I am using the term politics close to the work of Jacques Ranciere (1999, 2010), who presents in a number of texts the idea that politics emerges at the site of a 'wrong' when a clash or a confrontation in the name of equality arises between the police order and some event or mode of being that reveals discrimination, victimisation or marginalisation. Can the aphetic forcework of art similarly illuminate 'pedagogical wrongs' and thereby transform the commodification of learning, by revealing the way in which teachers and learners are produced as pedagogised subjects in art education contexts? These pedagogised subjectivities are produced through the power of established practices such as assessment, practice methodologies, examination and inspection. Art's forcework may rupture the capture and regulative power of established aesthetic or educational criteria employed in pedagogical work and, in doing so, we can be challenged to rethink practice, learning and teaching. How might we rethink the idea of the learner and, consequently, the teacher through the disrupting effects of the forcework of art? Ziarek writes:

> The idea of art as an object, constitutive of aesthetic reflection and pivotal to the logic of commodification, distorts the most significant aspect of artworks, concealing the very force that makes art artistically and socially significant (Ibid, p. 19)

Art practice thus becomes a field of force relations that are not constrained or regulated by established frameworks; arts forcework is disobedient to these and, through such force, it has the potential to reconfigure social relations (pedagogical relations), ways of seeing, thinking, feeling and acting. Again, historically perhaps, we can see the impact of Ziarek's term forcework and its transformative effects when we reflect upon moments of rupture in art or other modes of practice when established frameworks of practice were reconfigured. The work of Duchamp, the Situationists, or Joseph Beuys, for example, is frequently cited as generating forces of rupture and transformation. In literature, the writing practices of James Joyce and Gertrude Stein invoked similar radical forces that precipitated transformative effects. Such transformative events, following Ziarek, did not confront the power of established parameters of practice in order to establish alternative power structures, but rather, moved practice into a different space of practice, a space of non-power whose aphetic nature of release and enabling whilst exposing the working of power offered different, more emancipatory possibilities for practice.

In the context of school art education, we can enquire into the power-oriented forms of being and identification that are reflected in assessment criteria or practice methodologies; forms that are sedimented in our understanding of representation and practice and which mould our understanding of learning and practice. Many years ago, when I began to think more intensely about how young children make drawings and paintings, I had frequent conversations with John Matthews who has made extensive and intensive studies of these early practices. I learnt a great deal about the power of established theories, particularly from developmental psychology but also other fields, to identify and categorise these practices and to construct a kind of teleology of representational practice from, in crude terms, scribble to perspective. These taxonomies of early practices are equivalent to what Deleuze and Guattari call molar assemblages. But the conversations with John coupled with my expanding experience of observing children draw and paint punched through these assemblages of categorising early drawing practices and opened up a much more rhizomic and molecular world of practice, in which I became aware of the often sophisticated and novel ways in which children's drawing practices emerged and how they became invested with meanings and forms that were not recognisable within the molar assemblages of developmental psychology. These early practices showed me other ways of understanding children's drawings that cut beneath the power of academic regulatory discourses; they created a more aphetic space of release and enabling. In other words, I experienced a different kind of relationality with these drawings whose force transformed my ways of seeing and thinking. I was not interested in the drawings as objects, but as events and processes of expression and meaning-making particular to the relationalities that composed each context of practice.

These early explorations of what we might call the immanence of children's art practices compared to how they were classified within transcendent academic taxonomies in subsequent years informed my interest in taxonomies of assessment and how these discourses produced what I called *pedagogised identities* in the context of school art education (Atkinson 2003) that constitute important molar assemblages with secondary school education. Again, my interest was to explore emerging forms of practice that were immanent to a learner's learning encounter, each learner's evolving sensibilities, but which the transcendent criteria of assessment assemblages sometimes marginalised or ignored. One way of thinking about the force of the immanence of practice and its emerging forms of expression is through the force of appearing—or what in Greek is given the name *poiesis*. According to Agamben (1999), the Greeks made a clear distinction between the terms *praxis* and *poiesis*. Fundamental to *praxis* is the notion of a will that is expressed in action, while *poiesis* denotes a process of appearing, a coming into presence, a movement from non-being to being, from concealment to full view. The essential nature of *poiesis* is not concerned with productive action according to a will, but with the emergence of a truth as an unveiling (*alethia*). The materiality of *poiesis* is process, becoming, whilst the materiality of *praxis* rests on production by a prior will or idea. Another way of conceiving the difference between *praxis* and *poiesis* is that *praxis* is grounded in transcendent relations whilst those of *poiesis* are immanent.

Ziarek contrasts this idea of *poiesis* that is characteristic of the forcework of art to the Heidegerrian notion of technicity and its equivalent forcework. Technicity refers to the revealing of the world as *technic*, that is to say, where the world is conceived as a resource for human exploitation. Heidegger gives the example of a power plant on the Rheine where the river itself, before the onset of industrial construction, is already conceived as a resource that can be controlled, regulated and exploited. Thus, the forcework of technicity is grounded in relations of power and control in contrast to the poietic forcework of art that is grounded in the non-power of aphesis and actively letting be. As Ziarek argues (Ibid, p. 41), this does not imply that art is simply free from power or its influence, frequently, the reverse is the case as art practice and its objects are captured by technicity and its power of commodification. The point is that art as a poietic force may sometimes rupture and transform the dominant relations of technicity, and thereby transform relations beyond the grip of power. In reference to Adorno's comments on arts inversion of social powers of control and regulation Ziarek states:

> Art becomes socially "meaningful" precisely when it breaks with the aesthetic and political functions that society establishes for it, when it alters the power formations that regulate society and that society wants to stamp or project onto artworks. Instead, what art inaugurates is a different forcework, a different disposition of forces...(p. 41)

Such forces pass beyond the power of 'categorial determinations invisibly stamped on reality (Ibid, p. 42)', but they are not reducible to what we might call art's social or critical function (as adopted, it might be argued, in multicultural or visual culture modes of art education). The transformative event of art's forcework, of art's poietic materiality, points towards a world beyond art, to practices and a people yet to come, and it does not lie in art's power to criticise, but to the event of a world becoming otherwise or pointing towards such possibilities. This is the affirmative poietic force of art, the affirmational drive towards a world and a people yet to come.

Perhaps we might see this force of affirmation in a couple of art practices. In 1992, the artist Fred Wilson made an intervention at the Maryland Historical Society entitled *Mining the Museum* (1992), in which he subverted the idea of the truth of the museum exhibits by 'questioning' whose truth was being displayed. In the installation entitled *Metalwork 1793–1880,* the usual display of silverware was 'disrupted' by a pair of iron slave shackles. Though this intervention challenged underlying racist attitudes inherent to museum displays by juxtaposing objects of wealth and affluence with objects that made such affluence possible, I think that the force of the intervention was not primarily a force of social criticism, though this was certainly provoked, but a more affirmational and poietic force that pointed beyond the art objects to a possibility of a world and people yet to come, a possibility still yet to arrive.

A second art practice I want to mention was produced a few years ago by a Master's student for his final exhibition at Goldsmiths University of London. The work consisted of a giant assessment pro-forma measuring about two by one metres. Such pro-formas are commonplace in secondary school art department assessment and evaluation processes, but are usually no larger than a single page. This giant exhibit gently mocked the power of audit that is so pervasive in schools in England, whereby the device of assessment replaces—almost sublimates for the audit system—the actual learner. In displaying this apparatus of assessment, the student was also in a way challenging his university tutors to assess him. Again, the primary force of this artwork was not its power as a critical object, though this was obviously not to be ignored, but its undermining of the power of audit, of assessment and commodification in educational contexts, and a pointing towards the possibility of a different kind of pedagogical world of learners and teachers.

We can read this work as pointing towards the inherent technicity of educational practices, the fact that learners and teachers are assumed to be intrinsically calculable and commodifiable as a resource for future employability and the world of economic ambition. The technicity of educational practices therefore produces specific pedagogical relations grounded in measurement and audit. Ziarek writes:

> When beings come to be disclosed as "resources," natural, mineral, human, or otherwise, it means that they are constituted in their very essence in terms of power, that is, as intrinsically disposed toward being manipulated and (re) produced and thus articulated as part of the general flow of power, or, in other words, as preprogrammed to take a form or a value that "makes" them what they are by virtue of "making" them participate in the intensification of power. (Ibid, p. 62)

The power of technicity in our world today is manifested in the notion of digitality, whereby everything becomes intrinsically subject to being digitised as information—as data. Nevertheless, the poietic force of the work also cuts beneath the power of technicity in order to postulate the possibility of different kinds of pedagogic relations more concerned with drawing alongside the immanence and difference of learning in order to support and develop it in its local terms.

The Event of Art

We might conceive the poietic event of art further as a problematical process that opens up what might be possible (where we imagine the constitution of the world from the relationship between event and multiplicity). Lazzarato (2003) writes:

> Representation is [...] founded on the subject-work paradigm. In this paradigm the images, the signs and the statements have the function of representing the object, the world, whereas in the paradigm of the event, images, signs and statements contribute to allowing the world to happen. Images, signs and statements do not represent something, but rather create possible worlds.

Here, the event can be viewed in terms of the process of building a life, or a collective, and the pedagogical task is not to treat the event according to 'established answers' for they will 'miss' the event. We therefore need to view the force of art in art practices not in terms of representation of a world, but rather as trying to make a world happen. Art practices therefore 'are constitutive of reality and not its representation (Lazzarato, Ibid)'. This would seem to demand a different ontology to one grounded in representation, an ontology grounded in potential and which raises the issue of ethics and politics in relation to becoming rather than the issue of the relation between representation and judgement. It also raises the issues of obedience and disobedience. *Dispositifs* of obedience, their transcendent framings of practice, structure, value and discourse, lie in contrast to the immanence of local processes and capacities for transformation and power (in Spinoza's sense) beyond such *dispositifs* that establish new relations with self and others, that delineate the domain of an immanent ethics and politics emerging from such events rather than a transcendent ethics or politics imposed from outside.

Returning to Spinoza, the event of art is resonant with what he called active affects in contrast to passive affects. Active affects arise in interactions that enhance our ability to act. Passive affects (or passions) arise when we are affected by things in such a way that our power to act is decreased. As Lazzarato states, we might see the emergence of passive affects due to 'the invasive forces of advertising media that inscribe their images, words, sensibilities in our bodies; where advertising now has global effects (but where only a small minority can actualise its worlds)'. The force of art is a force that leads to action that passes beyond the grip or effects of established parameters of practice, representation and judgement. It is a force that can precipitate new ontologies and their potentials beyond the obedience to established *dispositifs* of practice. Daniel Smith (2012), writing on Deleuze and the emergence of the new, captures this ontological shift:

> Thus, at every moment, my experience [...] is objectively problematic, which means that it has the structure of a problem, constituted by virtual elements and divergent series, and the exact trajectory that "I" will follow is not predictable in advance. In a moment from now I will have actualised certain of those virtualities; I will have, say spoken or gestured in a certain manner. In doing so I will not have "realized a possibility" (in which the real resembles an already-conceptualised possibility) but will have "actualized a virtuality" – that is, I will have produced something new, a difference. (p. 253)

This idea of the problematic as indissoluble from the event of art when applied to a learning encounter in the context of art practice raises some tricky issues. If the force/event of art is a radical transformative force as discussed above, then how might we develop pedagogical practices in art education that embrace this force when, by implication, it seems anathema to them? This question is answered, not exclusively, through the idea of uncertainty, by the fact that the event of art produces moments of uncertainty, of disequilibrium, a feeling of not being sure how to proceed. Yet this notion of uncertainty is not to be viewed in negative terms, but as part of a creative process or, as Whitehead would say, the creative move into novelty. Here, the state of uncertainty is allied to the notion of disobedience, whereby opportunities arise to pass beyond established parameters. The temporality of this phase of uncertainty can be considered through the notion of *kairos*.

Antonio Negri and the Temporality of Kairos

In the book *Time For Revolution*, Antonio Negri (2013) discusses the Greek term *kairos*. I will provide a brief commentary on this discussion and its implications for considering the event of art and then proceed to say something about its relevance to processes of teaching and learning building upon my earlier commentary of Spinoza's writing and its relevance for pedagogical work. In simple terms, according to Negri, the term *kairos* refers to the opening of becoming to that which is yet to come but which is also grounded in the eternal of the past. Negri describes it as 'anticipating and constructing on the edge of time (Ibid, p. 146)'. Put another way, *kairos* denotes a process of something being 'called' into existence; when something new emerges and is grasped by a combination of the force of affect and the morphology of a word, a mark, an image, an action, a sound. It is a dynamic and intense event, like the event of learning and its immanence.

> In the classical conception of time, kairos is the instant, that is to say, the quality of the time of the instant, the moment of rupture and opening of temporality. It is the present but a singular and open present. *Kairos* is the modality of time through which being opens itself, attracted by the void at the edge of time, and it thus decides to fill that void. (p. 156)

Negri characterises *kairos* as an 'adventure beyond the edge of time (p. 156)', which links with the idea that the temporality of the event of art or the event of learning is rooted in that mode of existence in time that is *kairos*, since such events involve a shift into new or modified (yet-to-come) ontological and epistemological phases. Tim Ingold (2011, p. 72), writing about animacy, captures something of the environment of *kairos*:

> We are dealing here not with a way of believing about the world, but with a condition of being *in it*. This could be described as a condition of being alive to the world, characterised by a heightened sensitivity and responsiveness in perception and action, to an environment that is always in flux, never the same from one moment to the next.

He writes further:

> In an animic ontology, beings do not simply occupy the world, they *inhabit* it, and in so doing – in threading their own paths through the meshwork – they contribute to their ever-evolving weave. (Ibid, p. 71)

So *kairos* denotes a particular mode of existence in time, on the edge of time, looking out into the unknown, the not-yet-known, when beings make their pathways into the not-yet-known, yet grounded in an eternal past. This seems to capture the restlessness and inventiveness of the emergence of learning; the event of a new form of expression of a concept, a movement, a sound, an image or a form of practice. Negri (Ibid, p. 160) links the event of *kairos* with the power of imagination as he recalls, 'in Spinoza the imagination has the ontological function of recomposing the strata of being'. Though of course, for Spinoza, images of things lead to inadequate ideas (see Lord 2010, pp. 73–81). Thus, the mode of existence of *kairos* may involve ontological, epistemological, ethical and political recompositions in relation to whatever context or practice is involved.

Time and Kairos

In general terms, we tend to think of time as a linear and homogeneous process linking past, present and future, but with the temporality of *kairos* the past and the future are more complex. A common idea of the future conceives it as a continuation of the present, the present running on into the future. But the event of *kairos* is a creative moment occurring on the edge of something *to-come*. Negri writes, 'The passage to the to-come is always a difference, a creative leap (167)'. *Kairos* initiates a force of invention in the form of an action, a concept, an image, a way of seeing.

The past is often considered as a series of previous events that form a kind of sedimentation or condensation of experience, but again, as regards *kairos,* what went before can only emerge in the present and so the past like the future, for *kairos,* is a creative event. It is a process of imagination similar to the creative production of that which is to-come. Thus, the inventive mode of existence called *kairos* produces that which went before and that which is to-come. Negri writes, 'Every instance of life of what has been and what will be is a creative act (ibid, p. 168)'. The inventive moment of *kairos* and the expressive forms produced is the production of a world. This implies that subjectivity does not exist before *kairos,* in the sense that there is no prior ontological or epistemological pre-eminent subject who 'knows'. This idea, as Negri states (ibid, p. 175), is the product of a transcendental illusion which contradicts the ontological experience of *kairos* in which a subject emerges by joining that-which-once-was with that which is to-come. Subjectivity and practice are therefore a continual process of invention. Negri writes:

> The philosophies of the subject place the determination of the meaning 'here' (in the materialist field) in the act of knowing that perceives and reflects. But this epistemological pre-eminence of the subject, this ontological supremacy of the subject, is the product of a transcendental illusion and is immediately in contradiction with the ontological experience of *kairos*. For subjectivity is not something that subsists: it is – on the contrary – produced by *kairos*. Subjectivity is not before but after *kairos*. (Ibid, p. 175)

The uncertainty, restlessness and inventiveness of the event of art and learning denote the orientation of *kairos* as a mode of being opening towards that which is to come. And inherent to this orientation is a kind of resistance or disobedience that precipitates a leap beyond already existing patterns and values of being. If we think of the process of events of learning as a manifestation of *kairos*, then we must also think of the evolution of learners and teachers as a continual creative and materialist process whilst simultaneously not allowing established ways of understanding learning and teaching to dominate and structure our thinking and acting. Put another way, pedagogic work has to avoid or reduce the controlling force of those transcendent operators of established practice that might delimit action and therefore miss the generative event of learning. Such work needs to develop an eternal vigilance of the power of control and also acquire a sense of militancy in practice.

Tim Ingold (2015, p. 97) again seems to be describing the orientation of *kairos* when he writes about the artist 'standing forever at that sliding moment', when the world, 'is on the point of revealing itself, such that the perpetual birth (of the artist's awareness) is, concurrently, the perpetual birth of the world (my bracket)'. We experience, we learn, *with* the world (a walk in a landscape, a storm, a social occasion, and so on); such learning involves what Ingold terms an 'affective mingling of our own awareness with the turbulence and pulsations of the medium in which we are immersed'. There is a correspondence between mind/body and world that occupied, in different ways, the thought of Spinoza and Whitehead.

Force of Art and Poietic Materialism

The notion of uncertainty allied to the idea of disobedience in a time of *kairos* thus forms a creative nexus through which capacities to act and think, to see and make may be expanded, and where potential is affirmed but also conserved. Agamben (2005) calls this time of *kairos* the 'messianic moment' (see Lewis 2010)

> . . .an incoherent and unhomogenous time, whose truth is in the moment of abrupt interruption, when man, in a sudden act of consciousness, takes possession of his own condition of being resurrected. (Agamben 2007, p. 111)

This moment of interruption Agamben refers to as a 'state of exception' (1999), which destabilises established parameters and boundaries and opens up new possibilities for action. Such moments of interruption or disobedience to established orders, internal or external, can be conceived in terms of a *poietic materialism,* which is constituted through a series of encounters, and denotes a coming into being that is an amalgam of relations between human and non-human actants, a coming into being that precipitates new relationalities and potentialities for learning and its ontogenesis. The event of art as an appearing. . .as *poiesis*. . .is not subjective or objective, but *intra-active,* involving human and non-human actants such as feelings, thoughts, memories, materials such as paint, paper, metal, wood, digital technologies, performances and more. The pedagogical imperative of a *poietic material-ism* is to extend our grasp and potential of what it is to be human, or put in the words of Spinoza, to extend our compass of what a body can do.

(We can witness this poietic materialism at work for example in the process of painting viewed as an assemblage of heterogeneous parts in which body movements, thinking, affects/feelings, paint, brush, canvas/ paper, emerging marks, etc. intra-act...it involves an ongoing appearing, mutable-stable, changing process).

Whereas *praxis* is teleological, initially predicated upon a determinate idea towards specific outcomes, the process of *poietic materialism* involves a kind of paradox, a knowingness of the unknowing of practice which involves an affirmation of becoming as well as a carrying forward of the unknown and its potentialities, what might be termed poietic attractors or allures. Poietic materialism liberates *praxis* from the already known or possible-real linkages, so provoking a not-known future dimension of becoming.

A poietic materiality defines an *event* of becoming, an event of learning as it happens within the different temporalities of experiencing. The emphasis therefore is not upon a predetermined pathway for learning, but upon singularities or *haecceities* that enable invention into existence. In a strange, also paradoxical sense, one *becomes* a learner without *being* a learner—that is to say without those established *constructions* of being a learner which define (represent, theorise), and at the same time constrain what a learner is. The same goes for teaching. This illustrates the creative and mutable dynamic of *poiesis*, which has the potential to puncture existing comprehensions of learning that become inscribed upon pedagogical bodies and practices.

The poietic force of art practice precipitates an appearing, a letting go of normalised relations and practices as these are manifested in forms and practices that hold us... it is an assemblage of intra-actings, not a determined space but, as discussed earlier, a space of aphesis (letting go, release), a becoming which cannot be predicted, not a space of power but a space of enabling and affirmation. The trick is to not allow the outcomes of this aphetic space to turn into precious objects or practices, which in turn territorialise and control.

It's not that difficult to witness the poietic force of art in children's drawing or painting practices before these become subjected to the influences of aesthetic production and commodification that emerge in institutional sites. Such practices invent new worlds and possibilities, they are often events whose materiality involve desires, thoughts, speech, memories, affects, paper, crayons, paints, lines, marks, shapes, body movements and more...a poietic assemblage of intra-actions in which human and non-human actants become entangled.

An illustration of the force of art emerged on the MA Artist Teacher and Contemporary Practice at Goldsmiths a few years ago. The video produced by Rose Wong and her partner is entitled *Ceaseless* (2013, You Tube uploaded August 29, 2013). Rose worked with 23 Chinese students to collect their memories, expressions and understanding of 'Chineseness'. Many of these contained politically sensitive material for those living in China, such as evidence of attending the Tiananmen Memorials, anti-communist material and news articles. The idea for making the video was to capture memories that were oppressed by state politics by placing them in boxes reminiscent of reliquaries. The boxes of memories are taken to a beach in England and their contents are burned before the ocean. Turning the memories into ash is a way to dissolve the recognisable form of the materials so that they could be transported back to the most politically sensitive place in China...Tiananmen Square. Burning is also a form of dissolution in many religious cultures, burning the dead is a way of sending them to the afterlife instead of destroying them. In other words, burning is a process *of* a new becoming. The scene shifts from an English beach to Tiananmen Square in Beijing. A girl holds open a box of memories in their burnt form and the ashes are transported in the wind before the seat of power.

The poietic materialism of this video not only deals with power and resistance to power, injustice and persecution but more than that I argue that its force as event opens a space of non-power, a space of aphesis. The act of burning invokes a release, an enabling and affirmational force of becoming that seems to open a new space of potential, a space for new relationalities to emerge beyond the reach of power, a space for a people yet-to-come. The video moves beyond art practice as socio-political critique, though this is important, into another space of open potential. I don't think that the materiality of this 'work' is totalised by the determinate will of a critical *praxis*, it is also constituted by a poietic assemblage of relationalities taking account of memories, affects, documents, oppression, water, horizons, bodies, fire, ash, ritual, political power and more whose materiality is realised in a vital becoming. The non-violent imperative is not to 'empower', but to pass beyond power into a state of aphesis, of release and enabling so as to be able to contemplate new forms of becoming and relation.

PART TWO

The Force of Art, Disobedience, Virtual Ecologies

In the chapter entitled *Machinic Orality and Virtual Ecology* from the book *Chaosmosis*, Felix Guattari (1995) is concerned with modes of being and becoming that are able to escape prescribed and regulated forms of existence, particularly those promoted by machinic capitalism and its production of passive subjectivities and desires. Guattari suggests that the pre-semiotic, pre-verbal and pre-textual deterritorialised domain of affect or blocks of sensation is able to extract being from, 'banal perceptions and states of mind, from self-presence and standardised ways of being', and open up pathways that may produce 'radically different forms of subjectivity (p. 89)'. He considers performance art, though this term is not given further elaboration, as one domain that can effect such pathways, by putting on one side the 'semiotic net of quotidianity, (p. 90)' and rubbing 'our noses up against the genesis of being and forms, before they get a foothold in dominant redundancies, of style, schools and traditions of modernity (p. 90)'. Although he does not give illustrations of performance art, he argues that its practice, or its force, can engender what he terms 'mutant subjectivities' that disturb existing codes and structures and may lead to an enrichment of the world.

More generally, Guattari argues that *aesthetic machines* provide an effective means by which the force of affect, the force of art can interrupt and transform subjugated modes of being. We might consider the performance work of Maria Abramovich or Francis Alys, or the very recent *Touching Contract* by Jesse Jones and Sarah Browne as exploring, in their respective ways, this potential for transformation. A key aspect of such work is not necessarily the actualisation of practice, but what Guattari (p. 91) calls a *virtual ecology* of practice that might 'engender conditions for the creation and development of unprecedented formations of subjectivity that have never been seen and never felt (p. 91)'. Such ecologies have the potential therefore to bring about new or modified ethico-political and aesthetic practices. They cannot be 'understood' through representation, but apprehended through 'affective contamination,' apprehensions that invent new or modified existential territories and their different rhythms. It is as though such virtual ecologies and their potential for new aesthetic and ethico-political compositions have the potential to carry us beyond our 'familiar existential territories (p. 93)'.

It is worth referring again here to the ontological difference between actual and virtual, in contrast to the real and the possible as described by Deleuze (1988) in *Bergsonism* and *Difference and Repetition* (2004). This difference has clear implications for the ontological texture of the force of art. I will quote a complex passage from *Bergsonism* pointed out to me by Simon O'Sullivan (2006), in which Deleuze describes this ontological difference.

> The possible has no reality (although it may have an actuality); conversely, the virtual is not actual, but as such possesses a reality ... On the other hand, or from another point of view, the possible is that which is 'realised' (or is not realised). Now the process of realisation is subject to two essential rules, one of resemblance and another of limitation. For the real is supposed to be in the image of the possible that it realises. (It simply has existence or reality added to it, which is translated by saying that, from the point of view of the concept there is no difference between the possible and the real) And, every possible is not realised, realisation involves a limitation by which some possibles are supposed to be repulsed or thwarted, while others 'pass' into the real. The virtual on the other hand, does not have to be realised, but rather actualised; and the rules of actualisation are not those of resemblance and limitation, but those of difference or divergence and of creation. (Bergsonism, pp. 96–97)

In this quote, the possible is viewed as a kind of representational template of a prior reality, but which gives the impression of promoting something novel, something different to what already exists. The problem then for the notion of the possible is that it is always constrained by a pre-existent real, although this does not appear to be the case. We might state that the possible-real relation is governed by the ideas of transcendence and identity, the possible is always already a mirror of a prior reality. On the other hand, the idea of the virtual, according to Deleuze, is rooted in the notion of difference and creation, and the actualisation of the virtual is a process of invention. The virtual can be viewed as an undifferentiated multiplicity, or perhaps a field of potential which is real but which awaits actualisation or a becoming. If we think about learning encounters in relation to the virtual-actual combination, then the outcomes of such encounters can be viewed as particular inventive actualisations of an encounter, which is not to say that they are absolute solutions, because the virtual remains, although transformed, as part of the actualised outcome. Put another way, we can say that a learning encounter, before any actualisations emerge, is a virtual realm out of which may emerge actualisations that take us beyond the human. We might apply this point to the force of art whose actualisations may take us beyond the human and which await a people yet to arrive. The force of art and its virtual ecologies can therefore take us beyond the boundaries of what exists and point out new existential territories and forms of social existence.

In the context of pedagogic work in the domain of art in education, a pedagogy of immanence is by implication a pedagogy concerned with supporting the virtual ecologies of learning, events of learning, encouraging this crossing of thresholds so as to expand the existential territories of learners. If we consider the immanence of learning in terms of blocks of affects and percepts, virtual ecologies and their respective local rhythms precipitating emerging forms of expression, where learning is a process that engenders an alterity to its established parameters, then we are concerned not with 'objects' formed by extrinsic forces and parameters but with 'assemblages of subjectivation giving meaning and value to determinate existential territories (p. 94)'. The notion of assemblage (and machinic assemblages) is important to unpack, in that it does not suggest the traditional idea of causation, of causal relations between humans, or humans and the non-human. It is much more a case of machinic relations between heterogeneous parts or entities.

The force of art to challenge established parameters, its disobedience to invent new flows of affect and modes of expression, can bring about new qualities of being, to invent 'mutant coordinates' and unthinkable qualities of being (Ibid, pp. 126–134). For Guattari (Ibid, p. 131) 'The work of art [...] is an activity of unframing, of rupturing sense [...] which leads to a recreation and reinvention of the subject itself'. The force of art lies therefore beyond knowledge and without criteria; it lies beyond the human in that it is composed of blocs of affects and percepts that are themselves non-human. This is to say that affects and percepts arise beyond the transcendent forms of the human. The radical ontogenetic value of *art practice* is that it lies beyond art, outside of art and thus, in some cases, it has the capacity to expand what it means to be human through the materialities of art practice, a becoming-paint, becoming-film, becoming-metal, becoming-other, through which percepts and affects are produced. For Deleuze and Guattari (1994),

Percepts are no longer perceptions: they are independent of a state of those who experience them. Affects are no longer feelings or affections: they go beyond the strength of those who undergo them. Sensations, percepts and affects are beings whose validity lies in themselves and exceeds any lived. (p. 164)

Furthermore Deleuze and Guattari state:

By means of the material the aim of art is to wrest the percept from perceptions of objects and the states of the perceiving subject, to wrest the affect from affections as the transition from one state to another: to extract a bloc of sensations, a pure being of sensations. (p. 162)

For Deleuze and Guattari, it's not a matter of 'being in the world', but of 'becoming with the world'. It is in the process of such becomings that affects and percepts are generated and become independent of such becoming. They often refer to Cezanne's paintings as creating autonomous blocs of percepts and affects, a becoming landscape; a kind of becoming through which the imperceptible becomes perceptible through the materiality of the painting, where affects and percepts precipitate a non-human becoming (Ibid, p. 173). We might think of landscape as something that has become invisible to us due to the fact that we have populated, controlled, manipulated and regulated it. In order to really experience a landscape then, if possible, we need to shed all our inherited or preconceived ideas, feelings and memories about it, which also means that we are in a sense stripping ourselves. According to Deleuze and Guattari, Cezanne's paintings of landscape create a series of percepts and affects that effect such a transformation and make us see what was invisible to us. Such percepts and affects constitute the force of Cezanne's landscape.

The painting *Rain, Steam and Speed* (1844) by the English painter J.M.W. Turner was painted at the time of the industrial revolution in which sail, horse-drawn transportation, hand production methods and other traditional forms of production were replaced by the power of steam and the ensuing mechanisation of production. The painting produces a new materiality of paint, not seen before; it produces a series of percepts and affects that capture the monumental events of a changing world. It is an *untimely* painting in the terminology of Nietzsche; it does not convey the artist's perceptions and affections as though they exist through time, but it transforms such processes into percepts and affects that are atemporal, but which have the force to effect new temporalities of seeing, thinking and feeling. Percepts and affects are therefore non-human, in the sense that they are not subjected to established forms of human transcendence but they have the force to effect new conditions of becoming human. Deleuze and Guattari (1994) write, 'The percept makes perceptible the unperceptible forces that populate the world, affect us and make us become (p. 182)'.

In more contemporary art practices such as those termed performance art, we are often confronted by situations in which our normal codes of conduct, our social habits and conventions, manners and customs are challenged so that we become destabilised or feel uncomfortable. Such challenges can produce forces that generate a series of percepts and affects that pass beyond emotional states and exceed what it is to be human. The early performance work of Joseph Beuys and later practices of Abramovich, Orlan, Alys and others would seem to generate such blocs of sensation and their compounds of percepts and affects.

Ritornello (Refrain) and Territory

The French word 'ritournelle' is translated by Brian Massumi, the translator of *A Thousand Plateaus,* as 'refrain', but this may be a little misleading, in the sense that we normally think of a refrain in musical terminology as a phrase that is repeated, connecting each verse in a song or a phrase of music that is repeated through a piece. Deleuze insists (*Dialogues*, Deleuze and Parnet 2002, p. x) that 'ritournelle' should be translated with 'ritornello' and not 'refrain', because a ritornello is defined by variation and it is not therefore a repetition of the same, rather, crucially it involves a differentiation (Kleinherenbrink 2015); moreover the composition of a ritornello seems to be more complex. I will therefore use the term ritornello rather than refrain in this section.

Guattari (1996, O'Sullivan 2006, p. 92) states that subjectivity is made up of a multiplicity of ritornellos, that is to say, phases within which our subjectivities become organised. Deleuze and Guattari (1988) give the famous example of the ritornello of a child humming in the dark to provide a sense of security. So a ritornello can be conceived as a spatio-temporal process, the creation of a territory or a zone of securiy and consistency through repetition, but repetition as differentiation. Our lives are constituted through a multiplicity of ritornellos that create such zones in the different, heterogeneous milieus we inhabit. A ritornello is a little territorialisation composed of specific rhythms and repetitions according to which we configure ourselves; it affords a local composition of becoming with a world. Each ritornello or mode of expression defines its own territorial motifs, or put in other terms, it defines its own ways of mattering in the varied contexts of living. Guattari gives examples from the rhythms of everyday life: we watch television, the phone rings, someone comes to the door, the kettle boils, and so on. The contents and rhythms of such moments hold and structure our attention. Thinking more widely, we can extend the notion of ritornello to political, pedagogical or amorous ritornellos, and so on. Ritornellos and their respective rhythms thus relate to and structure different aspects of being and becoming in our different and evolving social milieus. Territories and ritornellos are composed of rhythms that emerge from what we might call the chaos of life.

We might see the different moments, relations and situations in which we find ourselves as constituting different inter-connected or separated milieus and their respective ritornellos in which heterogeneous elements are drawn together or synthesised, such as when I make a drawing, listen to a piece of music, look out onto my garden, notice birds feeding; or working in a classroom with all its dramas, relations, conversations, actions emotions, and so on. So, in summary, we might say that a social milieu involves the local composition of a world from heterogeneous elements, but that there is always more to the world than this composition leaving open the opportunity for new compositions to emerge between and across milieus.

Rhythm relates to what we might call a communication between elements of a composition or between milieus, it does not refer to regularity, but more to the managing of variation within or between milieus, the managing of different compositions and territories in a classroom, for example. As Kleinherenbrink (2015, p. 215) following Grosz (2008) tells us rhythm is:

> ...something constituted by the capacities of a being in reciprocal determination with the affordances and events in its environment. Hence, rhythm 'runs through all of life' in connecting living things to both nonorganic and organic entities in a series of contingent encounters (Grosz 2008: 18). If milieus concern *what* happens *where*, rhythms are about *how* and *when* things within and between milieus happen, and hence the flexibility and survivability of a milieu is a rhythmic concern. If milieus primarily refer to spatial arrangements and the constitution of components, rhythms are the 'particular temporal form' that maintains a certain measure of continuity and coherence. (taken from Grosz 2008, pp. 47–48)

In order to create a territory (which is not simply a spatial entity, as we shall see) a milieu and rhythm are insufficient.

...we call a refrain (ritornello) any aggregate of matters of expression that draws a territory and develops into territorial motifs and landscapes'. (Deleuze and Guattari 1988, p. 323, my bracket)

The ritornello is therefore a mode of expression or expressivity that develops 'its own' rhythms, creating a territory and territorial motifs within the different milieus of habitation.

In order to avoid this terminology sounding vacuous, I like to think of these terms as referring to what we might call the creation of assemblages of spaces and times of living; that is to say compositions of places and times of living that acquire their particular forms of expression, correspondence and consistency, that invoke modes of territorialisation or ways of being and becoming. Each ritornello or mode of expression defines its own territorial motifs or, put in other terms, it defines its own ways of mattering in the varied contexts of living. As Kleinherenbrink (p. 216) states, 'Ritornellos are signatures in the world and the expression of such signatures entails the formation of a domain'. Territories are marked by modes of expressivity—ritornellos that are not planned in advance but emerge in the flux of practice. This means that we view territory not in terms of a spatial zone, but as a dynamic, intense process that forms local patterns of action (skills) (Deleuze and Guattari, 1988, p. 314). We can consider the relation of ritornellos and territory as producing subjectivity and its different modes of expression.

Ritornellos constitute both territorialising forms and forces as well as deterritorialising processes that lead to the production of new territories. We can view art practice in terms of the ritornello, in the sense of building what Guattari terms existential territories where such ritornellos can be seen in terms of what he calls mutant centres of subjectivation. We might think of early expressive practices, such as drawing or painting, as producing aesthetic ritornellos that shape subjective territories. These initial vernacular ritornellos set down stepping stones that structure early drawing or mark-making practices, that produce territorialisations, deterritorialisations and reterritorialisations of practice. Such practices constitute local processes of invention. As Elizabeth Grosz (2008, p. 56) suggests we can conceive the ritornello as 'fundamentally constructive' and, in relation to early mark-making, as synthesising a series of disparate elements: marks, gestures, rhythms, materials, affects, cognitions, to constitute a territory of practice and becoming. In children's early drawing practices ritornellos constitute the repetition, but also the deterritorialising of marks, forms and compositions. But having said this, repetition is not a repetition of the same but what

Deleuze refers to as a repetition of difference, it is repetition as differentiation. We can see this in the early line and rotational configurations that young children produce. They are hardly ever the same and seem to constitute a series of explorations that involve, as mentioned above, correspondence, consistency and consolidation. These terms permit us to consider these early mark-making practices not in hylomorphic terms of a child making a drawing, but in processual terms of a series of correspondences between body movements, thoughts, feelings, drawing implement, paper, emerging marks, reflections. These correspondences between body and materials acquire levels of consistency and consolidation but are open to new nuances and variation leading to new configurations. Making (drawing) therefore is not to be seen as the imposition of form by a maker, but as a series of correspondences, consistencies and consolidations between bodies, minds and materials (Ingold 2013).

Each ritornello, according to Grosz's reading of Deleuze and Guattari, consists of three basic components, which she summarises as a home, an outside and a way out. These translate into local schemas and their arrangement that introduce a sense of order, the construction of a territory or expressive world and the potential to break out and construct new territories. Thus, these visual ritornellos (though they are not simply visual but also function on cognitive and affective levels) in early visual practices are both constructive and disobedient. I am using the idea of disobedience here to refer to a breaking out from the capture of established forms of order, expression or control. These ritornellos may not constitute 'art', but they are to be viewed as constituents of visual practices that establish expressive territories that can open up new possibilities for making, thinking, seeing and feeling. In other words, their expressive force can be equated with the force of art as discussed above.

Deleuze and Guattari (1988, p. 312) use a more technical language to describe these territorialising processes that Grosz calls home, outside and a way out. An *infra-assemblage* refers to the emergence of a threshold of a territorial assemblage, an intensive centre, (the emergence of early marks and shapes), an *intra-assemblage* refers to the organisation of an assemblage according to a sense of order and composition, the forming of a domain (different visual compositions and their logics of sense); and *inter-assemblage* which precipitates a shift or rupture from established assemblages into others which may be unknown. It is this latter deterritorialising aspect that links with the force of art. Such assemblages are not to be viewed as existing discretely, but as forming different aspects of a territorial ritornello. Encounters with new experiences can project us onto new pathways that may break old habits or call for a restructuring as we undertake new adventures and experiment with new ritornellos in response to what Guattari calls new universes of reference.

Employing the notions of ritornello, rhythm and territory to develop a brief reading of children's early drawing practices offers a different account of these processes from established developmental accounts such as the work of Viktor Lowenfeld and others, influenced by the developmental psychology of Jean Piaget. The developmental reading of children's drawing practice according to a series of incremental stages of development has of course been challenged by many researchers in the field, including John Matthews (1999), whose extensive and intensive investigations into the local dynamics and sense of children's drawing practices provides a very different account that illustrates a more complex and variegated process through which children display modes of invention and meaning that earlier developmental schemas overlook. Matthews analyses these early processes of drawing or mark-making in terms of inter-weaving generational structures that facilitate the expression of meaning in early childhood. These practices can be viewed as early ritornellos, expressive phases around which a territorialising process emerges and which also have potential to leap out into new, more complex forms, to build new ritornellos, new phases of order and rhythm, new territories and adventures of deterritorialisation that arise within the local milieus and relations of each child. Matthews (2011) shows that the drawings or mark-making that emerge in early childhood, commonly viewed as scribble drawings, stem from a complex history of body interactions and cognitions or emergent concepts; that they possess an organisational and semantic structure that is far from the meaningless and random action which they are usually accorded. We might view these mark-making processes in Guattari's terms as emerging auto-poietic nuclei that produce forms of mental, physical and affective territorialisation that constitute ontogenesis. Yet the notion of *auto-poiesis* may need to be modified if we are to accept that creative practice involves the notion of correspondence, as discussed by Ingold (2013), and the ritornello proposed by Deleuze and Guattari. Both these terms suggest that creative practice does not simply stem from human initiation but from an evolving correspondence between a number of different elements or entities, human and non-human. Donna Harraway (2016) employs the term *sympoiesis* to denote such creative aggregation encapsulated by the term 'becoming-with'.

Fig. 8.1   Fairground drawing (With kind permission of the artist)

Let's look briefly at a little boy's early drawing practices and read them through the notions of territory, ritornello and deterritorialisation (disobedience). His early so-called scribble drawings appear chaotic, but if we look closely, we can detect clear structural components and zones of intensity. The drawing 'fairground' consists of large orange rotating, swirling lines in amongst which are discrete circular closed and semi-closed forms as well as a series of dense patches of marks that form irregular shapes in different colours. We might develop a more complex and sophisticated reading and analysis of this drawing to consider its syntactic structures and possible meaning for the boy. It is a drawing among many others that are produced at this age (3 years) that contain a range of linear structures and forms, such as spirals zig-zags, and wandering lines, ritornellos or modes of expressivity that effect a particular kind of organisation, rhythm and milieu of practice. The drawing can be viewed as a series of expressive functions (ritornellos) that begin to compose a territory, a dynamic process of local motifs of practice and meaning (Figs. 8.1 and 8.2).

Fig. 8.2   Spirals drawing (With kind permission of the artist)

At 3 years 7 months, the boy is making drawings of creatures that dominate his interest, a butterfly, lobster (4.4 years), dinosaur (4.4 years). In these drawings, there is a greater focus upon individual creatures and their composition, he is able to employ earlier formations of lines, zigzags, shapes, rotations and contours to compose and organise and the drawings seem to take on an iconic stature in relation to the boy's interests and fascination. A new ritornello building upon previous ones has developed inventing new expressive territories (Figs. 8.3, 8.4, and 8.5).

By adopting this kind of reading of early drawing practices, we might view them as emerging and transforming existential territories. A more detailed and extensive analysis and description of these practices, as that developed in John Matthews work, provides a more complex understanding of their early compositional and transformational processes. One important point I want to make is in relation to meaning. In these early practices (and in later ones), meaning is not something that is given to the drawing by the child but it is inherent to the practice composed of a series of

Fig. 8.3 'Butterfly' drawing (With kind permission of the artist)

correspondences, consistencies and consolidations. Meaning is not 'in' the drawing, but it is dependent on a series of attunements between thought, action, implements and materials forming a series of expressions. Expression is not imposed upon material, but is the outcome of an interweaving of these components.

To summarise briefly some of the above points, the force of art lies beyond knowledge and without criteria, beyond the human, in that it involves what Deleuze and Guattari (1988) call affects and percepts that are non-human, that lie beyond the transcendent parameters of what constitutes the human, but which can extend what it is to be human. The ontogenetic value of art practice is that it can lead to the production of such affects and percepts, but this involves an ontological difficulty mentioned by O'Sullivan (2006, p. 68). The outcomes of such practice often seem mysterious or surprising—disobedient. They are not meant to echo existing forms of practice or to appeal to an already informed audience. Such work is calling a people yet to arrive into existence, where we are encouraged

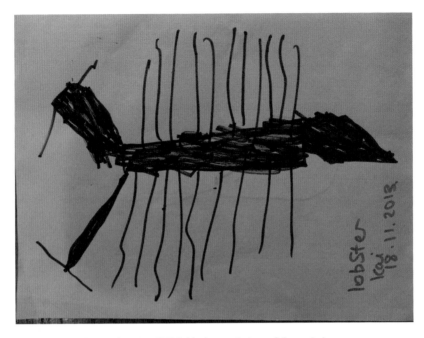

Fig. 8.4 'Lobster' drawing (With kind permission of the artist)

to think, feel, see and make in new ways. Lyotard (1984, pp. 71–80) states that an event of art always arrives too soon. And though for some the art practices of children and older students may not constitute what they consider to be 'Art', such practices—consisting of evolving ritornellos and territories as described above—can be viewed as practices in which new ways of thinking, seeing, making and feeling emerge; they are inventive visual-material practices that can project making (and viewing) onto new onto-semantic territories. The pedagogical value of such transformations lies in the potential to produce new aesthetic, ethical and political sensibilities that may lead to more convivial worlds, though this is not guaranteed.

Ethico-Aesthetics and the Force of Art

Whitehead's notion of the *fallacy of misplaced concreteness* alerts us to the point that there is no absolute registration between abstract knowledge and life, though we often fall into the trap of believing this to be so. To avoid

Fig. 8.5 'Dinosaur' drawing (With kind permission of the artist)

such delusion, Maria Hynes asks, (2013, p. 1934) quoting Zylinska (2009), how can we 'inject some life back into life'? Zylinska argues that art practice as a practice is concerned with 'experimenting with what counts as life', which we could rephrase as what counts as experience. In *Chaosmosis*, Guattari (1995, p. 107) tells us why an aesthetic paradigm is also an ethico-aesthetic and political paradigm, one suitable for dealing with the complexities and uncertainties of our world:

> The new aesthetic paradigm has ethico-political implications because to speak of creation is to speak of the responsibility of the creative instance with regard to the thing created, inflection of the state of things, bifurcation beyond pre-established schemas, once again taking into account the fate of alterity in its extreme modalities. But the ethical choice no longer emanates from a transcendent enunciation, a code of law or a unique and all-powerful god. The genesis of enunciation is itself caught up in the movement of processual creation.

This emphasis of ethical responsibility upon the *creative instance* would seem to bring the force of art, as an inventive force, into the domain of ethics, responsibility and relevance with regard to the process and outcomes of art practice. This is to recognise, as Hynes (Ibid, p. 1936) states, that with regard to the creative moment '. . .it is not 'I' who creates, any more than it is "I" who responds'. This shifts emphasis from a maker to making, from thinker to thinking, from seer to seeing, from viewer to viewing. This shift embodied in the gerund entails some important ontological implications. Indeed, the gerund as noun/verb is ontologically interesting in its fusion of stasis and movement, or object and process. It seems to accommodate both the actualisation of being and an open virtuality of becoming. In *What is Philosophy?* Deleuze and Guattari (1994) consider how art, as well as science think, they suggest that art is one mode of actualising the virtual, a realm of infinite potential that exists prior to any organisational framing. We might say that art practice, through the force of art, is a mode of composing the virtual into new percepts and affects that precipitate new materialisations of the world, or new sensibilities towards a world. We can think of such materialisations as passing beyond the human, that is to say, beyond established ways of thinking, making, seeing and feeling, into the non-human where new modes of existence might be developed. This engagement with the virtual and its creative potential is another way of thinking about ethical responsibility, discussed by Hynes and Guattari, as being attached to the creative instance or the movement of processual creation and not to a transcendent enunciation or ethical subject. The force of art expresses an ethico-aesthetic potential to explode the grip of such transcendent capture.

The force of art as an ethico-aesthetic and political force passes beyond representation or subjective experience so as to precipitate encounters with the non-human that problematize experience and from which new modes of being or building a life and their subsequent responsibilities might emerge. Put in Guattari's terminology, we might view the force of art as inventing new assemblages of enunciation, that is to say, new modes of subject production. In a lengthy quote, he expresses this creative potential:

> The incessant clash of the movement of art against established boundaries (already there in the Renaissance, but above all in the modern era), its propensity to renew its materials of expression and the ontological texture of the percepts and affects it promotes brings about if not a direct contamination of other domains then at least a highlighting and re-evaluation of the creative

dimensions that traverse all of them. Patently, art does not have a monopoly on creation, but it takes its capacity to invent mutant coordinates to extremes: it engenders unprecedented, unforeseen and unthinkable qualities of being. The decisive threshold constituting this new aesthetic paradigm lies in the aptitude of these processes of creation to auto-affirm themselves as existential nuclei, autopoietic machines. (Ibid, p. 106)

The last two sentences of this quote suggest to me an important pedagogical threshold that pertains to those moments of making and thinking with learners when their creative practices produce 'mutant coordinates' (we might see these as local ritornellos, as discussed above) that with confidence can lead to new existential territories. Art's virtuality points to its ontological difficulty, in that it is always more than its productions because it speaks to modes of life yet to emerge, it is always in excess of that which has been actualised. We can also think of these extreme mutant coordinates that engender unprecedented, unforeseen and unthinkable qualities of being which clash against established boundaries as emerging from some art practices and works produced in our contemporary world. I have already discussed the project *Rogue Game* in Chap. 2, where established boundaries, procedures and codes of conduct are fractured by unforeseeable and unpredictable interventions demanding new modes of being.

Such boundaries were explored, reaffirmed, opened or transgressed in the performative work organised by Tino Seghal at Tate London entitled *These Associations*. Seghal worked with a large group of volunteers who rehearsed a series of movements and encounters to confront and engage the public who assembled in the Turbine Hall (I did not witness this preparation). The volunteers struck up conversations with members of the public (who were not expected to reply), discussing personal, often quite private, experiences and then moved on into other group movements and then more individual encounters. Whilst some members of the public found the experience of the encounter challenging but engaging, even inspiring, others felt uneasy, experiencing differing degrees of threat and or intimidation. For me this practice illustrates a playful exploration, and play can be very serious, of intensity and relation in human affairs; it challenges the symbolic order or framing of relations, (the way we would normally or conventionally conduct ourselves in social contexts), perhaps asking us to reflect critically upon who we relate to and how, who we would not normally relate to and why. Its force as art allows us to view established codes and relationalities, to get a glimpse of who we are and how such codes and conventions make us who we are, precipitating a potential for rethinking or even challenging such conventions and their social boundaries. The appearance and dissolution of these random (or contrived) associations open up a potential for considering new or novel forms of subjectivation and collectivities.

Meditating on the notion of heterogenesis, Ranciere (2010) writes:

> I have tried to conceive heterogenesis through a type of thinking and activity that produces shocks between worlds, but shocks between worlds in the same world: re-distributions, re-compositions, and re-configurations of elements. (p. 212)

These Associations does not involve a meeting of people in the same time, but the heterogeneous times of people's lives being brought together, a disjunctive synthesis. We might view these heterogeneous encounters as producing shocks, resonances or convivialities between worlds in the same world, which precipitate a crossing of established thresholds that produces new ethico-aesthetic and political sensibilities. Equally, such encounters can invoke ontological barriers that resist the invitation to engage.

Beginning: Edith and Johanna

In relation to the notion of ethico-aesthetics developed by Guattari, and the generative force of art, I want to mention a work by a young German dance artist and choreographer, Johanna Knefelkamp, who worked with Edith Nagel, a Jewish woman who survived the Nazi occupation in the Netherlands but lost most of her family in concentration camps. The women met prior to the performance to talk about their lives, who they were, sharing experiences of their backgrounds, before agreeing to work together to make a performance that explored issues of trauma, guilt, obligation, friendship and care.

Johanna is developing her own form of dance practice based on 'direct contact improvisation'. This normally involves two participants who stay in hold or within touching distance for the duration of the performance. As such, the partners act in response to each other's movement, gestures and breathing to choreograph the event. Thus, the choreography is not pre-planned, but emerges as the two bodies form an evolving relation. Johanna, states, 'This combined rhythm of movement – sound and sight forms an interdependent bond between the dancers. In essence, the dancers become one – an entanglement of the physical and the intellectual'(email correspondence).

The performance begins with the two women facing each other a couple of metres apart. Edith moves tentatively and circumspectly towards Johanna and begins to 'inspect' and 'wonder' at Johanna, who stands almost motionless. She moves around Johanna's body touching and testing, looking and wondering, hoping, re-assuring but also uncertain. She stands behind Johanna and places her hands on Johanna's shoulders. Gradually Johanna begins to respond and they begin to walk tentatively together side by side, Johanna supporting Edith. Their bodies begin to support each other, there is a growing sense of shifting from a separation of being towards becoming-with, breathing with, listening with, watching with, feeling with, sensing with. They walk in tandem across the room towards a wall with a door. We don't know who might be at the door, who is calling, taking us back to those days and nights of fear when Edith hid from the Nazis in the homes of her friends. Edith seems uncertain, worried, she hesitates, whilst Johanna gradually persuades her to come away. A growing sense of togetherness, walking in unison, supporting, confiding, touching and caressing, discovering, embracing, entwining, celebrating, as they begin to dance, a dance of becoming-with, of folding and unfolding. Then they eventually separate and take up their original positions facing each other.

The performance points to unknown degrees of failing communication coupled with attempts to communicate and work together. Living with the failure of communication where there is no symmetrical exchange between two worlds of experience in this world. A desire to trust in a context of uncertainty where boundaries are unclear. An attempt to reciprocate, to absorb each other's energies through an evolving ecology of gestures (Fig. 8.6).

I asked Johanna to tell me more about how the work happened, and this is what she wrote in an email correspondence:

In this performance, each are attempting to find each other's place within the narrative of the Holocaust and in some way come to terms with its legacy. The research started by the question posed by Primo Levis's book (1947) *Is this a man?*. The question about humanity and identity was the main subject in the conversations between myself and Edith. In order to connect with the themes of Levi's narrative, both of us realised that we had to begin by exploring our own understandings of who we are– and most importantly – what made us

Fig. 8.6   'Beginning' (With kind permission of the artist)

who we are. We began to experiment with movement and catalogued a number of potential connections that we could explore. These connections were physical and intellectual. We shared our experiences and feelings about our identity. No words were spoken – just movement touch, sound and sight. This led us into another level of communication. Through our movements, through touching with each other and through the possibility of closing our eyes at any moment, we put ourselves into a vulnerable, sensible, caring and intimate situation. The one who lost her family and childhood during the Nazi-regime in Germany, the other who carries the burden of guilt and shame of the country she comes from. Together we share and sense our feelings through dance, help each other with the burden we carry and create an atmosphere of trust and humanity.

Edith gave me the space and the trust to talk to her through art. I learned, to let go of the artistic manner of thinking and to fall into the possibilities of communicating through dance to have this incredible experience. It felt like a space of equality and little miracles. In this space of art, I could confront my feelings and allow me to react. I felt human and as safe as in a womb.

One witness of the performance described how the combined sound of the dancers breathing moved him to tears. Here we had the embodiment of reconciliation – where victim and supposed perpetrator become one. However, the art in the work enables them to escape the narrative of victimhood and provides an avenue of hope and agency.

For both participants and for some of those observing the dance it is as though new existential territories developed, exploring what it might be to be human, or perhaps more to the point, exploring the in-human that precipitates new percepts and affects, thus extending capacities for becoming-with.

If we return to the idea of ritornello and territory, we might view the performance as the building up of ritornellos and their different and emerging rhythms of becoming-with that compose an evolving expressive territory, or to use Harraway's term, an expressive *sympoiesis* that opens up mutant coordinates for new existential territories.

If we consider the performance from the point of view of Guattari's ethico-aesthetic paradigm, then we must abandon humanist notions of ethics where ethical responsibility stems from the ethical subject, a transcendent position that precedes the events of the dance. In the performance, there is no such position of transcendence that 'guides' or 'monitors' the action. Guattari (1995, p. 107) tells us why an aesthetic paradigm is also an ethico-aesthetic paradigm in which a different, what we might term, anti-humanist, ethics is posited, I repeat the quotation cited above:

> The new aesthetic paradigm has ethico-political implications because to speak of creation is to speak of the responsibility of the creative instance with regard to the thing created, inflection of the state of things, bifurcation beyond pre-established schemas, once again taking into account the fate of alterity in its extreme modalities. But the ethical choice no longer emanates from a transcendent enunciation, a code of law or a unique and all-powerful god. The genesis of enunciation is itself caught up in the movement of processual creation.

In this statement, the idea that it is the creative instance and its correspondences that are responsible for the thing created, and which passes beyond established parameters of thought and action, is quite different from more humanist ethics where responsibility lies with the independent human agent. We can see in the performance that the responsibility for the creation of the dance cannot be aligned with one or other of the participants, but to a series of events of correspondence, consistency and consolidation, involving entanglements of bodies, breathing, touching, moving, sensing, watching, listening, and so on. We might view the performance as a confluence of actual and virtual domains where the virtual opens up potentialities for new experiences or materialities of sensation to emerge. Thus, the performance is not conceived in terms of subjective experience or as a representation of prior events or realities, but as an encounter whose force takes us beyond established ways of thinking, feeling and perceiving into new realms of experimentation and sensibility that open up possibilities for what Guattari terms new assemblages of enunciation, new forms of subject production and becoming-with. The performance precipitates new collective existential territories and it invites those observing to traverse their established thresholds of correspondence and consistency so as to embrace new experiential universes (Hynes 2013).

REFERENCES

Agamben, G. (1999). *The man without content.* Stanford: Stanford University Press.
Agamben, G. (2005). *State of exception.* Chicago: University of Chicago Press.
Agamben, G. (2007). *Infancy and history: On the destruction of experience.* London/New York: Verso.
Atkinson, D. (2003). *Art in education: Identity and practice.* Dordrecht/London/Boston: Kluwer Academic Publishers.
Deleuze, G. (1988). *Bergsonism.* New York: Zone Books.
Deleuze, G., & Guattari, F. (1988). *A thousand plateaus.* London: Athlone Press.
Deleuze, G., & Guattari, F. (1994). *What is philosophy?* London: Verso.
Deleuze, G., & Parnet, C. (2002). *Dialogues.* New York: Columbia University Press.
Grosz, E. (2008). *Chaos, territory, art: Deleuze and the framing of the earth.* New York: Columbia University Press.
Guattari, F. (1995). *Chaosmosis: An ethico-aesthetic paradigm.* Sydney: Power Publications.
Guattari, F. (1996). Subjectivities: For better or worse. In G. Genosko (Ed.), *The Guattari reader* (pp. 193–203). Oxford: Basil Blackwell.
Harraway, D. (2016). *Staying with the trouble: Making kin in the chthulucene.* Durham/London: Duke University Press.
Hynes, M. (2013). The ethic-aesthetics of life: Guattari and the problem of bioethics. *Environment and Planning, 45,* 1929–1943.
Ingold, T. (2011). *Being alive: Essays on movement, knowledge and description.* Abingdon: Routledge.

Ingold, T. (2013). *Making: Anthropology, archaeology, art and architecture*. London/New York: Routledge.

Ingold, T. (2015). *The life of lines*. London/New York: Routledge.

Kleinherenbrink, A. (2015). Territory and ritornello: Deleuze and Guattari on thinking living beings. *Deleuze Studies, 9*(2), 208–230.

Lazarrato, M. (2003). *Struggle, event, media*. In republic art. https://www.republicart.net/disc/representations/lazzarato01_en.htm

Lewis, T. (2010). Messianic pedagogy. *Educational Theory, 60*(2), 231–248.

Lord, B. (2010). *Spinoza's ethics*. Edinburgh: Edinburgh University Press.

Lyotard, J. F. (1984). *The postmodern condition: A report on knowledge*. Manchester: Manchester University Press.

Matthews, J. (1999). *The art of childhood and adolescence: The construction of meaning*. London/Philadelphia: Falmer Press.

Matthews, J. (2011). *Starting from scratch: The origin and development of expression, representation and symbolism in human and non-human primates*. London/New York: Psychology Press.

Negri, P. (2013). *Time for revolution*. London/New York/New Delhi/Sydney: Bloomsbury.

O'Sullivan, S. (2006). *Art encounters: Deleuze and Guattari, thought beyond representation*. London/New York: Palgrave Macmillan.

Ranciere, J. (1999). *Disagreement politics and philosophy*. Minneapolis: University of Minnesota Press.

Ranciere, J. (2010). *Dissensus on politics and aesthetics*. London/New York: Continuum.

Smith, D. (2012). *Essays on Deleuze*. Edinburgh: Edinburgh University Press.

Ziarek, K. (2004). *The force of art*. Stanford: Stanford University Press.

Zylinska, J. (2009). *Bioethics in the age of new media*. Cambridge, MA: MIT Press.

CHAPTER 9

Pedagogy and Events of Disobedience

Ritornello

Down in the valley where the mist settled, an uncomplicated scene perhaps a façade, or a dissemblance. Groups of people working together, a social coalition; adults, children, animals, tools and some early machines. Fields laced with hedgerows, a coat of corn rising above the gorge running towards a priory. Nearby they begin digging for coal; a presentiment of new assemblages, some may say a foreboding, a ruthless harbinger, an augury.

In the gorge by a river an iron structure begins to emerge, people stand and stare in wonder. A diviner amongst them warns, "soon these things will turn the world and we will lose our home, we will become immigrants." The vernacular will lose its ground. A voracious force will effect unimaginable lives.

The painter saw some of this like a comet. The demise of sail, an assemblage of new machines, in a new, unknown visual language; a monumental vision eclipsing, invading, pervading every tendril, capillary, every grammar and dialect, every niche and interior: an infinite disclosure. The fury of paint, the jolt of the new.

The bridge was completed and indeed it arched over the river but it also migrated from one epoch whilst listening for an answer to another. It was not only a local conduit but also primarily a seismic event through which different worlds collided and populations, their time, space, work, play, their entire existence regulated.

In the classroom they were learning about how to write a letter. Form, structure, content, expression and the expert's gaze. A panoptic pedagogy, a universal grammar unaware of the universal emerging from the singular. A pedagogy without dialect, Lego projects. Scripts returned embossed with

© The Author(s) 2018
D. Atkinson, *Art, Disobedience, and Ethics*, Education, Psychoanalysis, and Social Transformation, DOI 10.1007/978-3-319-62639-0_9

instructions, a palimpsest of red on black. A boy wants to know why so much of his letter has been crossed-through, eradicated. The teacher asks, "do you really say things in the way you have written them." "Yes," says the boy, "That's how we talk to each other." "Well" came the reply, "That is not the way we write letters."

Along a corridor in another register a teacher is astounded. He reads a piece of prose describing an experiment: enthusiasm, captivation and surprise. He recognises this in the student, he sees a fellow traveller. At the same time he knows the prose will not fit, he acknowledges its transgression, an epistemological breach, a disobedient event.

In the Courts of Justice a philosopher talks about belief. After the presentation as people were leaving he is approached by someone who listened, "I come from a world of education where there are teachers who lack belief in their work because they feel uneasy about the values being perpetuated by the educational system, how can we reconcile this?" The philosopher replies, "It is important that students believe that their teachers believe." But the interrogator persists, "Yes but what if the teachers do not believe, how can we resolve this?" The philosopher stared intensely at his interrogator and said with some force, "I am a philosopher and you are asking me a real question," and with that mercurial remark he marched away into the summer evening.

The executive's search for perfection continues at a pace, changing moulds every decade, hylomorphic engines churning out endless criteria, objectives and incentives for compliant practices. Native hues bleached by an intense force; nothing new under this sun. And yet . . .In between the slabs of stone small growths appear. In between the categories and frameworks of knowledge and virtue new worlds of disobedience begin to emerge beyond the raging paragons, beyond the human.

DISOBEDIENCE AS AN EVENT

In Chap. 8, disobedience was viewed as indissoluble from the force of art that opened up new possibilities for making, thinking, seeing and action. This chapter will pay more attention to thinking through the notion of disobedience in relation to pedagogic work. In doing so, importance is placed upon ways of knowing in practice that are immanent, to the ritornellos and rhythms of practice rather than knowing that accords with established territories of knowledge. Disobedience may function internally by crossing the thresholds of an individual's established ways of knowing and externally by challenging established forms of knowledge. For a teacher, disobedience towards personal frameworks of practice may be a difficult, perhaps intolerable process. We can think of disobedience in terms of a *disposition*, a moving away from established positions or patterns of being. Furthermore, we might think of existence itself as a process combining position and disposition, or obedience and disobedience, so that disobedience or disposition are immanent to events of becoming.

The recent exhibition at the V&A (2014) in London entitled *Disobedient Objects* displayed a wide range of artefacts, objects and practices produced by individuals, collectives, communities, resistance and protest groups. They included trade union banners, peace movement banners, the pan lids of striking farmers in Buenos Aires, umbrellas, barricades, photographs, tents, pamphlets for resistance tactics, lock-on devices, puppets and masks, magazines, posters, placards, badges, Chilean Arpilleras and more. Such disobedient objects have a long social history of protest, resistance and challenge. The exhibition illustrated the material cultures of these objects, their making and the 'range of object-based tactics and strategies that movements adopt to help them succeed'. (Flood and Grindon 2014, p. 11) The exhibition took place within the august and prestigious collections of the Victoria and Albert Museum; a rather ragbag exhibit of everyday objects used for purposes of protest and resistance in the midst of celebrated and almost consecrated objects of value.

After my visit, I thought about the notion of disobedient pedagogies amongst other things such as disobedient archives, disobedient methodologies, disobedient cartographies, disobedient languages, disobedient visualities, disobedient learning, disobedient teaching; the disobedience of questioning, thinking, seeing and making. I am using the term disobedience therefore not in the sense of being awkward or rebellious simply for the sake of it, but in terms of an *event* of non-compliance that opens up new ways of thinking and acting.

The exhibition reminded me of the disobedient work I mentioned—in the previous chapter—by Fred Wilson, whose intervention at the Maryland Historical Society entitled *Mining the Museum* (1992) subverted the idea of the truth of the museum exhibits by questioning whose truth was being displayed. In the installation entitled *Metalwork 1793–1880,* the usual display of silverware was 'disrupted' by a pair of iron slave shackles. Though this intervention challenged underlying racist attitudes inherent to museum displays and the visibilities that they perpetuate, by juxtaposing objects of wealth and affluence with objects that made such affluence possible, it also had, I think, a more affirmational aspect that pointed beyond the displayed objects to a possibility of a world and people yet to come, a possibility still yet to arrive in this world.

Another disobedient practice (which actually led to some tricky ethical issues) is the work of Andrea Fraser entitled *Museum Highlights* (1989). It involved her posing as a museum tour guide at the Philadelphia Museum of Art in 1989 under the pseudonym of Jane Castleton. During the performance, Fraser led a tour through the museum, describing art works in traditional aesthetic discourses but then also using similar discourses to describe a water fountain or an exit sign or a gallery café. Both Wilson and Frazer, in their different ways, problematised a particular ethos, set of discourses, identities and dispositifs of institutional practice.

The video *Hold Your Ground* by Karen Mirza and Brad Butler, in conjunction with the author China Miéville, presents a series of 'fugitive sounds' as a kind of disobedient speech accompanied by gestures. The work drew upon events in the Arab Spring in Cairo when the artists found a pamphlet of instructions entitled, *How to Protest Intelligently*, produced for pro-democracy demonstrators. The piece considers the 'semantics' of the crowd, and the performance of 'speech acts' whereby these fugitive sounds and gestures are performed as a form of speech of a people in transition.

An important aspect of the work of the German artist Joseph Beuys is concerned with challenging the notion of authority, not simply in terms of resistance but also, more affirmatively, with creating spaces for discussion and debate that open up possibilities for more equitable and emancipated forms of collective and institutional practice. Put in other terms, his work often interrogates the transcendent forces that impact upon and effect control over people's lives. In terms of art practice, Beuys argued that the idea of the artist should not only be accorded to traditional practices such as painting, ceramics and sculpture or more contemporary performance practices, but that it had universal significance, as he put it:

Every human being is an artist, a freedom being, called to participate in transforming and re-shaping the conditions, thinking and structures that shape and inform our lives. (Joseph Beuys, 'Every Man an Artist: Talks at Documenta 5', 1972)

Equally, Beuys insisted on the universal and transversal potential of creativity:

Creativity is not limited to people practising one of the traditional forms of art, and even in the case of artists, creativity is not confined to the exercise of their art. Each one of us has a creative potential, which is hidden by competitiveness and success-aggression. To recognize, explore and develop this potential is the task of the School. Creation – whether it be a painting, sculpture, symphony or novel – involves not merely talent, intuition, powers of imagination and application, but also the ability to shape material that could be expanded to other socially relevant spheres. (quoted in *Joseph Beuys* Caroline Tisdall, New York Thames and Hudson 1979, p. 278)

The notion of the school in this quotation is probably best understood in terms of the *potential of the school*, that is to say, with interrogating the nature of the school as an institution that shapes lives and trying to establish it as a space in which all learners and their ways of learning are valued and supported. Teaching, for Beuys, thus becomes a form of social sculpture where emphasis is placed upon developing individual and collective modes of living.

Beuys disrupts any prescriptive notion of what an artist is supposed to be, except, of course, to act and think critically and creatively in transforming the conditions that shape our lives. After his dismissal from the Dusseldorf Academy of Art in 1972 for opening his course to any student wishing to attend, a move that contravened admissions policy, Beuys established with Heinrich Boll the Free International University as a means of extending educational possibilities and potentials. This innovation, which later influenced similar 'free' educational projects in other parts of Europe and elsewhere, can also be viewed as an extension of Beuys artistic practice, whereby it becomes, as Jan Verwoert (2008) suggests, an artistic medium among others. Furthermore, Beuys's public lectures and talks can also be considered as forms of art practice in which his discourse becomes artistic material along with the writing and diagrams he placed on chalkboards in the installation *Richtkrafte* (Directional Forces 1974–1977).

The notion of public authority was challenged in a disobedient and humorous performance in 1967 (OO Programm), when Beuys introduced an orientation event at the Kunstakademie Dusseldorf to welcome new students. He stood at the microphone holding an axe whilst making strange noises for some minutes. This morphed an official academic function into an absurd event whilst undermining, but facilitated by, the authority invested in the position of academic professor. In performing this absurd act, Beuys pushed his authority to the very limit but at the same time, this event invoked a resistance and an opening for an interrogation of authority and the kind of relations and subjectivities it tends to perpetuate. The disobedience of the event was also charged with an affirmative potential. In a similar ludic manner perhaps we might push the limits of pedagogical work to open up its creative potentials, thus transforming and re-shaping parameters of practice.

Beuys had an intense interest in pedagogy as he expresses in the following quote from an interview with Willoughby Sharp (1969):

> To be a teacher is my greatest work of art. The rest is the waste product, a demonstration. If you want to express yourself you must present something tangible. But after a while this has only the function of a historic document. Objects aren't very important any more. I want to get to the origin of matter, to the thought behind it. (An interview with Joseph Beuys,', Willoughby Sharp, published in 'Artforum,' November 1969; as quoted in *Six Years: The Dematerialization of the Art Object from 1966 to 1972,* Lucy R. Lippard, University of California Press, 1973, p. 121)

Returning to the *Disobedient Objects* exhibition, I felt that the notion of disobedient objects and practices has a kind of resonance with teaching and learning contexts where you frequently come across what might be called disobedient objects and practices in art rooms. Of course, these practices and objects are not *intentionally* disobedient, they are not objects of protest or resistance but, as objects, they may be resisted or rejected by established pedagogical criteria or frameworks within which they *appear* to be disobedient. Such objects or practices often violate the pedagogical norms, particularly of prescribed pedagogies, that frequently create, in Butler's terms, 'the viability of the subject, its ontological and epistemological parameters'. I frequently experienced such objects and practices, for example, in the form of drawings and other practices that did not fit my pedagogical expectations. We often experience disobedient objects and practices when we are confronted by art practices that challenge our conceptions of art, precipitating a struggle to understand what is going on.

The notion of disobedient pedagogies therefore relates to an advocacy for those pedagogies that do not anticipate a prescribed onto-epistemic subject (teacher/learner), which in turn invokes an onto-epistemic invalidation of those practices of learning or teaching that do not fit the prescription. In many countries today, as I have already mentioned, the pedagogical subject of prescribed pedagogies is conceived almost completely in terms of productivity relating to economic ambition. Within this specific onto-epistemic prescription of learning and teaching, art practice fails to register significance and is therefore viewed as superfluous to requirements, hence the recent proposal to exclude art in secondary schools from the proposed

English Baccalaureate and the cutting back of art education provision in other countries. In this context, art education faces a struggle for survival.

Disobedient pedagogies, in contrast to those prescribed by Government, adopt the Spinozan notion that we don't really know what a body is capable of or what thoughts are capable of being thought, coupled with the notion of a pragmatics and ethics of the suddenly possible. Such pedagogies involve a continual inventive interweaving of ontology and ethics which, when confronting disobedient objects or aberrant ways of learning/practising, may open up new possibilities for practice and new ways of understanding learning, new ways of understanding art. It seems important therefore to ask for whom is the practice of learning relevant; is it the learner? The teacher? The government? For each of these suggest different agendas. This negotiation of relevance or the morphology of relevance is important in asking how something matters for a learner. Different agendas assume different ontological, epistemological, ethical and political grounds and different kinds of knowing.

We might consider events of disobedience in ontological terms whereby the process of becoming or individuation is viewed as a process or an *expression* of disobedience to established parameters of being; a mixture of stability and disobedience. This is close to Deleuze's thinking about the emergence of the new where, according to Smith (2012), the 'problematic' and 'virtuality' are synonymous in that problems can be conceived beyond actual solutions. One way of thinking about this is that behind any particular resolution there is always a potential for others that are disobedient to it.

Smith makes the point that every moment of our existence is 'objectively *problematic*' (virtual) and the exact way in which things develop cannot be predicted in advance. Let's think again about the reality of classrooms in which teachers and learners work together in an on-going flow of relations and differing rhythms. The problematic or virtual nature of teaching means that a teacher cannot predict precisely in advance how learners will *actually* respond to his or her pedagogical strategies nor how he or she will *actually* respond to their responses. In each relation, something new is produced, a difference. On each occasion, the problematic structure of the virtual will not dissolve because the next situation that the previous one bleeds into will consist of a problematic structure, but one that is modified by the previous actualisation. This means that the actualisation of the virtual also produces the virtual. It is crucial to acknowledge that the process of actualisation does not produce a new 'thing' (a new perception, for example) but a new relation, a disobedient relation in terms of former relations, and a difference of potential.

Smith writes:

> Thus, at every moment, my existence [...] is objectively problematic, which means that it has the structure of a problem, constituted by virtual elements and divergent series, and the exact trajectory that "I" will follow is not predictable in advance. In a moment from now I will have actualized certain of those virtualities; I will have, say, spoken or gestured in a certain manner. In doing so I will not have "realized a possibility" (in which the real resembles an already-conceptualised possibility) but will have "actualized a virtuality" – that is, I will have produced something new, a difference. (p. 253)

Stretching these points to a degree, we might suggest that the inbuilt instability of existence that Smith depicts in his notions of the 'objectively problematic' and the actualisation of a virtuality can, on occasions, involve events of disobedience that transgress what Smith terms 'already-conceptualised possibilities'. If we apply these ideas to pedagogic work and view it as 'objectively problematic', in the sense that a teacher is frequently faced with the challenge of trying to respond effectively to the diverse ways in which children or students learn, such challenges may precipitate events of disobedience that produce for the teacher an expanded pedagogical capacity.

EXPRESSION AND DIFFERENCE

I want to return to the notion of expression hinted at above and show how this notion is helpful for thinking about the idea of disobedience in pedagogic work. But before doing this, I need to revisit briefly Deleuze's reading of Spinoza and the ontological notion of univocity that Deleuze took initially from Duns Scotus. For Spinoza, there is but one world of substance and its attributes and their modes that are known through expression. Deleuze (2004, p. 39) replaces Spinoza's idea of one substance and its modifications with an always folding, unfolding and refolding *process*.

Kathrin Thiele (2008), following Deleuze, describes how univocity incorporates the equation essence=existence, it is a non-hierarchical interweaving of transcendence and immanence. Univocity is not to be viewed as unity, that is to say, a whole-parts relation, which implies transcendence; it does not refer or conform to anything outside its expression. Therefore, if we consider the relation of cause and effect, for example, this relation does not involve a transcendent cause but a relation of immanence in which a cause is in its effects and vice versa. Thiele describes Spinoza's univocity (though he does not use this term) of substance, attributes and modes, as a *one-all* composition, or put in other terms, being in infinite differentiation (not infinite perfection and finite imperfection). A univocal 'one' is manifested through difference and each difference is an expression of the 'one', the 'one' propagates difference. Thiele writes, 'Univocity is a oneness that because of its indivisibility (absolute infinity) is nothing but its own process of differentiation'. (p. 57)

For Spinoza, then, there is no hierarchy of being but an equality of being, and a crucial aspect of his ontology is what a 'one-all' might be capable of, or in other words, what differentiations become possible, what propagations or individuations emerge, what expressions become possible. The ontological unity of substance equals the qualitative plurality of its attributes. Thiele again:

> Substance, attribute, and modes are equal in the sense that attributes and modes [as modifications of attributes] equally express the essence of substance which in itself is nothing but these infinite expressions. (p. 58)

Expression is a key concept that Deleuze takes from Spinoza, particularly the idea of a substance that manifests itself in infinite expressions in qualitatively different ways. The term self-expression is frequently employed in art educational contexts; it tends to assume a prior transcendent unity (self, idea, feeling), that is being expressed. In broad terms, this notion contrasts with a Spinoza/Deleuze idea of expression in the sense that for Spinoza/Deleuze it is the expression itself that constructs a self. Expression does not mirror or represent something that pre-exists. Expression is therefore a process with potential for infinite genesis and differentiation. We might consider this non-representational idea of expression not as the representation of a prior reality or world, but as the *invention* of a world. Furthermore, if we annex the notion of expression as potential for infinite differentiation to the idea of multiplicity, this allows us to consider ontology as not existing in an already constituted space and time, and thus to established forms of organisation, classification and distribution, but as *producing* spatio-temporal realities. Expression thus becomes a creative event that can reconfigure space and time.

We can conceive the human then as an expression of being, with infinite attributes and modes (qualities) but equally, we might see that problems can arise when these attributes and modes are controlled and regulated according to particular agendas that govern educational practices. This tends to be the case in educational institutions whose modes of practice and assessment tend to prescribe learning and teaching according to specific agendas and, in doing so, produce specific forms of pedagogical subjectification. Such processes of subjection produce limited conceptions of the human such as when in our current epoch the human in pedagogical contexts is governed by economic ambition, the idea of *homo-economicus*. This process of subjectification even occurs within art education in schools and other contexts where there are tendencies to perpetuate particular methodologies and practices that function as transcendent operators pre-scribing what art practice is. If such predication is relaxed, we might see that art practice becomes open to infinite expression that may extend what it is to be human. It becomes open to infinite forms of disobedience!

We might view this difference between expression and prescription in the difference that Deleuze (2004) makes between two kinds of territorial distribution:

> We must first of all distinguish a type of distribution which implies a dividing up of that which is distributed: it is a matter of dividing up the distributed as such...A distribution of this type proceeds by fixed and proportional deter-minations which may be assimilated to "properties" or limited territories within representation...Then there is a completely other distribution which must be called nomadic, a nomad *nomos*, without property, enclosure or measure. Here, there is no longer a division of that which is distributed but rather a division among those who distribute *themselves* in an open space – a space which is unlimited, or at least without precise limits. Nothing pertains or belongs to any person, but all persons are arrayed here and there in such a manner as to cover the largest possible space. Even when it concerns the serious business of life, it is more like a space of play, or a rule of play, by contrast with sedentary space and nomos. To fill a space, to be distributed within it, is very different from distributing the space. (pp. 45–46)

The first kind of distribution, which Deleuze and Guattari later term the plane of organisation, and which Ranciere calls the distribution of the sensible, already presupposes a particular spatio-temporal organisation, forms of representation and categorisation awaiting that which is to be distributed. We might relate this kind of distribution to the organisation of knowledge in schools, universities and elsewhere and to their examination apparatuses that distribute learners according to assessment criteria. The second distribution has no set boundaries or prescribed criteria that divide what is to be distributed; in this spatio-temporality, participants distribute themselves in space according to their differences and relations, which are continuously emerging and changing. This more organic and variegated distribution requires a different, more nomadic or rhizomic approach to pedagogical work that can respond effectively to the diversity of expression. We might conceive pedagogical work in the first distribution as a pedagogy of transcendence whilst, in the second distribution, pedagogical work would demand a pedagogy of immanence.

In relation to this idea of nomadic or rhizomic pedagogies that attempt to correspond with the local ritornellos, rhythms and territories of children's and student's learning encounters, we might want to consider how such encounters may involve a becoming-disobedient so that established pedagogical vectors that configure the pedagogical relation are challenged. In pedagogical work, how much space for such disobedience do we permit? Can we contemplate the process of learning or the process of becoming a learner as a becoming-disobedient? Though the necessity for constructing curriculum content, methodologies and structures within institutions such as schools and other centres of learning goes without saying, can we also respond affirmatively to forms of practice that are disobedient or recalcitrant to these? Here, the need to resonate or to correspond to the specific rhythms of each learner's practice becomes important. Such correspondences imply the development of new relations being added to the local ritornellos and rhythmic relations of a leaner's practice, as well as the teacher's practice, and an open mind to what a learner can achieve. By adopting such a disobedient pedagogical attitude that facilitates ways of learning and questioning beyond expected parameters of learning and teaching, we may encourage the invention of new, unexpected, surprising and valued modes of becoming.

REFERENCES

Beuys, J. (1972). *Every man an artist: Talks at documenta 5.* Kassel: Documenta 5.

Deleuze, G. (2004). *Difference and repetition.* London/New York: Continuum.

Flood, C., & Grindon, G. (2014). *Disobedient objects.* London: V&A Publishing.

Sharp, W. (1969). An interview with Joseph Beuys. In L. R. Lippard (Ed.), *'Artforum,' November 1969; as quoted in six years: The dematerialization of the art object from 1966 to 1972* (Vol. 1973, p. 121). California: University of California Press.

Smith, D. (2012). *Essays of Deleuze*. Edinburgh: Edinburgh University Press.

Thiele, K. (2008). *The thought of becoming*. Zurich/Berlin: Diaphanes.

Tisdall, C. (1979). *Joseph Beuys*. New York: Thames and Hudson.

Verwoert, J. (2008). The boss: On the unresolved question of authority in Joseph Beuys' oeuvre and public image. *e-flux Journal, 12.*

CHAPTER 10

Pedagogic Work: An Ethics of Building a Life

We do not obtain knowledge by standing outside of the world. . . we know because
"we" are of the world. We are part of the world in its differential becoming.
Barad 2007, p. 185
We are not in the world, we become with the world. . . .
Deleuze and Guattari 1994, p. 169

THE ADVENTURE OF CONCERN

On the island of Sao Nicolau in the Cabo Verde Islands there is a mountain nature reserve. Not far from the summit we stopped to look at the beautiful and rich vegetation. One shrub called *Tortullho,* which had been virtually destroyed because of the need for fuel in earlier days, has now recovered and it covered the mountain slopes. Attached to the shrub branches is a woolly lichen. The lichen is not a parasite but forms a symbiotic relation with the shrub; it collects water from the surrounding mists and thus provides a source of water for the shrub. The symbiotic process, or symbiogenesis, is therefore dependent upon a convivial atmosphere for both shrub and lichen to thrive. As a metaphor for learning perhaps this little note prompts us to consider the kinds of atmospheres that we require to support each learner's materialising of their world and future potentials.

In Chaps. 8 and 9 I discussed the disobedience of the force of art not in terms of opposition or being obstinate for the sake of it, but in more affirmational terms, as a possibility for an opening, a resistance towards

© The Author(s) 2018
D. Atkinson, *Art, Disobedience, and Ethics,* Education, Psychoanalysis, and Social Transformation, DOI 10.1007/978-3-319-62639-0_10

normalisation through established modes of practice and a coming into existence of new ways of seeing, thinking, feeling and acting. Such disobedience through art practice makes a difference to the world it helps to compose. The pedagogical task in relation to such disobedience is to negotiate how a learning encounter matters for a learner, how it is felt, conceived and enfolded without imposing ready-made conceptions of what is happening so that this mattering for the learner becomes something else. The adventure of pedagogy therefore is to expand our comprehension of what art, teaching and learning can become. Established knowledge and practice may be delimiting as we are sometimes confronted with a learner's form of expression that does not fit our frameworks of understanding. We might view such moments in terms of what Lyotard terms the emergence of a *differend*, where there is a conflict between quite different value-form-practice systems as to what constitutes practice. Remaining open to the not known, may be a better disposition rather than the closure of knowledge. There is a sense that in such circumstances knowing, as an inventive practice, becomes indissoluble from ethics. I will deal with this indissolubility between the creative moment and ethics below. As I wrote earlier in Chap. 4, sometimes, all you meet are walls and then it is about trying to reveal your own foundations. Thus, a pedagogical imperative is to develop ways of living attentively with learners, to facilitate the continuous weaving of our lines of life, a process that, according to Deleuze and Guattari, always begins in the middle.

Tim Ingold (2016, p. 16) argues that individuals are not, 'bounded, entities, but sites of binding, formed of knotted trails whose loose ends spread in all directions, tangling with other trails in other knots to form an ever-extending meshwork'. Alongside this point, we can also say that art practice is not centrally concerned with the production of objects or the representation of entities or beings in the world, but rather, with experimenting and exploring to forge openings, correspondences and potentials for building new worlds, processes that, in Ingold's terms, are perpetually ravelling and unravelling within an unbounded matrix of relations. Our word 'understanding' suggests a predication on that which already exists and may sometimes blind us to other possibilities; we may therefore wish to abandon such hylomorphic thinking and replace it with a thinking that emphasises the processual lived relationalities of becoming, more precisely, of becoming-with. All these points seem to coalesce around the idea of the force of art as a force of becoming-with and the dynamic ontogenesis of new worlds. If these folding and unfolding processes are morphed into pedagogic work in art education, then attempts to respond to the ravelling and unravelling of lines of living and their different values and sensibilities within a multiplicity of relations, would seem to be indissoluble from ethics.

Learning processes vary as learners become enmeshed in the different worlds and milieus they inhabit and which afford different experiences and relations, different ways of knowing, valuing, expressing and feeling. Within such experiences, learners inherit contrasting demands and respond accordingly through ways of thinking, feeling, valuing and acting. We can say then that these varied ways of knowing and acquisition of skills arise from the different lines of living and their meshwork (Ingold) of relations that in their difference lead to local pathways of ontogenesis. The pedagogical task therefore is to have a concern for the ontogenesis of different lines of becoming and not to see that which is different or mysterious as a problem in the sense of being an obstacle, but as a problematic that opens up phases of the challenge of becoming-with. Pedagogical learning for a teacher would thus involve not only a reconfiguring of that which is problematic, but also a genesis of a new pedagogical reality. The pedagogical task as directed towards a learner would not primarily be to impart established blocks of knowledge or skill, but to create the conditions for effective learning to occur within each line of becoming-with and its local ways of knowing, and then for the teacher to integrate each learning complex to the learning encounter he or she initiates.

The idea of 'part of the world making itself intelligible to another', reminiscent of Whitehead's notion of prehension, has powerful implications for learning in that it is concerned with the specific onto-epistemic events of learning, their composition, correspondences and consistencies that include human and non-human actants. Such onto-epistemic events are indissoluble from ethics in the sense that knowing forges new ways of becoming-with, of building a life. Donna Harraway (2008, 2016) coins the term, *response-ability*, to highlight obligatory relations in processes of becoming-with.

Without wishing to refute Barad's notion of intra-action which I discussed in Chap. 2, but rather calling for a more discriminating use in order to avoid 'relational reductionism', Martin Savransky (2016) offers some insightful thoughts and judicious warnings in response to Barad's assertion that 'relata do not pre-exist relations'. For Barad, according to Savransky (Ibid, p. 6), things come into existence through their relations, which implies that they do not exist prior to them; that things *are* through the relations in which they are constituted. Barad (2003) writes:

...relata do not pre-exist relations; rather, relata-within-phenomena emerge through specific intra-actions', and furthermore, ...there are no independent relata, only relata-within-relations. (p. 815)

Such a position tempts us to conclude that relations are always prior to things and that the latter can have no being that is separate from the relations through which they emerge as things. However, Whitehead (1967) provides a different position on this issue, in *Adventure of Ideas* he writes:

...it must be remembered that just as the relations modify the natures of the relata, so the relata modify the nature of the relation. The relationship is not a universal. It is a concrete fact with the same concreteness as the relata. (p. 157)

While taking on board an apparent dualism of relata and relations, it is important to conceive their 'relation' within a world of process. Savransky's question in not wanting to adopt a relational reductionism is '*how*, in the configuring of a specific situation, both relations and relata come to matter and affect each other. (p. 6)?' Can we conceive of beings in Whitehead's terminology as *enduring*? Savransky argues that if the answer to such questions is affirmative, if we can conceive of entities as being in some way capable of enduring through their complex relations, which, as Whitehead indicates above, involves an on-going reciprocal evolution, then he asks to what extent can a being be,

capable of posing its own obligations, that is, of constraining – in the sense of both limiting and enabling – the manner in which a situation [...] might inherit it; its capacity to institute itself as a demand for a situation to "take responsibility for that which [it] inherit[s]" and for how it does so. (Barad Quantum Entanglements. p. 264), (Rhizomes, 30)

It is therefore important to recognise the historical constitution of the process of becoming, which is always a becoming-with, but without ditching or over-doing the notion of relationality. When we come to consider processes of becoming, we cannot ignore the generative force of intra-action but at the same time we cannot discount what Savransky, following Whitehead, terms 'the stubborn fact' of an entity's existence, its presence in a situation and its capacity to 'constrain the directions' of becoming. This is not to return to a metaphysics of individualism but, as Savransky writes, to:

...affirm simultaneously, the relational processes by which the different creatures of this world come into existence as well as the radical *irreducibility* of
the stubborn fact of their existence. (Rhizomes, 30)

The importance of Savransky's intervention for my purposes is the *concern*, and I am using this term in its Whiteheadian sense, for how, in
pedagogic encounters we become obligated by the different lines of learning we encounter, what such different modes of learning demand of us and
'the heterogeneous obligations that these pose as "stubborn facts"'. This
constitutes a matrix of problematic co-existence, or becoming-with, that
calls for a heterogeneity in the acts of being *response-able* towards the
different lines of learning that pose their own obligations and thus both
limit and enable how teachers inherit and respond to them. As already stated
in Chap. 6, how does a pedagogical relation take account of the obligations
posed by a learner? How does such a relation inherit a learner's way of
conceiving, of acting, how does it become response-able to this inheritance?

Taking on board Savransky's modification of Barad's notion of intra-
action, we might wish to think carefully about the nature of relations in
specific contexts and, where appropriate, how entities or beings in their
force or presence as 'stubborn facts' in the evolving reciprocities of becoming-with may limit or expand processes of becoming. This would entail
developing sensibilities to different modes of being and becoming, and
considering how things matter in such processes.

How then does the adventure of a learner's practice matter in a learning
encounter and how might we affirm and support this adventure and be
response-able to its mattering? How do the 'potential obligations'
(Savransky) that a learner may pose to the 'mode of mattering' of the
pedagogical relations in which a learning encounter comes to be configured,
affect such relations and their outcomes? The learner's practice develops a
response to a learning encounter in terms of how this matters; the teacher
inherits this mattering and makes a pedagogic response...a risky and inventive process, denoting a problematic co-existence or *mitsein* and a concern
for developing new ways of thinking and acting. It is this task of paying
attention to the different modes of mattering and the way in which they
compose their world in this world and then how such modes of mattering
can be challenged in order to expand learning that constitutes a pedagogical
ethics. In contrast, to adopt a one-way pedagogical practice in which a

teacher asks the questions and the learner is expected to respond is to assume this practice is obligated by nothing; that the teacher is the only one with the right to obligate. Such a pedagogical approach entails the submission of a learner to the teacher's pedagogical demands and assumptions, to the teacher's interpretation of the learning encounter whether or not this resonates with how an encounter matters for a learner. A problematic of becoming-with, making-with, learning-with, has a concern for modes of learning that may be recalcitrant to pedagogic assumptions or expectations and which may consequently invoke a transformation in pedagogic practice as it takes into account such aberrant modes. To repeat, the pedagogic imperative therefore is to consider how teachers might invent ways of inheriting and responding to modes of learning that lie beyond their frameworks of understanding? In relation to the task of responding effectively and ethically to that which appears recalcitrant to established modes of practice, William James (1897/1956, p. 209) writes:

> The highest ethical life – however few may be called to bear its burdens – consists at all times in breaking the rules which have grown too narrow for the actual case.

So in returning to Whitehead's point that relata emerge from relations but they also modify the nature of relation, the specific mode of mattering for a learner that emerges from a learning encounter (relation) and all its components (human and non-human), suggests what Ingold (2013, pp. 98–102) calls an on-going correspondence, a dance of animacy, as discussed in Chap. 6, which is composed of a contrapuntal weaving of body, mind, affects and materials. This constitutes the learners adventure of learning. For the teacher the learner's dance of animacy constitutes a proposition and obligation, another kind of dance and contrapuntal weaving of learning-with, making-with, sensing-with and feeling-with. In this kind of pedagogic scenario teachers and other educators have to be vigilant to the different obligations that a learner's dance poses. Perhaps it is worth considering what kind of relations are initiated or emerge within pedagogic work, or what kind of relations might emerge? What kinds of relations facilitate or limit learning?

These issues return us to the importance of relation and the 'stubborn facts' of pedagogical work and through them we enter not only an ethics of pedagogical work but also a politics and aesthetics of learning. If pedagogical work is not a one-way process in which educators initiate learning, where learners submit to the teacher's pedagogical demands but rather a problematic of co-existence in which lines of life are woven together in pedagogical work, this weaving involves a politics and ethics of negotiation and an aesthetics of becoming.

The process of building a life in pedagogic work constitutes a struggle that is often challenging, frustrating, enervating and invigorating and the morphologies of becoming-with, making-with, feeling-with, learning-with are complex. In the Post Partum *Document (1973–1979)* (*Documentation III, Analysed Markings and Diary-Perspective Schema, 1975*) by Mary Kelly we witness both the complexity of relations and the stubborn facts of existence of a mother and child relation over 6 years. We get a sense of how 'relata' emerge from relations but also how they modify relations. This sensitive and complex work has direct implications for the riskiness and the obligatory dimensions of pedagogical work. In the *Documentation III* we are confronted with a series of small diary charts each consisting of four forms of semiotic-material configurations denoting aspects of the mother's relations with her child. Three columns of text cover a child's scribble drawing. The first column captures the child's linguistic expressions on particular occasions and the mother's annotations, the second tables the mother's comments and thoughts on each utterance, the third presents a hand written 'diary' comment on memorable events. In one chart (27.9.75), the first column begins by noting the child's expression on wanting to fly a kite and the mother's annotation, 'Come'n do it' (wants to fly a kite), in the second column the mother's comment in upper case is 'I SAY IT WOULD BE NICE TO TAKE IT OUTSIDE AS IT'S VERY WINDY BUT IT'S ALSO VERY LATE SO I TRY TO CHANGE THE SUBJECT'. The next extract in column one is 'down dis, its falling'. (I'm pretending to fly a kite) accompanied in column two by the mother's comment, 'AS I STARTED THIS GAME OF PRETENDING TO FLY THE KITE STANDING ON A CHAIR HOLDING IT AND MAKING SOUNDS LIKE WIND, NOW I'M STUCK WITH IT'. The third extract in column one is, 'Ask daddy flying the kite, go ask him', (I say daddy will fly it tomorrow) followed in column two with, 'HE REMEMBERS PROM-ISES VERY WELL'. The fourth extract in column one says, 'Go potty now' (asking me to get pot), followed in column two, 'WHY DOES HE ASK ME TO GET THE POT THEN REFUSE TO SIT ON IT'. The last extract in column one states, 'Where 'tories gone' (trying to postpone bedtime),' followed in column two with, 'HE SEEMS TO SPEAK LESS CLEARLY NOW BUT MORE OF IT'.

In column three, there is a more extended handwritten diary statement by the mother dated a few days later about an incident when the child drank some liquid aspirin and was taken to hospital, but with no ill effects. The child was diagnosed as having tonsillitis and the extract continues to express the never-ending worries of motherhood (Fig. 10.1).

Though not directly concerned with pedagogic work, and by no means wishing to imply a direct similarity, this extract from the Post Partum *Document, Documentation III*, as well as the entire body of the work, does seem to resonate with the many, often conflicting obligatory dimensions and dispositions of pedagogic work. It seems to echo the affective-cognitive morphogenesis of pedagogical relations. The child's expressions of desire, the mother's strategies for fulfilment or evasion, and then having to work with the consequences (now I'm stuck with it), the promises that will need to be kept. These 'little moments' seem to me to capture the

Fig. 10.1 Post partum document (1973–79) (Documentation III, analysed markings and diary-perspective schema, 1975) 27/9/75 (Reproduced by permission of artist Mary Kelly)

intricate entanglements (ritornellos) that form the ongoing shifting relations of pedagogic work and ensuing strategies. The hand-written statement by mother has a strong affinity with statements made by student teachers as they reflect in their teaching practice journals upon incidents in their teaching, expressing their anxieties, frustrations, sense of failure or moments of encouragement and excitement. It is in such periods of reflection on practice, but also sometimes in the heat of practice, that a teacher allows the disturbances of practice to alert her to her obligations to the relevance for a learner of how something matters.

As well as invoking an ethics of relevance, how a teacher responds to such obligations involves a politics and aesthetics of relevance. How? In order to tackle this question Susan Buck Morss's notion of a *pragmatics of the suddenly possible* seems important, but also the notion of an ecology of practices advocated by Isabelle Stengers (2005).

ECOLOGY OF PRACTICES

Stengers makes an immediate ontological point that no practice can be defined like any other.

> This is how I produced what I would call my first step towards an ecology of practice; the demand that no practice be defined as 'like any other', just as no living species is like any other. Approaching a practice then means approaching it as it diverges, that is, feeling its borders. (2005, p. 184)

Approaching learners is a little like approaching a series of different territories, each composed of different rhythms and intensities; different ritornellos, ways of seeing, feeling and thinking. It would seem then that an approach made, often through questions and conversation, cannot afford to assume anything about what is happening, but to pay attention to the particularity of a learner's practice. Questions are creative tools for exploration that a learner may find relevant to her practice; they are not tests (as in a litmus test) for preconceived outcomes. When teachers enter into pedagogic work with learners, it seems important that the foreclosures of assumptions or habits need to be resisted, as Stengers writes, 'what is at stake here is giving to the situation the power to make us think, knowing that this power is always a virtual one, that it has to be actualised (p. 185)'. Something happens to make us think. Relevant questions try to actualise the power of a learner's practice, its particular concern or mattering for the learner. Such questions and precipitant outcomes may expand pedagogic work.

Stengers views this ecology of practice, this process of feeling its borders, as functioning in a minor key whereby we address practice through the Deleuzian/Guattarian notion of thinking 'in the middle'. Thinking in the middle is therefore not grounded in pre-determined outcomes that 'capture' practice or through which practice is recognised. Ecology is fused with an ethology, so that in pedagogic work, the very way in which learners are approached constitutes a formative aspect of their learning, it affects the *ethos* of their learning. This again introduces ethics into pedagogic work and the learner's task of building a life. However, it is not a matter of trying to deal with things 'as they are' but more significantly with how things (learners and teachers) might become.

> An ecology of practices does not have any ambition to describe practices 'as they are'; it resists the master word of progress that would justify their destruction. It aims at the construction of new 'practical identities' for practices, that is, new possibilities for them to be present, or in other words to connect. It thus does not approach practices as they are – (art practice for instance) but as they become. (p. 186, my bracket)

Stengers makes a profound point concerning ethics, relevance and responsibility (obligation) that has important implications for a pedagogy of immanence in contrast to pedagogies of prescription or transcendence. She quotes Leibniz as saying that the only general moral advice he could give is 'to say why you chose to say this, or to do that, on this precise occasion'. She maintains that by adhering to this principle does not suggest that we have the power to define the situation or have clear reasons for acting. It is more a case that when approaching pedagogic work, it is not a matter of employing general principles but of taking some time to *imagine* the particularity of a situation, and if sometimes things don't work out or go in unanticipated directions, you cannot be responsible for what follows or for the limitations of your imagination.

> Your responsibility is to be played in the minor key, as a matter of pragmatic ethos, a demanding one nevertheless – what you are responsible for is paying attention as best you can, to be as discerning, as discriminating as you can about the particular situation. That is, you need to decide in this particular case and not to obey the power of some more general reason. (p. 188)

The probability of misunderstanding in pedagogic work, as approaches to the territory of a learner's practice are made, is always present. A teacher's questions form part of the milieu of a learner's practice and therefore 'intervene in the ethos' of the learner. What matters therefore is that as teachers, whenever possible, we put aside general reasons that authorise our approach to the specificity of each learner's learning encounter when we take the risk of approaching it. The problem with treating a learner's practice according to general categories of practice that apply, for instance, to established techniques or skills, is that such action may delegitimise a learner, on the other hand it may inspire. In other words, such action raises the issues of belonging and attachment. In pedagogical contexts, feelings of belonging and attachment matter and facilitate the process of becoming able, a confidence and independence of practice. Whitehead's gentle advice, 'have a care' for learners' concerns is not to be under-estimated here in terms of facilitating each learner's process of becoming able.

Stengers links the idea of concern with the notion of 'cause' in the sense of, 'you do not think without a cause (p. 191)', so that 'causes are causes for those who are obliged to think by them'. The warning here from the perspective of an ecology of practices, is that in pedagogic work we do not try to manipulate a learner's cause according to a teacher's categorisations, in other words employ a hylomorphic approach because we cannot predict or take for granted how learners might become able in their particular mode of learning. Pedagogic work is thus a matter of learning-with and feeling-with in a process of contrapuntal weaving. A learning encounter for a learner is a practical problem involving how something matters. Pedagogical work from the perspective of an ecology of practices is also full of practical problems and obligations that arise from the risk of approaching the territory of a learner's practice. The task is therefore not to achieve some kind of commonality between a teacher and learner but a kind of reciprocity-in-difference, perhaps a dance of animacy as proposed by Ingold, in which teacher and learner each take their respective meanings and achieve their respective advances in building a life in the pedagogic relation. Respectful of ontological difference, adventures of pedagogies of immanence may foster what Stengers calls 'an experimental togetherness' or a becoming-with, a pragmatics of the suddenly possible enabling new practical identities and their respective becoming.

GUATTARI'S THREE ECOLOGIES

Felix Guattari, in the article *The Three Ecologies* (1989, New Formations No. 8) writes, 'We should perhaps not speak of subjects, but rather of components of subjectification' (p. 131). I would prefer components of subjectivation, in the sense that subjectification seems to denote a power to subjectify, whereas subjectivation suggests an action or capacity for invention, a creative process of becoming-with. Furthermore Guattari, in advocating the need for ethico-aesthetic paradigms to inspire new ways of living, thinking and making together, argues that 'both individual and collective subjective assemblages have the potential to develop and proliferate far beyond their ordinary state of equilibrium' (p. 133). In parallel to this advocacy for ethico-aesthetic paradigms and potential for invention lies the requirement to evolve commensurate pedagogical practices that try to align with the evolving sensibilities of learners, a requirement that becomes more pressing in a world of increasing speed of technical invention, production and communication as well as multiple events of social and cultural disruption, precipitating vast movements of migration and displacement. Writing in 1989, Guattari states with a sense of prescience,

> ...the ecology I propose questions the whole of subjectivity and capitalist power formations – formations which, moreover, can by no means be assured of continuing their successes of the last decade. Not only may the present financial and economic crisis lead to substantial upheavals in the social status quo and the media-based imaginary that underpins it; at the same time, neo-liberal ideology may well be hoisted on its own petard, as it espouses such eminently recuperable notions as flexible working hours, deregulation, etc. (p. 140)

In order to consider what I have termed building a life in such circumstances, Guattari offers three inter-linked ecologies through which to contemplate a reconstitution of social and individual practices within an increasingly problematic and at times frightening world: social ecology, mental ecology and environmental ecology.

Guattari lists a number of social and environmental disasters affecting the world and its peoples, including pollution, the deterritorialisation of the Third World, property developers whose actions lead to thousands of families being condemned to homelessness, the growth of child labour, the disappearance of 'the words, expressions, and gestures of human solidarity' (p. 135). Over two decades since he listed these social and environmental issues we can also add the wars in the Middle East that have involved many Western countries, the uprisings in the Arab Spring and the mass migrations of people from Syria and other parts of the Middle East as well as Africa into mainland Europe. Rather than appealing to what Guattari terms pseudo-scientific paradigms for possible resolutions, these are rejected due to their totalising logics in favour of what he terms an eco-logic or a logic of process and intensities (p. 136).

> Process, which I here counterpose to system and structure, seeks to grasp existence in the very act of its constitution, definition and deterritorialisation; it is a process of 'setting into being', instituted by sub-sets of expressive ensembles which break with their totalising frame and set to work on their own account, gradually superseding the referential totality from which they emerge, and manifesting themselves finally as their own existential index, processual lines of flight... (p. 136).

Guattari is making an appeal to develop new 'existential configurations' and 'universes of value' beyond existing social frameworks that in his eyes have become redundant or oppressive and inoperative for many. He warns of the deterritorialising flows of capitalist power that has extended its grip across social, economic and cultural zones as well as 'infiltrating the most unconscious levels of subjectivity' (p. 138). The task ahead therefore is to try to 'confront the effects of capitalist power on the mental ecology of everyday life' (Ibid.). The real challenge being to avoid what he terms, 'a mind-numbing and infantilising consensus', or what, as I write, is termed 'populist politics', and create a kind of 'dissensus and the singular production of existence'. In a simple but profound appeal, particularly in the light of emerging reactionary and nationalist politics, Guattari writes:

> Our objective should be to nurture individual cultures, while at the same time inventing new contracts of citizenship: to create an order of the state in which singularity, exceptions, and rarity coexist under the least oppressive possible conditions (Ibid, p. 139).

There is a need for such contracts at national and international levels to agree upon particular values and modes of conduct, for example, within the complex relations of the United Nations. It seems to me, if such agreements cannot be attained and honoured, however difficult, the terror of the bully is not far away. Equally, the struggles involved in emancipatory mental and social ecologies are struggles in which marginalised singularities aim to achieve existence in political, aesthetic and ethical terms. Guattari likens the logic of such struggles to art practice in which accidental events can sometimes transform the artist's initial vision and produce a totally unanticipated outcome.

In relation to mental ecologies, it is the creation that arises beyond the boundaries of established ways of thinking that matters and the form of this mattering that matters. One catalyst for such emancipatory change is art practice or, as discussed in Chap. 8, the emergence of aesthetic ritornellos (mutant forms of ontogenesis) and territories that create new pathways striking out from established modes of thought that in turn become deterritorialised by art practice. Through the singularised processes of art practice there is a potential to effect new ways of thinking, seeing, making and feeling that lead to new valorisations.

GUATTARI'S ETHICO-AESTHETIC PARADIGM

In his book *Chaosmosis* Guattari argues that to meet the growing challenges facing existence, human and non-human, we may be better placed to adopt what he terms an ethico-aesthetic paradigm than to rely upon the scientific-technical assemblages of enunciation that, 'place emphasis upon an objectal world of relations and functions, systematically bracketing out subjective affects', and giving precedence to 'the finite, the delimited and the co-ordinatable' (1995, p. 100). The phrase assemblages of enunciation refers to the different kinds of processes in which subjectivity is composed, scientific, aesthetic, technical, biological, political, and so on. Guattari's point is that an ethico-aesthetic paradigm is more suitable, more attuned to dealing with the unpredictabilities and uncertainties of existence and the potentials of creative innovations. In support of Guattari, Maria Hynes (2013) as discussed in Chap. 8, argues in relation to ethical responsibility that an ethico-aesthetic paradigm shifts such responsibility 'from an attribute of a pre-existing ethical subject to the idea of a potential mobilised within particular creative instances' (2013, p. 1931). Here the practice of ethics is not tied to established codes or to unified subjects, but to creative or inventive instances and to forms of life yet to emerge. Thus, an ethics of building a life is effected not through the individual subject, but through creative events; what I have described, after Ingold, an on-going contrapuntal weaving of entities, human and non-human. Hynes asks: 'What would it mean for an ethics of life to function as a discourse that genuinely encounters life in the newness of its forms, rather than seeking to secure the future against the throes of change?' Pedagogic work, curriculum methods or educational policies understandably assume normative attitudes toward teaching and learning and may exert a closure upon inventive pedagogic evolution in favour of established values and practices. Can we re-imagine pedagogical contexts in terms of an openness to the potential of the new and a pedagogical ethics that tries to respond to that which is not yet known, or put differently, the non-human?

Whilst Guattari argues for a relaxation of the dominance of scientific-technological assemblages of enunciation, in educational contexts it could be argued that the dominant assemblage is that pertaining to the economic-scientific-technological. This is not to dismiss the importance of science, technology or economics, but to put the case for other forms of subject production, other assemblages of enunciation, in educational contexts that may be more appropriate and convivial for building a life and collective forms of existence. If we try to embrace life, or in the contexts of pedagogic work, processes of learning and teaching, as sometimes encountering the not-known rather than always functioning according to established frameworks, then teaching and learning become exposed to the virtual and its force of potential. In this scenario, pedagogic work confronts by implication forms of teaching and learning that are yet to emerge.

Pedagogical practice can be viewed as an inventive practice that engages in working-with, making-with, thinking-with and feeling-with learners; it is a practice that speaks *from* a world (series of assemblages) that exists (knowledge, skills, practices), but also *to* a people and worlds yet to emerge (virtual), as each learner builds a life. In an ethico-aesthetic paradigm, a teacher is someone who we might say functions from assemblages of knowledge or know-how but who also remains open to the unforeseen or the unthinkable, the virtual potential of modes of practice that learners may employ. In a strange ontological sense the teacher operates from the 'human' but is also open to the 'non-human', the 'creative instance itself' (Hynes, p. 1931) and its relevance for a learner, for we can view this instance as the emergence of a new subjectivation. A teacher's ethical responsibility is not towards the learner-as-subject but, as Hynes writes, to the creative moment, or as Guattari (1995, p. 107) puts it, 'the movement of processual creation' through which new modes of subjectivation follow. The teacher's ethical responsibility is not driven or monitored by a transcendent code or practice but it evolves in the genesis of new forms of enunciation, in other words, such responsibility is immanent to the creative moment. In this scenario pedagogic work as well as the task of learning for a learner are viewed as processes of experimentation.

Moving the idea of ethical responsibility from a pre-existing subject to a concern for the 'potential mobilised within particular creative instances' thus suggests that ethics is not to be viewed as a body of established principles that informs action or thought, but an inventive aesthetic practice that attempts to respond to the open or virtual potential to create new subjectivations and collectivities.

WHITEHEAD: A CREATIVE AND FALLIBLE ETHICS

In relation to processes and adventures of building a life, and particularly in the context of pedagogic work, let me return to Whitehead. In much of his writing, he takes up the issue of ethics not emerging from pre-established principles or some objective point of value. In *Modes of Thought* (1968 p. 14), he writes, 'There is no one behaviour system belonging to the essential character of the universe, as the universal moral ideal'. As we have seen in Chap. 5, Whitehead's metaphysics is a metaphysics of process that conceives the world as an on-going inter-dependent and inter-connected process. For Whitehead, existence is concomitant with value, there is no vacuous or valueless existence. All beings, organic and inorganic, have value in themselves relating to their structure and organisation. Human beings are not separate from other beings; they are not to be conceived as independent or transcendent beings that accord value to other beings or entities, they are part of the process of life in all its variety and diversity. In *Modes of Thought* (p. 111), he writes, 'Everything has some value for itself, for others, and for the whole'. Thus, we see that for Whitehead the correlation of being or becoming with value establishes equivalence between ontology and axiology.

In pedagogic work, questions of axiology are almost indissoluble from questions of ontology. A fundamental position of a pedagogy of immanence is that all learners have value, but this will vary with respect to their life worlds and different evolving sensibilities and how these are structured and organised and how things matter. An important pedagogical task therefore, as stated previously, is to ascertain how things matter for a learner in a specific learning encounter, which involves an appreciation of value. Trying to understand such axiological relations may sometimes invoke a politics as when such relations and their modes of concrescence do not fit with accepted or expected modes. Equally, this raises a question of aesthetics in that by acknowledging as legitimate what were once perceived as recalcitrant concrescences, such acknowledgment may expand and enrich pedagogic experience. The realisation of value in what was once deemed recalcitrant expands both the learner's and the teacher's task of building a life. Of course, such realisation may not occur. Pedagogic work is fallible. The axiological and ontological dimensions of pedagogic work are therefore determined through processes of thinking-with, making-with, feeling-with, questioning-with, projecting-with and learning-with. This complex dynamic of weaving together on a number of levels and through a variety of practices also sheds a different light onto what Whitehead called an individual.

Whitehead's notion of an individual does not refer to the more traditional idea of a conscious, independent subject. Rather, for Whitehead, an individual includes a self, other or others and a whole. The idea of an individual therefore implies a becoming-with. In other words, an individual is always inter-dependent and inter-connected (perhaps intra-dependent and intra-connected) with others and the whole within each specific situation. In a processive universe self, other and whole are constantly intra-acting on numerous levels (molecules, cells, organs, bodies, collectives) such that we might say that an individual is at once in the world and the world is in the individual. This on-going creative advance is captured by Whitehead in his unusual aphorism, 'the many become one and are increased by one' (1985, p. 21). These ideas relating to the individual conceived in terms of inter-dependent processes seem to resonate with the later work of Jean Luc Nancy (2000) in his book, *Being Singular Plural,* and his notion of being-with, which he views as ontologically prior to being. Being-with and the notion of being singular plural are both notions that posit the multiplicity of being, that is to say the necessity of being as multiple. Nancy (p. 30), writes, 'if Being is being-with, then it is, in its being-with, the 'with' that constitutes being; the with is not simply an addition'.

It is within the weaving together in pedagogic work that we may sometimes find ourselves in what Nietzsche called the *untimely,* where we might lift the mantle of present conditions and determinants of practice in order to embrace that-which-is-not-yet, in other words, forms of practice which appear recalcitrant or strange. As hinted at above, pedagogic work is not infallible, nor is the process of building a life. We might consider then the point that the approach to pedagogic work I have tried to advocate throughout this book, based on a pedagogy of immanence, is inherently fallible. Brian Henning (2005) discusses in detail the issue of ethics and fallibility persistent in Whitehead's philosophy of process. The pedagogical predicaments mentioned above in relation to the fallibility of pedagogical work should not be viewed in terms of a problem, but rather in terms of an opportunity to expand thought, feeling and action.

There is no Archimedean position dictating the practice of pedagogy, though some may feel there is; there is no perfect pedagogical system nor can we gain a complete overview of pedagogic requirements. Fallibility has to be taken into account in the practical realities of pedagogic work and, as stated, seen in terms of possibility rather than problem. Thus, it is not always certain in particular pedagogical situations to know which course of action to take because every pedagogical situation is ontologically and axiologically different. Pedagogical work cannot afford to work exclusively from pre-scribed principles and must be open to revision when experience throws us beyond established values and practice. Henning makes the point that,

> ...every situation is ontologically unique because every actual occasion brings together the diverse elements of its actual world in just this way, just here, and just now. Furthermore, because every situation is ontologically unique, it is also morally unique in the sense that the values obtainable in a situation are never strictly identical. (p. 139)

In respect of pedagogic work and the task of building a life with others, such work does not exist in a vacuum but in relation to its contexts and the values and sensibilities of learners, hence the need to appreciate the situated nature of such work in each of its situations and the obligations that arise for a teacher. In reference to Whitehead's claim that everything that exists has value Henning (p. 146), makes the point that if this is so then every individual places an obligation on us to take it into account. I have already mentioned the importance of obligation in pedagogic work in Chap. 6 and Henning (p. 146), helps by constructing a number of inter-related obligations that I apply to pedagogical work. The first and most important is to act to achieve the greatest possible value for participants in each pedagogical situation. Next is an obligation to maximise the intensity and harmony of one's own experience and the experience of others. Finally, the obligation to expand our capacities and sensibilities to think, act and feel. Henning makes a crucial point in relation to the importance of developing a sensibility of value, for example, in terms of how things matter for a learner in a particular learning encounter. The first step in pedagogic work then is the task of trying to comprehend, 'the value of the individuals involved in a given situation', for the success of such work will depend our capacity to do so. If this cannot be achieved, and it is no easy task, then we may obstruct the growth that is possible. Put in other terms, an excessive or stubborn reliance upon established parameters of practice can inhibit our practices of living with present situations. The task of building a life and helping others to do so is an aesthetic pursuit in which we try to ascertain the values of others and how they are affected by our words and actions. The fact that many education systems are geared to what Henning (p. 152), calls an 'egoistic pursuit of ever greater material acquisition' and economic competition that promotes particular capitalist values makes it difficult to develop an ethics of creativity and a pedagogy of immanence that advocates a more integrated valuing of self, other and world.

How do we treat learners? Are they viewed as instruments towards particular ideological ends, disguised by fake or misguided intentions towards equality? Are they conceived as commodities? Do we appreciate and foster their diversity and act accordingly? Do targets that satisfy already established ends preoccupy us? The idea of a learner being supported to find his or her own expression on whatever level seems deeply important for pedagogic work, but the reality of such work is constantly bedevilled by other forces, established refrains, that demand obedience. With all such issues in mind it seems important to recognise the obligations that arise in pedagogic work and to respond as best we can to the 'demands' and 'objections' of learners. Such work thus requires that we try to act inventively to such demands and this may involve developing pedagogies of disobedience. These points take me back to Chap. 8 and the discussion of ritornellos, a coming into existence of forms that may forge new connections in contrast to the more settled and sedimented forms of practice.

In her PhD thesis, Carolina Carvalho Palma da Silva (2017, p. 68) made an intense study of museum and gallery programmes in the UK and the USA that develop work in the gallery with young people. Carolina's research focussed on the programmes developed by the Youth Forum at the Whitechapel Gallery in London. The intention of these programmes is to create learning environments, learning collectives, in which participants engage with artists and the issues they deal with in their work in order to experiment, explore and produce work together by developing ideas collectively towards negotiated outcomes. When Carolina asked one participant called Hari in a workshop how it felt to be part of a collaborative project without knowing the outcome, this is what he replied:

I think it's (...) a bit challenging because you don't know the end product (...). With Ruth's work it was sort of like going into a darkness with only a little glow stick, no flashlight so you can't see where you're going, just a little glow stick to let everyone know where you are, that's it. And once you are more inwards, inwards, inwards, the light starts turning on a little bit more.

Working with learners in pedagogic work is a little bit like trying to acknowledge and respond to their individual 'glow sticks' which they evolve during learning encounters in order to 'know where they are and where they are going'. Hari's words are deeply resonant of the affective struggles of learning and they bring to the fore the pedagogic imperative suggested by Whitehead's profound advice, 'have a care, here is something that matters'. And heeding such advice may often lead teachers to produce pedagogic ritornellos that help them to cope with the unknown, like children in the dark who hum to summon courage.

Coda

I need a body, a bit long and fat. I'll do some eyes, big eyes, have you got some scissors? I need scissors, have you got scissors?
Ok I'll do that while you do the eyes, right?
(Time passes, some cutting, some measuring.)
No that's not what I want, the shape's not right it needs to be fatter and more curved.
(He looks annoyed and frustrated)
Do you want me to help make another?
Ok ...if you like (He is not convinced)
(A second version emerges but it's obvious in the boy's eyes that it's not what he wants but he hesitates to say so and smiles. Does he know what he wants? What image is he working from? Can he realise what he wants to achieve? The adult puzzles over the boy's demands. What does he want?)
When I say fatter and longer I mean *this* way.
(He draws a diagram on some paper but it's not clear to the adult.)
But isn't that what we made the first time?
No! It wasn't right; you missed a bit here.
(He points to a very small area of the body.)
It needs to have a little bump here or it's not right.
Oh I see, Is that better?
(Adding the bump)
Yes its ok ...but now you have to make it all right all over.

These negotiations-in-practice continue along complex trajectories of becoming with: making-with, questioning-with, feeling-with, talking-with, seeing-with, guessing-with, risking-with and learning with. It is a process of co-existing in which relations and 'objects', demands and obligations impact upon each other folding, unfolding and refolding, constituting practices of negotiation and learning. The intensity of the boy's vision and demands, the adult's obligation to respond: adventures of making-with. Each of these relational processes may have the capacity to expand or dilute our capacities to experiment, think and act. They have the potential to open up new assemblages of practice and new modes of experimentation.

References

Barad, K. (2003). Posthumanist performativity: Toward an understanding of how matter comes to matter. *Signs: Journal of Women in Culture and Society, 28*(3), 801–829.

Barad, K. (2007). *Meeting the universe halfway: Quantum physics and the entanglement of matter and meaning.* Durham: Duke University Press.

Deleuze, G., & Guattari, F. (1994). *What is philosophy?* London: Verso.

Guattari, F. (1989). The three ecologies. *New Formations, 8*, 131–147.

Guattari, F. (1995). *Chaosmosis: An ethico-aesthetic paradigm.* Sydney: Power Publications.

Harraway, D. (2008). *When species meet.* Minneapolis: Minneapolis University Press.

Harraway, D. (2016). *Staying with the trouble.* Durham/London: Duke University Press.

Henning, B. (2005). *The ethics of creativity: Beauty morality and nature in a processive cosmos.* Pittsburgh: University of Pittsburgh Press.

Hynes, M. (2013). The ethic-aesthetics of life: Guattari and the problem of bioethics. *Environment and Planning, 45*, 1929–1943.

Ingold, T. (2013). *Making: Anthropology, archaeology, art and architecture.* London/New York: Routledge.

Ingold, T. (2016). From science to art and back again: The pendulum of an anthropologist. *ANUAC, 5*, 5–23.

James, W. (1897/1956). *The will to believe and other essays in popular philosophy.* Mineola: Dover Publications.

Nancy, J. L. (2000). *Being singular plural.* Stanford: Stanford University Press.

Savransky, M. (2016). Modes of mattering: Barad, Whitehead and societies. *Rhizomes: Cultural Studies in Emerging Knowledge, Issue, 30*, https://doi.org/10.20415/rhiz/030.e08

Silva C. C. P. (2017). *Youth forums in contemporary art museums: Mapping untimely entanglements.* Unpublished PhD thesis, Goldsmiths University of London.

Stengers, E. (2005). Introductory notes on an ecology of practices. *Cultural Studies Review, 11*(1), 183–196.

Whitehead, A. N. (1967). *Adventures of ideas.* New York: Free Press.

Whitehead, A. N. (1968). *Modes of thought.* New York: Free Press.

Whitehead, A. N. (1985). *Process and reality.* New York: Free Press.

ENDNOTE

What is the value, if any, of making a book on pedagogy when I see pictures on my television that depict unimaginable brutality and desperate struggles for life and safety? Surely, there are and must be other priorities! In our current world, we witness famine, pollution, violence, genocide and incomprehensible atrocities. Dogmatism in silos of nationalism, religious affirmation and self-interest seems endemic, diluting or dissolving willing cooperation, sharing and the hard task of working together towards convivial relations and the success and fallibility of such pursuits.

Can pedagogic work do anything positive to achieve such relations? Well, it must be possible; we have to believe that it can make a contribution, but I think it will demand the courage for a different kind of pedagogy than that which tends to dominate schools in many countries today; pedagogies that promote new ways of understanding ourselves and being together and our relations to the world. To begin such a difficult journey, pedagogical work requires an ontology that Nancy describes as 'being-with' but which we can easily extend to the praxis, poiesis and ethos of becoming-with.

Perhaps we need to think of becoming-with in terms of knots and weavings, not blocks and sections, but knots where lines grow and weave from a complex middle, from a crucible of relations and correspondences in which learning emerges, unfolding and refolding along mutant pathways, openings and closures. Weavings of living, lines of becoming-with.

The eternal dialectic between systems of order and control and the desire to pass beyond them in politics, education and other social domains seems to be locked into what Alain Badiou (2005) calls an 'expressive dialectic'

© The Author(s) 2018

D. Atkinson, *Art, Disobedience, and Ethics*, Education, Psychoanalysis, and Social Transformation, DOI 10.1007/978-3-319-62639-0

that prevents our ability to evolve new ways of thinking and acting. Expressive forms or positions, that which can be expressed according to parties, theoretical positions and 'isms' of various colours.

The disobedience of events of encounter emerges in their singular-plurality (Nancy 2000): the singularity of the evental moment and the plurality in the moment of possibilities for something new to emerge in contrast to the codes and regulations of established orders of practice. Here, tradition and novelty come together and care has to be taken to prevent the novel from dogmatism and its subsequent constraints and perversions. Perhaps we require a step further, what Badiou calls a 'non-expressive dialectics,' referring to those ontological mixtures or multiplicities that cannot be named but which designate that-which-is-yet-to-arrive, beyond established codes and labels, calling for processes of experimentation and invention and the courage to take a leap. This suggests that we do not try to impose the power of the norm that admits or excludes, that names or ignores, that recognises what exists and, by implication, is blind to what is aberrant to such existence.

There are two relations of desire to established codes and practice; a desire that is controlled by tradition so that the latter delimits desire to what we might call normal desires. Then there is a desire to strike out beyond established parameters of knowledge, of collectivities, of practice—a desire for that which does not yet exist, a desire for invention beyond the capture of conservative forces. Badiou argues that a crucial task is to give this force of invention a symbolic form (symbol is a term originally concerned with the practice of bringing together) or, in his words, to seek for a new fiction beyond the capture of tradition, predatory capitalism or reactionary appeals to old hierarchies and identities. For Lacan, truth is always in the structure of fiction. For Badiou, truth is an event occurring within a situation that transforms it according to new egalitarian principles; it is a matter of persevering with or holding true to such principles and to work with others to achieve them. For Deleuze, truth is not simply actualised in the sense of verification, but is coupled with interest and intensity that may open up virtual potentialities or virtual worlds that may precipitate, for example, political and ethical possibilities, and the task is to act discriminatively and apply such potential to actual practices.

Emphasis is therefore to be placed not upon a closure of meaning, but upon a constant inventive dynamic of experimenting and consolidating. Effective pedagogies of immanence rely upon such dynamics and their always evolving outcomes, their successes and their fallibilities. In Spinoza's terminology, the dynamics of events of learning involve what we can already do, our established capabilities, but also, crucially, that which we do not yet know we are capable of. The latter tends to emerge during what I have called learning encounters, or events of learning, in which something unforeseeable happens and propels a learner or teacher into modes of acting, feeling and thinking that were unknown prior to the encounter. Such dynamics involve established modes of practice, but also disobedience towards them, a wondering and wandering, an experimenting. There is the capacity to act but also a disobedience to engage with the not-yet-known, to pursue an adventure into unknown territories and relations, and an important disposition in such adventures is to try to maintain grace in such moments and beyond.

Perhaps the task is to relax genres or 'isms' of pedagogic practice and pay more attention to pedagogies that emerge from the immanence of relations that happen in the different ecologies of pedagogic work. To develop a pedagogic discrimination that allows us to evolve that which extends capacities for action, feeling and thought in contrast to that which restricts or delimits capacities. This requires a craft of nurturing (Stengers 2008), and a speculative trust that may at times run against established codes of practice. Today, there is a need to reclaim this craft in the light of the capture of educational practices by the constant pressure of economic refrains.

REFERENCES

Badiou, A. (2005). *Politics: A non-expressive dialectics.* London: Urbanomic.
Nancy, J. L. (2000). *Being singular plural.* Stanford: Stanford University Press.
Stengers, E. (2008). Experimenting with refrains: Subjectivity and the challenge of escaping modern dualism. *Subjectivity, 22,* 38–59.

INDEX

© The Author(s) 2018

D. Atkinson, *Art, Disobedience, and Ethics*, Education, Psychoanalysis, and Social Transformation, DOI 10.1007/978-3-319-62639-0

Printed in Great Britain
by Amazon